Counterpoetics of Modernity

In memory of Seamus Deane, 1940–2021.

"... *Pen's mark*
lives on, but not the mouth that sang."
Trevor Joyce, *Rome's Wreck*

Counterpoetics of Modernity
On Irish Poetry and Modernism

David Lloyd

EDINBURGH
University Press

Edinburgh University Press is one of the leading university presses in the UK. We publish academic books and journals in our selected subject areas across the humanities and social sciences, combining cutting-edge scholarship with high editorial and production values to produce academic works of lasting importance. For more information visit our website: edinburghuniversitypress.com

© David Lloyd, 2022, 2023

Edinburgh University Press Ltd
The Tun – Holyrood Road
12(2f) Jackson's Entry
Edinburgh EH8 8PJ

First published in hardback by Edinburgh University Press 2022

Typeset in 10.5/13 Adobe Sabon by
Cheshire Typesetting Ltd, Cuddington, Cheshire,
and printed and bound by CPI Group (UK) Ltd, Croydon, CR0 4YY

A CIP record for this book is available from the British Library

ISBN 978 1 4744 8980 5 (hardback)
ISBN 978 1 4744 8981 2 (paperback)
ISBN 978 1 4744 8982 9 (webready PDF)
ISBN 978 1 4744 8983 6 (epub)

The right of David Lloyd to be identified as the author of this work has been asserted in accordance with the Copyright, Designs and Patents Act 1988, and the Copyright and Related Rights Regulations 2003 (SI No. 2498).

Contents

Preface

Counterpoetics of Modernity is dedicated to Seamus Deane, who passed away in May 2021, even as this book was in its last stages. The epigraph, the last lines of Trevor Joyce's *Rome's Wreck*, renders the Irish proverb "Maireann lorg an phinn, ach ní mhaireann an béal a chan." Those who knew Seamus not only through his unmatched writings on Irish literature and critical theory, but also through his voice, his wit and conversation, and his laughter, will feel deeply the truth of that saying.

My dedication of the book to Seamus is inspired not just by the untimely moment of his passing, but also by my regret about a conversation that never did take place. Trevor once remarked that he "would love to see stuff done on Field Day *and* SoundEye," imagining a possible encounter and discussion between the cultural and political work of the Derry-based cultural and political organization that Seamus directed over many years and the poetry festival that Trevor co-founded and ran for some twenty years in Cork. Though the former evolved out of a theatre company and the latter's focus on poetry intersected with related avant-garde cultural interventions, The Avant and Cork Caucus, both initiatives sought to reinvigorate thought and imagination in Ireland, and opened Irish intellectual and creative life to multiple currents and possibilities from around the world. Their cultural practice represented something sorely lacking in Ireland, the space in which to further the rigorous critical reflection on which both the political and the aesthetic imagination has to draw. The very fact that SoundEye and Field Day seem so at variance in their projects and their aims only means that the conversation Trevor imagined could have sparked an unprecedented and invaluable colloquy, one that might have spawned critical engagements that would have lasted years rather than days.

Sadly, with Seamus's death, the opportunity for that conversation is gone. Nevertheless, though this book can never substitute for the conversation that might have been, I was struck in the course of assembling its final shape by the realization that in a peculiar way it brings together two distinct aspects of my own work over many years that represent respectively ongoing critical dialogues with Seamus and Field Day and with Trevor and SoundEye. That is perhaps unsurprising from one perspective. My first encounters with both Seamus and Trevor took place when I was still an undergraduate studying in Cambridge, stepping tentatively into the field of Irish Studies that was just about to be transformed by new energies and new approaches, many of which were pioneered and sustained by Field Day. Those meetings gave rise to what is now over forty years of conversations that have been my deep good fortune to enjoy. But though poets—Seamus Heaney, Tom Paulin, and Derek Mahon—were intimately involved with Field Day's work from an early point, and though Seamus himself began his writing career with the publication of three volumes of poems, poetry was never a principal focus of his work. Nor, indeed, has poetry very often formed the object of the critical tendency in Irish Studies most closely associated with the overall project and outlook of Field Day, that is, postcolonial theory. In particular, the contemporary poetic work that has been understood as carrying forward the modernist impulse of the poets of the 30s—Samuel Beckett, Brian Coffey, Denis Devlin, and Thomas MacGreevy—and that interests me most in the second part of this book, has fallen entirely outside the purview of postcolonial criticism.

In Chapter 4, I try to come to terms with the peculiar ways in which experimental or innovative poetics have seemed to be incompatible with postcolonial or race critical theory. But it will remain surprising to many readers that throughout this book I read not only poets like Mangan and Yeats—who have often enough been understood in relation to anti-colonial nationalism—but also the most innovative of Irish poets, Trevor Joyce himself, Maurice Scully, and Catherine Walsh, in a way that consistently holds the colonial nature of Irish modernity in mind. In fact, however, the thing that should surprise is that they have not been read in this light. This is not only a matter of their content, which consistently engages with Ireland's past, with the Irish language, with the destructiveness of modernization in Ireland and elsewhere, and with alternative imaginings of social life. It is also a question, which I try to answer in Chapter 1, as to why the modernist impulses that shaped the literary work of the Revival, from Synge and Yeats to Joyce and O'Casey, were eclipsed in the wake of Ireland's partial decolonization. The anti-nationalist reaction against the Free State was also an anti-modernist one and both tendencies remain dominant in our own time, in writing and in criticism. But it should seem odder than it does that a postcolonial criticism that took for its principal texts the advanced modernist work of Yeats and Joyce should have neglected the poetry of the most formally inventive of contemporary poets. I hope that *Counterpoetics of Modernity* will contribute to remedying that curious oversight.

This may be the first book-length study of Irish poetry to devote chapters to each of Joyce, Scully, and Walsh and to regard them, along with Ciaran Carson and Medbh McGuckian, in a postcolonial framework and in the context of a broader meditation on the forms of modernization that shaped Irish culture. But it would have been impossible without the pioneering work of two critics in particular, J. C. C. Mays and Alex Davis. Any critic working on what Davis calls "the broken line" of Irish modernist poetry is indebted to their critical work. But my debt to each is also personal. It was Jim Mays who, with generous hospitality and a little mischievous humor at my expense, welcomed me into his home, shared books with me, and above all introduced me to the work of younger Irish poets that he had consistently supported, by his writing and by his attentive reading. At the time, I was just a student looking for material for an Irish issue of what was then still the undergraduate magazine, *Granta*, but Jim has remained an unfailingly generous resource ever since and an unflaggingly insightful critic of poetry. Alex Davis was the first to identify a "neo-avant-garde" in Irish poetry and to devote a chapter of his book on Denis Devlin to the poets he identified as belonging to that tendency. This book could not have been written without his work or the volume on Irish modernism in the 1930s that he edited with Patricia Coughlan. But I am particularly grateful for his generous comments on the drafts of some of this work, and especially for his comments on the first chapter which owes so much to his thinking.

The work has benefited also from the insights of Joe Cleary, whose work on Irish modernism and postcolonial writing brings with it an internationalist breadth of reading and theoretical insight that has invigorated Irish criticism for over two decades. Over and above what I have learned from his thinking, which will be evident especially in Chapter 1, his specific feedback has been invaluable to me. Maureen Fadem's just and critical editorial eye saved me from many an unwieldy sentence and gave me intellectual encouragement just as my energy was flagging. But beyond such specific debts, I am aware of many others less easy to identify. Irish Studies lives, as everyone knows, through conversations in which ideas are formulated and tested long before they are written—if, indeed, they ever are. Over many years I have gained in more ways than I could name, from such conversations with friends whose intellectual generosity has been an always sustaining pleasure: Luke Gibbons, Lee

Jenkins, Heather Laird, Breandán Mac Suibhne, Conor McCarthy, Victor Merriman, Emer Nolan, Alexandra Poulain, John P. Waters, and Clair Wills.

But it is, of course, to poets that this book owes most: to Trevor Joyce, whose invitations to participate at SoundEye were an incomparable gift, restoring to me conversations and friendships that had long been broken off; to Fergal Gaynor, whose commitment to making new things happen never ceases to amaze me; to Billy Mills and Catherine Walsh, who reached out to me so kindly many years ago and have remained an inspiration ever since; to Maurice and to Mary Scully, whose welcoming home has always been a haven of good food and great talk; and to Geoff Squires and Randolph Healy, whose work forms an essential part of the ongoing "infinite conversation" that constitutes the spirit of SoundEye.

Several editors who published the first versions of chapters of this book, as listed below, gave me not only indispensable opportunities to "road test" my thinking, but also feedback that improved them greatly. My thanks are due to Jimmy Cummins, Eric Falci, Kenneth Keating, Niamh O'Sullivan, Mark Quigley, Sinead Sturgeon, and Rachel Warriner.

The final stages of assembling a book can often prove the most arduous and taxing. I am deeply grateful to Soraya Zarook for her indefatigable editorial and research assistance and her long-suffering patience and good humor, without which this book would hardly have seen the light of day. And, for the second time and with equal pleasure, I have to thank the editorial team at Edinburgh University Press for the great attentiveness, patience and care for producing beautiful books. In particular, I have to thank Eliza Wright for her painstaking editing of the manuscript, without which many more errors and infelicities would have survived than those for which I bear the sole responsibility. Finally, many thanks to Clare Counihan for producing an index that could serve as a subterranean map of the whole book!

For many years, Sarita See has shared with me the pleasures of living and the pains and panics of writing. She has an uncanny capacity to be right. For her insights, readings, laughter and a companionship that makes life rich, I am daily thankful.

Permissions

Versions of these chapters have been previously published as follows. I am grateful to the editors and publishers for permission to reprint them here.

Chapter 2: "Crossing Over: On Mangan's 'Spirits Everywhere,'" in *Essays on James Clarence Mangan: The Man in the Cloak*, edited by Sinead Sturgeon. Basingstoke: Palgrave Macmillan, 2014, pp. 14–32. Reproduced with permission of Palgrave Macmillan.

Chapter 3: "1913–1916–1919," in *Modernist Cultures*, vol. 13, no. 3, Autumn 2018, pp. 445–64.

Chapter 4: "'To Live Surrounded by a White Song,' or, The Sublimation of Race in Experiment: On the Margins of Susan Howe", in *Journal of British and Irish Innovative Poetry*, vol. 5, no. 1, 2013, pp. 61–80.

Chapter 5: "New Things That Have Happened: The Cultures of Poetry in Contemporary Ireland," in *Irish Literature in Transition: 1980–2020*, edited by Eric Falci and Paige Reynolds. Cambridge: Cambridge University Press, 2020, pp. 44–64.

Chapter 6: "Intricate Walking: Scully's Livelihood," in *A Line of Tiny Zeros in the Fabric: Essays on the Poetry of Maurice Scully*, edited by Kenneth Keating. Swindon: Shearsman Books, 2020, pp. 36–67.

Chapter 7: "*Rome's Wreck*: Joyce's Baroque," in *Essays on the Poetry of Trevor Joyce*, edited by Niamh O'Mahony. Bristol: Shearsman Books, 2015, pp. 170–94.

Introduction: Counterpoetics and Colonial Modernity

The successive modernist moments that punctuate Irish literature, defined by their response to the colonial conditions of Ireland's modernity, are no new thing, even if they always seems to take new forms and require new declarations. Modernism in Irish poetry, a quality inseparable from its precocious experience of the violent and disruptive impact of modernization and the inroads of colonialism, cannot be understood apart from that history. The Irish poet Trevor Joyce concluded an essay on "alternative poetries" in Ireland with the following remarks:

> The tug of [James] Joyce, Beckett, and other poets of the '30s has been strong enough for us to feel free of all hegemonies, whether from Britain, America, Europe or elsewhere, and to confirm to us that writing in Ireland can be radically innovative and independent without privileging any external authorities. We seek from nowhere the franchise to regard ourselves as innovators, or to provide a living alternative to those tendencies we find most intimately oppressive.[1]

The political echoes that reverberate in this poetic "declaration of independence," with its insistence on the specificity and anti-hegemonic nature of an "alternative" Irish writing, are hardly accidental. They draw on a long and still fraught history, a history that distinguishes a specifically Irish modernist impetus from the mainstream of Anglo-American writing and, no less, from the "intimately oppressive" conformity of an Irish anti-modernism that has sought to establish its own untroubled backwater within that mainstream.

The traits of that alternative poetic modernism, from fragmentation to the suspicion of representation or of originality, can already be tracked in nineteenth-century work and respond to the rapid and unsettling effects of colonial modernity, from language loss to political violence. Irish poetry becomes modernist by virtue of its haunted awareness of loss: its inventiveness is driven not by poetic innovation for its own sake, but by the need to find formal means to engage with historical conditions that take from the writer the customary certainties of cultural continuity, autonomy, personal voice or even unmediated access to experience. To read Irish poetic work in this light is to move away from the divisions between traditionalism and modernism, mainstream and margins, formalism and experiment, that have tended to organize critical approaches to date, usually at the expense of the most vital and innovative work being written in Ireland.

Only quite recently, and still largely on the critical margins, has it been recognized that an alternative body of poetic work, challenging and inventive in its formal and linguistic innovations, has long existed in Ireland.[2] This delayed reception, too, is hardly accidental: Trevor Joyce's invocation of Beckett and the poets of the '30s (Brian Coffey, Denis Devlin, and Thomas MacGreevy) belies an awareness that he and other radical poets of his generation often express, that their discovery of their forebears came after they had already, and on their own terms, begun to write a poetry independent of the conventional modes of Irish writing. The overworked notion of influence and its agonistic anxieties, especially in the oedipal version promoted by Harold Bloom, may disguise the ways in which poetic *affiliation*, displacing the family romance of filiation or genealogy, lends itself better to reading the work of poets in cultures that do not claim the continuity of a "major" tradition, but constitute minor disruptions of the very notion of tradition and of the conceptions of subjecthood and representation that inform it.[3] Affiliation is a notion that well describes the process by which a group of Irish poets, who were unfamiliar with one another prior to the 1996 New Hampshire conference, "Assembling Alternatives" to which Joyce is responding, came to form a critically recognizable constellation.[4] As I argue in the first chapter of *Counterpoetics of Modernity*, the actuality of discontinuity, a distinct consequence of colonial conditions, constantly interrupts every effort to forge an Irish poetic tradition. In the most critically conscious writers, however, this does not lead to an effort to constitute fictive filiative continuities, but is absorbed into the form their writing takes, as an index and a response to those conditions, in their contemporary as in their historical effects.

This is not only true of the Irish context but links it to the wider, global legacies of colonialism. Cultures shattered by what Kenyan writer Ngũgĩ wa Thiong'o once called the "colonial bomb" must, as Black Caribbean poets Kamau Brathwaite and Marlene NourbeSe Philip have shown, forge their "nation-languages" or "i-mages" out of hybrid sources, twisting and torquing them in the process. They tend to disarticulate poetic form and its language—"l/anguish;" in Philip's pointed pun. Such cultures do not so much "lack" continuity as have little need of it, preferring to consider the phenomenon of their broken-ness as a means to openness, "poreux à tous les souffles du monde," as Césaire put it.[5] Discontinuity with the past, in this light, becomes a guarantee of a poetics that embraces incompletion and provisionality rather than the perfect enclosures of form and the patrimonies and authority of lineage and heritage. Whether by avocation or historical necessity, porosity is their resource and they take their cues not from traditions and progenitors, but from the potentials identified in their willful assemblage of hints and inventions from an array of writers who happen to serve the furtherance of their projects. The modes of reading they elicit are likewise archipelagean in form, seeking configuration, constellation and relation, rather than the continuity and totality of the unified work or the coherent tradition. The desire to restore continuity then appears as the reactive effort of the minor to "perform a major function" in Deleuze and Guattari's sense, and to disavow the occa-sions for thinking and making otherwise that nest in the ruined edifices of the past.[6]

The aim of *Counterpoetics of Modernity* is not, then, to seek to establish the persistence of a continuous modernist tradition in Irish poetry, to bridge the "broken line"—in Alex Davis's apt phrase—that leads from the Irish poets of the 1930s who affiliated themselves, if only temporarily, with the radical and iconoclastic energies of European modernism to the contemporary Irish "neo-avant-garde" (again, in Davis's phrase).[7] For it is clear that any connections between the work of the poets focused on in the second part of *Counterpoetics of Modernity*—Trevor Joyce, Maurice Scully, and Catherine Walsh—and that earlier generation, the "poets of the '30s," are indeed retrospec-tive constructions, assumed long after the formers' poetic independence from the dominant Irish lyric mode had been declared. Poetic lineage and cultural continuities, especially in the Irish context, are almost always belated constructions, forged as poets—or their critics—become self-conscious with regard to the constellation of past or present writers in relation to whom they seek to be read. Likewise, what now seems the obvious grouping of a set of writers who have become known loosely as the "SoundEye poets," after the international festival organ-ized by Joyce for twenty years in Cork, is a no less belated appearance, their acquaintance with one another's work having been occasioned by their chance meeting at that by now almost legendary conference, "Assembling Alternatives" to which Joyce's essay responded.[8] To seek now to invent such a tradition would be to impose the institution of a canon upon writers whose innovative energies derive in good part from their recalcitrance to the canonized modes of Irish poetry, which persists even at the cost of marginalization.

Nor does *Counterpoetics of Modernity* seek to confine itself to writers who, under various rubrics from experimental to innovative to "neo-avant-garde," have been identified explicitly—and often dismissed—as Irish poetic modernists. The available terms just cited, all of which have been applied to the work of these poets at various times, and even on occasion been embraced by them, fail adequately to capture the specificity of their work, principally on account of the peculiar history out of which Irish literary and, more broadly, aesthetic institutions emerged. Likewise, emphasis on the "broken line" that has been taken to connect them to the poets of the 1930s distracts from the distinctive characteristics of Irish modernism that so many Irish poets "since Yeats" and so many of their critics have turned away from with distaste. Insofar as Irish modernisms have found their condition of possibility in the peculiarities of Ireland's forced and colonial modernization, the flight *from* modernism, which—as I show in the first chapter—has been the dominant recourse for Irish poets, is at the same time their acquiescence, if at times nostalgic, in the normalization of a general process of modernization that continues apace. The fact that since the 1960s the ongoing project of capitalist modernization has been embraced by Ireland's political and economic elites does not make it any less an imposed and often violent process, determined by circumstances not of our choosing. Colonial modernity prepared the way for the neoliberal and dependent modernity that fulfills and supplants it.

My earlier invocation of poets from the Caribbean was not a merely casual reference. The conditions of twentieth-century Irish poetry, which emerges from societies that have been, north and south of an imposed postcolonial partition, subject to equally imposed regimes of modernization, do resemble those that determine what Caribbean poet and critic Édouard Glissant has called a *forced poetics*: "Forced poetics exist," Glissant says, "where a need for expression confronts an inability to achieve expression."[9] One factor in forced poetics is that which Irish poet Thomas Kinsella equally foregrounded in his seminal essay, "The Irish Writer," loss of a language: as Glissant put it, "It can happen that this confrontation is fixed in an opposition between the content to be expressed and the language suggested or imposed."[10] But language loss is not the only situation out of which a forced poetics emerges. It may also be that the poetic language in dominance, or the forms that have gained currency through their naturalization, cease to be adequate to the matter that needs to be expressed. If the legitimation of those forms as norms derives from the critical expectations and assumptions of a more powerful culture whose language the poet shares or feels obliged to use, then too a forced poetics may emerge: Caribbean writers, from Glissant to Brathwaite and Philip, have been especially alert to this predicament.

For the poets discussed in Part II of this book, "New Things That Have Happened," what Joyce calls "the standard Irish bag of tricks," that is, "lyrics of description and expression dressed in the most transparent of formal attire," has become a mode of unreflective and therefore unproblematized forced poetics that masquerades as spontaneous and authentic self-expression.[11] The Irish lyric, with its artfully naturalized naturalism, assumes an air of free responsiveness to experience that in its very form, that of packaged units of neatly processed if sometimes pained subjectivity, reproduces the state of heteronomy that it disavows, even where its content may be haunted by actual losses deeper than its assumed formal autonomy could ever register. It seeks by its form to affirm the persistence of the self-possessed and possessive subject even in the face of a general condition of dispossession. Its apparent accessibility derives from its instant delivery of satisfactions predicated on the well-crafted simulation of "the common experience of seeming to act freely and spontaneously, while even a minimal self-awareness reveals that the freedom is to a great extent generated and governed by forces and concerns in which one has had no hand, act, or part."[12] For the writer drawn to extend the form and language of poetry to address the complexities of contemporary social life, such lyric modes are, unlike the modes of writing that might exert their hegemony from outside, "intimately oppressive."

Against such simulations, which can only succeed in so far as the conditions of poetry and its production remain largely unproblematized, the poets focused on here—despite the heterogeneity of their modes of writing—share a willingness to confront the conditions of poetic writing without the specific molds and dictions into which Irish poetry has tended to slip. Maurice Scully long ago abandoned the bag of tricks of the Irish lyric, refusing, as he has often declared, to "write poems," preferring instead to assemble books. As he describes them, "the books are not 'collections' of disparate 'poems,' but pieces, tesserae, that make up a larger shifting picture, or thought-sound-world."[13] Even still, his work evokes the most traditional of forms—ballads, sonnets, rounds, marching songs, elegies—only to shatter their generic enclosures for the sake of composing networks of echo and correspondence "fibrously" across the terrain offered by the extended scale of the book format. At the same time, his work constantly explores the dialectics of living, labor, and leisure that shape the conditions for writing, transforming "occasion" into a motive for interrogation and perception into a mode of self-displacement rather than accumulation. Where Scully's work appears improvisational and constantly projective, in a sense I argue to be very different from Charles Olson's usage of that term, Joyce tends to embrace constraints and procedures that range from translation and writing through others' texts to the generation of poems from spreadsheets. Far from eschewing formal frameworks along with the expressive lyric, his poems are a constant investigation of the relation between forms of constraint that condition contemporary subjectivity and the potentialities for the generation of poetic texts that reside in constraint itself. And if, like Scully's, Walsh's work seems provisional and anti-formalist, she also subjects herself in her best-known volume, *City West* (2005), to a condition resembling the white noise of a continual and unrelieved "overhearing" determined by the saturation of the contemporary soundscape with injunctions, exhortations, clichés, and phatic locutions that hem the subject in on all sides with preformed expression. The later volume, on which I focus in Chapter 5 and in the Conclusion, *Optic Verve* (2009), links these conditions of enunciation to a larger context of ongoing modernization, from the destruction of rural lifeways to the displacing violence of urban "renewal" and the penetration of domestic life by routines of labor and mechanization.

At this juncture, the modernist precepts to "make it new" or to "purify the dialect of the tribe," or the formalist intent to employ the aesthetic estrangement of appearances to shatter the hold of perceptual habits and see the world afresh, seem obsolescent and inadequate to the universalization of heteronomy. Forced poetics is no longer a condition imposed only upon the formerly colonized; it is the condition of writing itself, as Beckett presciently grasped in the wake of the Second World War in a phrasing uncannily similar to Glissant's, if even more radical in its recognition "that there is nothing to express, nothing from which to express, no power to express, no desire to express, together with the obligation to express."[14] What genuinely resonates between these contemporary Irish poets and Beckett (or his fellow poets of the '30s) lies less in the question of influence—his work is a surprisingly marginal presence in any of their writing—than in a shared disposition to incorporate a problematization of the conditions of writing into the very fabric of that writing. This problematization is occasioned by what Beckett himself called "the new thing that has happened," the breakdown of the lines of communication and of the certainties of the subject–object relation on which the traditional lyric reposes.[15] In the creative-destructive process of modernization, the "new thing" happens not once but over and again, imposing on the attentive poet the perpetual injunction to engage anew with the constraints it imposes. Rather than adopt the somewhat unhelpful labels of "experimental" or "innovative" poetry, or—for reasons I elaborate in the next chapter—the literary historical categories of "[late] modernist," "postmodernist," "avant-garde," or even "neo-avant-garde," I have chosen to regard the work of these Irish poets as representing, after Glissant's term, a *counterpoetics* of modernity, one always cognizant of and vigilant towards the forced conditions of their production. But where, for Glissant, the fact that a "forced poetics or counterpoetics is instituted by a community whose self-expression does not emerge spontaneously, or result from the autonomous activity of the social body," leads to "a kind of impotence, a sense of futility," the counterpoetics I trace defines itself over against the claim to autonomy and spontaneity that continues to undergird the subjective lyric that is the norm for Irish poetry.[16] It is a self-consciously interrogatory poetry, forged in Ireland's own version of "The irruption into modernity, the violent departure from tradition, from literary continuity" that Glissant locates in the Caribbean.[17]

In an essay unsurpassed for its unfolding of the situation of poetry and the predicament of the poet in the wake of and in the face of all civilization's barbarities, Paul Celan speaks of a certain persistence of poetry as "the poem holds its ground on its own margin. In order to endure, it constantly calls and pulls itself back from an 'already-no-more' into a 'still-here.'" The need to persist against the unutterable violences of modernity, before which so much has been disappeared, whether by the administrative technologies of genocide or by the devastations of colonialism, demands of the poet and poetic language an intimately dialectical attentiveness: it requires "language actualized, set free under the sign of a radical individuation which, however, remains as aware of the limits drawn by language as of the possibilities it opens." Such responsiveness and such persistence, the "still-here" of the poem, are realized only "in the work of poets who do not forget that they speak from an angle of reflection which is their own existence, their own physical nature."[18] This individuated "angle of reflection" is not to be confused with the free-floating autonomy or putative political independence of the poet, nor with the "singular voice" much prized by poetry criticism. None was more aware than Celan of his own situatedness, "mindful of all his dates," or of the brutal historicity that had made him and unmade so many others. "Racked by reality and in search of it" (*wirklichkeitswund und Wirklichkeit suchend*), as he elsewhere puts it, he speaks out of that "innermost narrowness" (*allereigenste Enge*), from the crevasse or ravine that haunts his poetry as the determinate space in which history has placed him. Out of that situated attentiveness, the poem can "give voice to what is most its own: its time," while also staking itself as a "word against the grain."[19]

The work I foreground in *Counterpoetics of Modernity* tends to occupy such a highly individuated angle of reflection always mindful of its specific historical conditions and committed to a sense of the poem as a word against the grain, or, to invoke Walter Benjamin's famous expression to which Celan alludes, as brushing *history* against its grain. Their attention to and engagement with the long and ongoing history of modernization that remakes Ireland and ties it to the larger circuits of European colonialisms and the brutalities of the Atlantic world, rather than their correspondence to any particular poetic or aesthetic movement, is what drives what I have called their counterpoetics of modernity. Irish postcolonial criticism has to date paid much less attention to poetic work, with the exception of Yeats, than it has to the novel, drama, and the visual arts. This may have had much to do with the regular protestations of poets and critics alike that poetry is an apolitical art, protestations that betray a rather impoverished notion of how the relation between poetic and political language might be conceived.[20] Poetry, taken at its own word, might seem an asocial genre more divorced from the material formations of colonial society than the novel or the theatre. To the contrary, this book maintains, not only the concerns but the forms of poetic modernisms are shaped by their dialectical relation to the transformative impact of modernity, even as those forms critically refract the experiential through their own "angles of reflection." Thus, while it might seem counter-intuitive to place James Clarence Mangan or Yeats at the head of a book that then turns to Irish American experimental poet Susan Howe, and to Scully, Joyce, and Walsh, what matters is to grasp the work of these earlier poets as a refractory response to modernity as it appeared in their moment, haunted by the potentials its voracious advance threatened to consume.

The four chapters in Part I of *Counterpoetics of Modernity*, "Specters of Modernity," stand awry to the historical model that has been implicit in the accepted critical account of Irish poetic traditions. Chapter 1 offers an "overture" that seeks to understand the historical conditions out of which that critical account emerged: Irish literature and criticism, and in particular the poetic tradition, have been haunted by a sense of their discontinuity. I argue that this anxiety about discontinuity and rupture is derived from an anti-modernism that is inseparable from the anti-nationalism of the established literary discourses that emerged in the first place among writers who reacted against the conservatism of the Free State. In doing so, however, they sought to forge what I call a "weak universalism" against the modernist experiments of the

Revival and post-Revival writers. The formal conservatism that that effort entailed persists into the later academic critical models that have dominated Irish culture since. Accordingly, rather than consider W. B. Yeats as a kind of bulwark of formally conservative poetic modes, as a "last Romantic" whose work effectively banishes modernism to the margins of the Irish poetic tradition, I seek to understand Yeats's work as an intrinsic element in the longer trajectory of Irish counterpoetics.

The subsequent chapters track that modernist impulse in Irish poetics back into the nineteenth-century and Mangan's seminal work. Mangan's critical translations pose the kinds of question regarding language, identity, and spirit that necessarily haunted a "semi-colonial" and emerging nation that had already begun to feel the full force of capitalist modernization in cultural destruction and violent demographic and economic transformation. As I have argued at length elsewhere, his selective recruitment to the cause of Young Ireland's cultural nationalism and his later sentimentalization as a plangent balladeer has obscured the profound problematization of Romantic poetic modes that his work performed.[21] In Chapter 2, I return to one of Mangan's principal means of problematization, translation. Chapter 3 goes on to consider Yeats's poems of commemoration, written across a critical decade for Irish nationalism whose centenary is still being commemorated, as a linked series of meditations on violence, memory, and modernity. Turning finally to Irish American poet Susan Howe, this section ends with recent debates about the relation of experimental poetic work to race or identity, unsettling what it means to think of "Irishness" in relation to poetic modernism, given the fluidity of Irish identity and its transatlantic movements and the supposed tendency of innovative poetry to abstraction from materiality and experience.

Chapter 1, "Overture: The Burden of Discontinuity: Criticism, Colonialism, and Anti-Modernism," argues that despite the fact that rupture and discontinuity insist on perpetuating themselves in history and culture, critics of Irish poetry, together with the poets who participate in the critical conversation, have not abandoned the effort to establish lines of continuity. In order to contextualize the anti-modernism that characterizes the predominant stance of critics and poets alike, I offer a somewhat speculative account of the modes of aesthetic institutionalization that prevailed in Ireland's anti- and postcolonial societies. The anti-modernist turn that Irish writing mostly took in the wake of the Revival, and that continues to prevail, occludes any recognition that what Ireland's key modernist moment, the Revival, actually represented was a modernism seeking to counter a modernizing process. In the context of the political and cultural failures of both post-partition states, anti-modernism cast itself as a universalizing transcendence of nationalist insularity. It thus foreclosed the vantage point that might have registered that the Revival's version of modernism had been neither insular nor backward, but part of a wider social movement that sought to trace the possibilities of an alternative path within modernity. The continuing influence of this reaction on Irish academic criticism has marginalized the alternative poetries which extend the potentials of that modernist moment and which I describe as constituting a "counterpoetics of modernity."

Chapter 2, "Crossing Over: On James Clarence Mangan's 'Spirits Everywhere'" reads Mangan's practice of translation as an allegorical questioning of the afterlife or "living on" through the destructive conditions of colonial modernity that anticipates a fully modernist set of concerns. As I conclude in the chapter, minor or anachronistic as his practice might seem, Mangan's work continues to foreshadow insights whose pertinence only becomes apparent many decades after he wrote. Lodged in a space and a time where the question as to what languages could authentically bear, of spirit or of cultural material, was of increasing political urgency, Mangan also wrote at a moment in which it was possible to witness the fading of one language into the shadow of another, transformed by the evolving capitalist marketplace overwhelmingly into a means of exchange. These are the conditions that led Glissant to speak of forced poetics, and Mangan's peripheral and minor location gave him a peculiarly privileged vantage point on modernity, and on the fate of language in modernity, that anticipates many of the concerns and poetic strategies of later modernists.

Where Mangan's practice of translation proves to be burdened with dates and their afterlives, Yeats's own poems of commemoration, written across a critical decade for Irish nationalism whose centenary is still being commemorated, furnish a linked series of meditations on violence, memory, and modernity. Beyond that, Yeats's acts of commemoration also open up a space for the contemplation of potentials, of encounters and afterlives that were not historically actualized but nonetheless resonate as missed but not exhausted possibilities. Unrealized possibilities secrete alternative histories that, however counterfactual, live on as a kind of spectral penumbra around losses that must be commemorated. Chapter 3, "1913–1916–1919: Yeats's Dates," explores the spectral resonances around missed encounters between Irish Marxist James Connolly and Rosa Luxemburg in Germany and links Yeats's modernist poetry of commemoration with Celan's belated commemoration of Luxemburg in his posthumous volume *Schneepart*. Commemoration, as opposed to acts of nostalgia or piety, appears as a distinctly counter-modernist practice that seeks to find in the wake of destruction, in the afterlives of futures imagined in the past, a way to speak of other possible modes of living on and in common.[22]

Chapter 4, "'To Live Surrounded by a White Song,' or, The Sublimation of Race in Experiment: On the Margins of Susan Howe," pursues further the ways in which modernity is haunted by the speculative possibilities of the past—precisely by the "might-have-been" of the counter-factual potentials that remain unrealized. This chapter examines "Melville's Marginalia," one of the American poet Susan Howe's innovative works that deliberately engages with the Irish and transatlantic dimension of her poetic and intellectual formation. The chapter takes on recent debates about the relation of experimental poetic work to race or identity: contemporary criticism has begun to challenge the assumed dichotomy between poetries that deal with race or identity and the innovative or experimental, between a poetry all too often read for a quasi-sociological interest or for an affirmation or exposition of identity, and an experimental or avant-garde poetry. The latter is rigorously critical of identity formation, suspicious of groundings in experience or of representation, understood in the restricted but connected forms of the presentation of personal experience or of "speaking for" a community. Here I explore the question of the relation between poetic practices that fundamentally challenge the stability of identity and voice and the continuing force of material histories and their colonial and racial effects, challenging the dichotomy so often imposed between historical experience and poetic experiment. Mangan haunts Howe's "Melville's Marginalia" as the spectral Irish absent presence behind Bartleby. Both signify the trace of a subjected racial matter disseminated through the formal operations of her work, haunting its procedures even as the specters of colonial modernity continue to shape what the unworked-through entailments of modernity might mean in the Irish context.

The second part of *Counterpoetics of Modernity*, "New Things That Have Happened," traces the emergence of a contemporary counterpoetics of modernity not from the inheritance of past instances of poetic innovation, but rather from the conditions of the successive waves and modes of modernization that Ireland has undergone since the early 1960s and in the work of poets who have been willing to work against the grain both of the homogenizing force of global capitalist culture and of the associated critical conventions and poetic practices that emerged across this period.

Chapter 5, "New Things That Have Happened: Forms of Irish Poetry," challenges the ways in which the academic critical industry has promoted the conventions of Irish lyric practice since the 1970s, with scant regard to the pressures that either the spectacular political violence or the "slow violence" of neoliberal capitalist development during recent decades has placed on the forms and language of poetry. The chapter focuses on three poets whose work has pushed against the constant reproduction of "well-made poems": Ciaran Carson, Medbh McGuckian, and Catherine Walsh. Carson's signal achievement was to break with what was by then the empty formal shell of the epiphanic lyric in order to develop the long, sinuous, mostly blank-verse line that proved capable of integrating the colloquial rhythms of bar-stool or barbershop conversation with a playful, associative, and often tongue-in-cheek intellectuality. He forged a formal means to enact the attitude of ironic suspicion, visceral threat, and restless movement that are the conditions of survival as of a poetic critical address in a situation of state as well as paramilitary terror.

McGuckian, all too often cast as a poet of the "rich inner world of feminine sensibility" and as an unusually obscure writer who draws on private or hidden allusions to render the enclosed world of women's experience, likewise emerges as a poet whose writing, far from privileging the personal lyric of self-expression, meditates on the ways in which quotidian language is charged with cultural and political burdens.

Working under the very different economic and political conditions of the Republic, but no less under the shadow of neoliberal capitalist developments that shaped Ireland's "Celtic Tiger" boom, Catherine Walsh deploys in her 2009 book-length text, *Optic Verve*, a mixed repertoire of dismantled lyric forms, prose passages she calls "commentary," and diaristic notations to confront which she nicely designates "rattled subjectivity." Drawing at times on traditional women's labor, at others on the commodity culture and real estate speculation of the present, her work reminds us that formal innovation is the means to imagine or recuperate "structures of feeling" and forms of living that resist the unfreedom of universal commodification, producing a medium that itself defies easy consumption even as it insists on remaining open to the traces of past practices whose implicit alternative values live on into the present as an almost physical residue that has survived destruction.

Chapter 6, "Intricate Walking: Scully's *Livelihood*," focuses on the volume that forms the centerpiece of Maurice Scully's massive, eight-volume poetic work, *Things That Happen*, composed over twenty-five years. Scully's departure from the traditional lyric was explicit, even as his work constantly reflects on fundamental elements of the lyric tradition and its relation to singing or humming, ballad or sonnet, forms that he thoroughly deconstructs. Critics have noted often enough Scully's antipathy towards the "well-made poem" that he dismisses as "the Gem

School" or "bottled poetry" and whose characteristics he satirizes more than once in *Livelihood*. But there is more at issue than the anecdotal matter of poems that perpetually reiterate the conditions of deracination that has affected an agricultural economy undergoing rapid modernization, only to reassure the reader of the snug fit between the modern subject and the rural past. Ultimately, Scully's critique is more about the inadequacy of a reproducible and widely reproduced poetic mode to the economic and social conditions of the present: the so-called well-made poem reproduces the preset pattern of formation of the subject that integrates individual autonomy with the appropriation of the world. Scully's work, with its commitment to a processive mode of composition, working always at the edge of attention and in the moment, effects a continual letting-go rather than an appropriation of what passes into the poem. It is a work that withdraws from all those forms through which writing has participated in the domination of the world and of the reader, and offers us an unprecedented poetics of displacement and of dispossession. We might say that therein lie both the Irishness and the modernity of Scully's work, so long as we recognize that, conditioned by a colonial modernity shaped by domination and expropriation, Irish modernism has always been a counter-modernity.

Chapter 7, "Rome's Wreck: Joyce's Baroque," extends my argument about the relation between poetic innovation or experiment and the invention of forms adequate to Ireland's colonial modernity. I situate Joyce's poetry and its critical practice in relation to Mannerism and the Baroque, not as anachronistic art-historical practices, but—following Arnold Hauser's argument in his *Mannerism* (1965)—as stylistic modes that emerge in times of rapid and violent political or economic transition. From his earliest collection, *Pentahedron* (1972), whose poems at least appeared to be lyric in form, to *Rome's Wreck* (2014), a "translation" into monosyllables of the Elizabethan poet and colonial administrator, Edmund Spenser, I trace Joyce's deployment of elemental figures—stone, water or river, ash—and the recurrence of an allegorical mode that registers the effects of a contemporary intensification of reification to constitute a mannerist mode of colonial baroque. Counterpart to other forms of colonial baroque in Latin America and elsewhere, and sharing in their sense of ruination and melancholic refusal to abandon the fragments that history has stranded, Joyce's Irish baroque constitutes a counterpoetic with its own broken and dispersed lines of transmission. The ruination that afflicts it is not only an effect of its procedural destruction of all naturalized models of reference and representation, but also an echo of unrelenting historical catastrophe such as has haunted Irish modernity and Irish modernisms since the nineteenth century. As with Mangan, translation, an infusion into the present of a refracted image of the past, furnishes the means to accommodate that haunting.

In the "Conclusion. Conduits for the Humane: Walsh's *Optic Verve*," I return to Catherine Walsh's *Optic Verve*, which deploys a variety of poetic forms, from "lyric" fragments to prose commentary and narrative verse, in a complex meditation on the long and destructive history of Irish modernity and—as she puts it in the later work *Astonished Birds* (2012)—the "repetition from one / dominant cultural context to / another" of modes of dispossession and enclosure, "imparkation / of what was held / common."[23] Against the vexed conditions that sustain and impede the work of writing and the colonization of daily language by commodification and bureaucratic euphemism, Walsh forges a mode of writing that allows her to draw together the destructive impacts of contemporary neoliberalism with the survival of practices of mutual aid and life in common that persisted through the destructiveness of an earlier colonial mode of modernization. They come together in constellations of instants and languages that recall Walter Benjamin's dialectical images, where past and present converge.

Walsh's work proves exemplary of the ways in which Irish modernist and experimental poetry has continually shown itself capable of inventing forms and languages adequate to Irish conditions a century after the nation's partial decolonization. The plural is critical: the poets considered in this book form neither a continuous lineage stretching from Mangan through Yeats to Walsh nor a self-conscious poetic tradition, any more than the later "SoundEye poets" have forged a movement with a common voice or set of formal procedures. But collectively these poets, for too long at the margins of Irish culture, have succeeded in finding ways to address the predicament of a society whose apparent freedom is, as Trevor Joyce suggested, "to a great extent generated and governed by forces and concerns in which one has had no hand, act, or part." They do so without purveying nostalgic lyric compensation or affecting the naturalistic common language or common sense that have become the hallmarks of contemporary poetic convention, though for the most part their work is full of colloquialism, overheard speech, the self-assured clichés that pass for collective wisdom, but always suspended in a configuration with multiple other modes of language use or discourse. At a time when Ireland, North and South, is undergoing radical shifts that have produced a new sense of cultural openness together with an appreciation of what Irish traditions of counter-modernity may still have to offer in a moment of crisis, the counterpoetics of such poets could not be more timely or in more urgent need of revaluation and dissemination. In short, of reading and rereading.

Notes

1. Trevor Joyce, "Irish Terrain: Alternative Planes of Cleavage." *Assembling Alternatives: Reading Postmodern Poetries Transnationally*, edited by Romana Huk. Wesleyan University Press, 2003, p. 166.
2. J. C. C. Mays furnishes a comprehensive set of reasons for the marginality of these poets, from their supposed difficulty to the demands of the publishing and bookselling industries and their recalcitrance to classroom teaching. See his essay, "The Third Walker." *Irish University Review*, vol. 46, no. 1, Spring/Summer 2016, p. 56.
3. Harold Bloom, *The Anxiety of Influence*. Oxford University Press, 1973. On the distinction between filiation and affiliation, see Edward W. Said, "Introduction: Secular Criticism." *The World, The Text and the Critic*. Harvard University Press, 1983, pp. 16–24. Said's further remarks are quite relevant to the situation of Irish poetry and its diverse affiliations: "What I am describing is the transition from a failed idea or possibility of filiation to a kind of compensatory order that ... provides men and women with a new form of relationship that I have been calling affiliation but which is also a new system." On minor literature in the Irish context and its deviance from or disruption of the canon and "major work," see David Lloyd, *Nationalism and Minor Literature: James Clarence Mangan and the Emergence of Irish Cultural Nationalism*. University of California Press, 1987.
4. In addition to the poets directly addressed in *Counterpoetics of Modernity*, Trevor Joyce, Maurice Scully and Catherine Walsh, attendees at the Assembling Alternatives conference included Randolph Healy, Billy Mills and Geoffrey Squires. For essays on their work, see the *Irish University Review*'s special issue on "Irish Experimental Poetry," vol. 46, no. 1, Spring/Summer 2016.
5. Ngũgĩ wa Thiong'o, *Decolonising the Mind: The Politics of Language in African Literature*. James Currey, 1986, p. 3; Kamau Brathwaite, "History of Voice." *Roots*. University of Michigan Press, 1993, pp. 266–73; Marlene Nourbese Philip, "Introduction: The Absence of Writing or How I Almost Became a Spy" and "Discourse on the Logic of Language." *She Tries Her Tongue, Her Silence Softly Breaks*. Ragweed Press, 1989, pp. 10–25 and 56–9; Aimé Césaire, "Cahier d'un retour au pays natal" ("Notebook of a Return to the Native Land"). *The Collected Poetry*, translated by Clayton Eshleman and Annette Smith. University of California Press, 1983, p. 68 (translated as "porous to all the breathing of the world," p. 69).
6. Gilles Deleuze and Félix Guattari, *Kafka: pour une littérature mineure*. Éditions de Minuit, 1975, p. 50.
7. For the titular phrase "broken line" and for a discussion of what he calls the "Irish neo-avant-garde," see Alex Davis, "Coda. 'No Narrative Easy in the Mind': The Irish Neo-Avant-Garde." *A Broken Line: Denis Devlin and Irish Poetic Modernism*. University College Dublin Press, 2000, pp. 159–76.
8. See, for example, Trevor Joyce's account both of the New Hampshire conference and the relation of his New Writers' Press to the '30s poets in

Marthine Satris, "Interview with Trevor Joyce." *Journal of British and Irish Innovative Poetry*, vol. 5, no. 1, 2013, p. 13.

9. Édouard Glissant, *Caribbean Discourse: Selected Essays*. University Press of Virginia, 1989, p. 120.

10. Glissant, *Caribbean Discourse*, p. 120; Thomas Kinsella, "The Irish Writer." *Davis, Mangan Ferguson: Tradition and The Irish Writer*. Dolmen Press, 1970, pp. 57–71. I discuss this essay of Kinsella's further in Chapter 2.

11. Trevor Joyce, "The Phantom Quarry: Translating a Renaissance Painting into Modern Poetry." *Enclave Review*, vol. 8, Summer 2013, p. 6.

12. Joyce, "Phantom Quarry," p. 6.

13. Marthine Satris, "An Interview with Maurice Scully." *Contemporary Literature*, vol. 53, no. 1, 2012, p. 14.

14. Samuel Beckett, "Three Dialogues with Georges Duthuit." *Disjecta: Miscellaneous Writings and a Dramatic Fragment*, edited with a foreword by Ruby Cohn. Grove Press, 1984, p. 139. It should be noted that, citing Kafka, Deleuze and Guattari locate in this inability to express the fundamental condition of a minor literature: *Kafka*, p. 29.

15. Samuel Beckett, "Recent Irish Poetry." *Disjecta*, p. 70.

16. Glissant, *Caribbean Discourse*, p. 121.

17. Glissant, *Caribbean Discourse*, p. 146.

18. Paul Celan, "The Meridian." *Collected Prose*, translated by Rosemary Waldrop. Carcanet Press, 1986, p. 49. In his earlier "Speech on the Occasion of Receiving the Literature Prize of the Free Hanseatic City of Bremen," Celan had remarked on how, through the catastrophe of Nazism, war and the Holocaust, language had ended up *angereichert*, paradoxically enriched but perhaps also "stretched" (*reichen*): see *Collected Prose*, p. 34.

19. Celan, "The Meridian," pp. 50 and 40 and "Speech," p. 35.

20. Typical and possibly authoritative is Edna Longley's pronouncement in *The Living Stream: Literature and Revisionism in Ireland*. Bloodaxe Books, 1994, p. 9 (citing her earlier *Poetry in the Wars*), that "'Poetry and politics, like church and state, should be separated.' By politics I meant predatory ideologies, fixed agendas and fixed expectations." Apart from the fact that the critic here betrays an exceptionally limited experience or consideration of actual engagement in politics, so narrow a definition of the political virtually reduces the pronouncement to a vapid tautology. But the utterance of truisms easily gains the uncritical assent that sustains the circulation of clichés. Anne Mulhall offers a dismal catalog of more recent such pronouncements, sufficient to convince anyone of the anti-intellectual function played by the conventional allergy of poets to what they misconstrue as "politics," in her essay "The Ends of Irish Studies? On Whiteness, Academia, and Activism." *Irish University Review*, vol. 50, no. 1, Spring/Summer 2020, pp. 94–5.

21. See Lloyd, *Nationalism and Minor Literature*.

22. On the relation of commemoration and haunting in Irish political as well as poetic culture, see E. Molloy, "Racial Capitalism, Hauntology and the Politics of Death in Ireland." *Identities: Global Studies in Culture and Power*, 2019, pp. 1–18. In conclusion, Molloy remarks that "commemoration practices signal both an attempt to lay the ghosts of the past to rest as

well as highlighting the unfinished business of anti-colonial struggle." He goes on to point out that the ambiguity of commemoration thus disrupts "any attempt to present a simplified teleology leading inexorably to the present" (p. 15).

23. Catherine Walsh, *Astonished Birds* and *Cara, Jane, Bob and James.* hard-Pressed Poetry, 2012, n.p. (34 and 39).

Part I:

Specters of Modernity

Overture. The Burden of Discontinuity: Criticism, Colonialism, and Anti-Modernism

Irish culture is burdened by an apprehension of its discontinuity that recurs as rhythmically as the pulsations of the unconscious, irrupting periodically and in relation to the most diverse phenomena with all the force of unfinished business. This apprehension is as old as the effort to forge a nation and a tradition that could unify a people divided by sect and national origin and by an ongoing historical violence of which the memory was, if Ernest Renan's famous formulation on the nation and forgetting is to be credited, too alive to permit a redemptive narrative of integration and unity.[1] The succession of conquests and catastrophes lacked what one Young Ireland leader called "the unity and purpose of an epic poem."[2] In comparison to the apparently continuous evolution of the British constitution, as it was rendered in both Whig and Burkean histories, Ireland's story seems one characterized by rupture and antagonism:

> One of the great social bonds which England—in fact, every other nation but ours—possesses, is the existence of some *institution* or *idea* towards the completion of which all have toiled in common, which comprehends all, and renders them respectable in each other's eyes. Thus her *history* knits together all ranks and sects in England ... Each has erected the story of the constitution. They value each other and acknowledge a connection. There are bright spots in our history; but of how few is the story common! And the contemplation of it, *as a whole*, does not tend to harmony, unless the conviction of past error produces wisdom for the future. We have no institution or idea that has been produced by all.[3]

One hundred years after partial decolonization, as commemoration hesitates on the brink of summoning the ghosts of civil war and partition, whose legacy remains the unresolved matter of the present, charged with restive memories and the potential for resurgent violence, Ireland remains haunted by the absence of a continuous narrative and a "common story."

That haunting may be—again, like the rhythmic pulsations of the unconscious—an effect produced precisely by the desire to let the past go, to "move on" from or repress the divisive and unresolved traumas of the past. As Renan saw, the memory of past violence, as much as the recurrence of violence in the present, troubles the legitimacy of any nation state whose foundations inevitably lie in that violence. The desire for a fictive continuity, for tradition itself, pairs the will to forge a common story with the equally compelling will to forget. Hence the impulse to forget past violence constitutes a civil violence in the present: the common story can only be sustained by the consignment of whatever does not fit the official narrative to oblivion or, what amounts to the same thing, to irrelevance for the present. In this respect, as the most astute theorists of nationalism have taught us, the continuous story that establishes the epic of tradition is none other than the progressive narrative of modernization: nationalism is the Janus-faced door through which the colonized enter into their modernity.[4] Tradition selects what, out of the polymorphous repertoire of cultural practices, will serve the project of national modernization. The frustration of the state that every successful nationalism institutes, no less than that of the colonial state that preceded it, lies in the obstinate persistence of those elements that live on long after they have been relegated to the past. Those elements represent the persistence in the modern of the counter-modern, whose unfulfilled potentials fracture the triumphalist tale of progress by laying their claim to be the alternative possibilities of the present. They hold open, and pass through, the gaps that the destructive violence of modernization, which is the brutal underside of progress, has left in its wake.

Discontinuity by no means precludes transmission. The uncanny phenomenon that the young IRA organizer Ernie O'Malley observed with some consternation in the countryside in 1920 may hold true for the culture at large:

> Areas of the country had a habit of going to sleep. They would wake up after a century or more and step into a gap. This unexpected quality was there in what I knew to be a bad area. It might awaken of itself: the times and situation might start the spark.[5]

Like the waters of Yeats's emblematic stream that "Run for a mile undimmed in Heaven's face / Then darkening through 'dark' Raftery's 'cellar' drop, / Run underground, rise in a rocky place . . .," transmission occurs in and through discontinuity.[6] This sense of discontinuity not as loss, but as the gapped fabric through which potentialities emerge unexpectedly and in new forms, impelled by the needs and conditions of the moment, offers another way to think about the phenomena of living on, transmission, passage, and invention that inhere in any culture. Such phenomena are no less intrinsic to that dimension of the culture that we think of loosely as its poetic tradition.

Irish poetry has notoriously been as marked by the specter of discontinuity as has the political culture. Pained expressions of this sense of the Irish poetic tradition's fragmentation and rupturing in consequence of colonial destruction, language loss, and lack of institutional transmission range from Thomas Davis's lament in the 1840s that there were "great gaps in Irish song" to Thomas Kinsella's backward look in the 1960s that revealed to him an insuperable gulf:

> I simply recognize that I stand on one side of a great rift, and can feel the discontinuity in myself. It is a matter of people and place as well as writing— of coming, so to speak, from a broken and uprooted family, of being drawn to those who share my origins and finding that we cannot share our lives.[7]

Davis, on the cusp of a new cultural nationalism's push to forge an Irish cultural consciousness and make it "racy of the soil," as *The Nation*'s banner famously proclaimed, imagined filling in those gaps through the willed artifice of translating what remained of "Irish Song" and inventing what he felt ought to have been found there. Thus the missing "unity and purpose of an epic poem," of a distinctive Irish culture worthy of an independent nationhood, might be restored. Kinsella, with a lived sense of the failure of the nationalist project fifty years after 1916 and with a close and jaundiced eye on the neocolonial developmentalism the recent opening of the Irish economy to global investment portended, finds no option for the poet but to embrace the historical "mutilation" of the culture as the very condition of writing: "The continuity or the mutilation of traditions becomes, in itself, irrelevant as the artist steps back from his entire world, mutilations and all, and absorbs it." Or, as he concludes the essay, mutilation itself is the matter of the work: "I am certain that a great part of the significance of my own past, as I try to write my poetry, is that the past *is* mutilated." Nor is this condition one that afflicts—or enables, as the case may be—only the Irish writer: "every writer in the modern world—since he can't be in all the literary traditions at once—is the inheritor of a gapped, discontinuous, polyglot tradition."[8]

From this perspective, a continuous literary and cultural tradition becomes itself an insular possession. The formerly envied unbroken story of the English poetic tradition comes to seem a sheltered preserve: it is, in Sean Golden's words, "an extension of the generally stable and balanced life lived against a Constable background" and a reactionary hedge against the "instability of the Modern period" that had "disrupted and displaced that balanced life permanently." Rather than a valued resource, poetic continuity becomes "essentially nostalgic, is an anti-Modernism disguised as traditionalism and constitutes a reactionary trend."[9] By contrast, Ireland's colonial history of violently imposed modernization, carried out by dispossession and famine, military occupation and Coercion Acts, eviction and enforced migration, and institutionalized by the most advanced and thorough set of state apparatuses in the Empire, "a project of modernisation . . . mediated by a state not of its own choosing," appears precocious and—in the context of global colonialism—more typical of modernity than any imagined continuous tradition with its civilly policed and well-groomed "Constable background" could be.[10] Kinsella's musings resonate powerfully with the great anti-colonial poet of negritude, Aimé Césaire: "all that was ever mutilated / has been mutilated in me." Like Césaire's Caribbean, Ireland was, in Declan Kiberd's words, "no provincial backwater" but, rather, "a test-case for modernity," even if that was the modernity of a culture whose own "moments of animation . . . have all been created in the face of possible extinction."[11]

Yet despite the availability of such insights, and the obstinacy with which rupture and discontinuity seem to insist on perpetuating themselves both temporally and spatially, critics of Irish poetry, together with the poets who participate in the critical conversation, have not abandoned the effort to establish lines of continuity. The fissures they seek to suture are multiple and not confined to the "great rift" that Davis and Kinsella both, in different ways, identified between an Irish language tradition mutilated by colonialism and the halting emergence of an Irish poetry in English across the nineteenth century, culminating in Yeats. But Yeats himself only constitutes a new rupture, as in study after study Irish poets "after Yeats" are seen to react against him but never quite to escape his shadow.[12] The agonistic reaction against Yeats, indeed, often seems to take the form of self-mutilation, as if the effort of rejection exhausts poetic promise, leading, for example, from Patrick Kavanagh's formally quite innovative if mind-numbingly misogynistic *The Great Hunger* (1942) to the inept (and no less misogynistic) ballads and later satires that Kinsella accurately characterizes as "a slapdash verse frequently not 'bothering' to say it, or to say it right."[13] Whatever permission Kavanagh offered to later Irish poets by the example of a less patrician and high-handed mode, its "parochial" voice came too often at the cost of adopting a stridently anti-intellectual stance and a poetic language that, while affecting a common speech, entirely accommodated the weakest legacies of Wordsworth's revolutionary poetics, filtered down though English Georgian and Movement poetics. As Coleridge long ago pointed out, with devastating precision, even Wordsworth's claim to have adopted "the language really spoken by men" and grounded in "low and rustic life" was a delusion that masked the fact that his diction was almost everywhere "the general language of cultivated society."[14] Coleridge's observations hold true, *mutatis mutandis*, for the work of virtually any Irish poet who claims Kavanagh as a forebear. What persists is an anxious familiarity, the need to appear as socially accessible as poetically legible, that disavows the facts of modernity: the atomization of society, the ever-increasing division of labor, and the consequent differentiations of its specialized languages that defy any pretension to a common language. Appeals to common language and the common reader stand revealed as threadbare invocations of a compensatory universality that colonial-capitalist modernity long ago put out of reach. In this light, the rejection of the later Yeats, that is, the refusal to come to terms with the rigorous violence and deconstructive force of his poetic language, is at one and the same time, as I will argue further, the disavowal rather than the contestation of modernity and its impact.

As numerous critics, including Kinsella, have indicated, the alternative lineage to that of Yeats finds its fountainhead not in a poet but in a prose-writer, James Joyce. In Kinsella's quite typical view, Joyce "simultaneously revives the Irish tradition and admits the modern world." Accordingly, where "Yeats stands for the Irish tradition as broken, Joyce stands for it as continuous, or healed—or healing—from its mutilation."[15] Significantly, Kinsella himself does not embrace that healing, but chooses to inhabit the mutilation. In general, however, the permission that Joyce offers lies far from the linguistic and formal innovations of his work that produced the difficulty and polyvocality of *Ulysses* and *Finnegans Wake*, resting instead on a reductive version of *Dubliners* and *A Portrait of the Artist as a Young Man*. Neither the polemical naturalism of the former nor the stylized symbolist aesthetics of the latter radically impacts Irish poetry, leaving only a diluted strain of naturalist mannerism to filter through. Joe Cleary has pointed to this pattern in both the Irish poetry and the fiction that assume Joyce's legacy:

> Naturalism's ascendancy in poetry was marked by Patrick Kavanagh's *The Great Hunger* (1942); it was Kavanagh, not Yeats, who became the dominant model for Irish poets during the second half of the twentieth century. In narrative fiction, it was the early naturalistic Joyce of *Dubliners* and *Portrait of the Artist*, and not *Ulysses*, that exerted by far the most decisive influence on the development of Irish writing in the post-Independence period.[16]

Cleary goes on to identify the "aesthetic conservatism" that afflicted post-independence Irish writing in every genre, its retreat from "the altogether more outward-looking and experimental modernists" that led to its replication of "the very condition of backwardness or inward-looking provincialism that their own works protest."[17] The aesthetic conservatism, or timidity, that seems to overtake Irish culture even before the deaths of Joyce and Yeats doubtless correlates with a general antagonism to the figure of the artist as iconoclast or antagonist of social normalization, a suspicion militantly expressed by Kavanagh's comrade-in-writing Flann O'Brien in a hilarious but ultimately quite pathetic attack on Joyce, "A Bash in the Tunnel," that is more diagnostic of O'Brien himself and of the writerly culture around him than of the isolated and solipsistic artist whose satiric portrait he seeks to paint.[18] The very invocation of the early Joyce in preference to Yeats as "progenitor," to borrow Kenneth Keating's term, thus spells—*pace* Kinsella—not so much a healing or restoration of continuity as yet another mode of discontinuity, insofar as it legitimates a refusal to carry forward the logic of Joyce's specifically Irish modes of literary experimentalism and suspends the possibility of conjoining aesthetic radicalism and anti-colonial cultural innovation. This is not, despite O'Brien and Kavanagh's moralizing aesthetic conservatism, so much a question of individual tastes or preferences as it is one of the modes of aesthetic institutionalization that prevailed in Ireland's anti- and post-colonial societies. I will return to this point shortly.

As Kenneth Keating has suggested, Irish poetry "since Yeats" never attains the movement of agonistic rejection that leads, in Harold Bloom's famous argument, to the furtherance of a continual process of poetic innovation that he considers the attribute—in an unfortunate phrase—of the "strong poet."[19] The constant iteration of ruptures in transmission across the history of Irish poetry furnishes an overarching pattern against which a variety of other forms of discontinuity stand out. Some of those regard what Kinsella obliquely termed "a matter of people and place as well as writing":[20] they include the marked rural–urban divide that perhaps more accurately pits the Dublin-based literary and journalistic establishment, along with the hegemonic political and economic institutions, against other regions or provinces, including smaller cities and towns, as an effect of the Republic's endemic centralization. This effect of bureaucratic and institutional concentration may in part account for the peculiar convergence of aesthetic conservatism and a vociferously anti-establishment strain in the predominantly rural poetics that Kavanagh's influence promoted and in relation to which Dublin poets, like Kinsella or Austin Clarke, suffered a critical eclipse.[21]

Yet more significant than the fallout of Ireland's cultural and geographical antagonisms is the less easily explained phenomenon of critical indifference. Louis MacNeice and Denis Devlin, whose publications bridged the 1930s and 1940s and who had, in very different modes, the substance and intelligence as well as the formal gifts to offer an alternative poetic model to that of Yeats, were almost entirely ignored at a moment when their work might have offered new possibilities to younger poets working in Ireland. The reasons for their lack of reception and influence are surely complex and made all the more perplexing by the evident compatibility of their modes of writing with the simultaneously emerging critical tenets of English Practical Criticism and its US counterpart, the New Criticism.[22] Both combined exacting, even metaphysical complexity with poetic formalism, furnishing modes of conservative modernism that could already have sustained the kinds of reading practice that eventually came to dominate the Irish critical establishment from the 1960s. Doubtless their residence outside Ireland, MacNeice in London and Devlin the diplomat in New York and Rome, at a time when Ireland had become increasingly inward looking, had a significant role to play in the critical neglect of their work. But it was scarcely inevitable. If, on the one hand, it is difficult for any society whose most vital artists and intellectuals migrate under economic if not social pressure to maintain an ongoing critical dialogue with itself, on the other hand, the sense of cultural isolation that extensive emigration produces must be counterpoised by the consequent potential for cultural openness and porosity to exogamous possibilities that migration furnishes. An island is not necessarily insular; the sea is a mode of transport and communication as much as it marks a boundary and a barrier. But, as I shall discuss, the institutional context for their reception was lacking in Ireland at the time, especially in the South, and they had little impact on the direction taken by what became the dominant Irish mode and the more or less established lineage that leads across partition from the "one and only bard" Kavanagh to Seamus Heaney.[23]

Heaney's debt to Kavanagh, and his own emergence as a global poetic phenomenon, suggest that discontinuity across partition and the rural–urban divide were far less marked in the distinct Northern Irish poetic "renaissance" that took shape in the 1960s, highlighting yet another spatial discontinuity, that between the separate cultural contexts of Northern Ireland and the Republic. We need not dwell here on the reasons for and dynamics of that post-partition phenomenon of separate development, which mainly exacerbated an already existing set of regional disparities.[24] In terms of both poetic context and publishing history, however, it may have been decisive for the continuing asymmetry between poetic cultures North and South. Dillon Johnston has painfully recorded the struggles of Dublin-based (or oriented) poets like Kinsella and John Montague to bridge the contradiction between seeking publication, audience, and critical recognition from England's far larger reading public and developing specifically Irish modes and materials in opposition to dominant English styles.[25] To the contrary, Johnston suggests, Northern Irish poets joined the wider circuits of British publishing, not least because their work accorded aesthetically with the conservative poetics of the Movement anti-modernism that their celebrated teacher at Queens, Philip Hobsbaum, advocated.[26] As I argue in Chapter 5, it is precisely the violent breakdown of state institutions and the consequent counter-insurgency campaign—a distinct form of state-directed modernization—that transformed Northern Ireland in the 1970s and shaped the context for formal innovation among some of its poets. Not only Northern Ireland's integration within the United Kingdom, but also the continuing cultures of resistance to that integration established the conditions for a poetic practice that differed from those that prevailed in the South with its waning postcolonial consciousness and distinct path to globalization and economic dependency.

We need not belabor further the well-documented phenomenon of the anti-modernist turn that Irish writing mostly took in the wake of the Revival and that continues to prevail. Nonetheless, it is important to specify the mode of modernism against which, in the first instance, it reacted, especially given that such a reaction could be regarded, as Frank Hutton-Williams has pointed out, "as part of a broader international reaction against modernism," especially in the anglophone world.[27] In the most general sense, modernism can be understood as the radical extension of art's claim to autonomy that cuts across the periodization of Romanticism, realism, and modernism. Theorized in time with the first revolutionary upsurge of Romanticism and with the circum-Atlantic political revolutions of the United States, France, San Domingo/Haiti, and Ireland, the emancipation of art in this moment concerned principally its social function and its corresponding mode of production.[28] The artist ceased to produce in the service of Church, State, or even patron, and became a free agent, producing artworks that were considered ends in themselves and that rendered the image of the newly emancipated individual of bourgeois society as likewise an end in itself. Art nonetheless retained a social function, that of representation in the broadest sense. On one level, the artwork, whether the lyric poem or the realist novel, Wordsworth or Balzac, represents the individual in contradictory relation to both the natural world and the social one that is defined by its opposition to nature. The nature of the earth and the nature of the individual as natural born person stand over against what Georg Lukács called "second nature," "the nature of man-made structures," with which the bourgeois novel-hero comes to integrate.[29] On another level, art seeks the reconciliation of these contradictions, written into its own social being, riven as it is between the ideal of autonomy and its status as commodity, in the production of representative subjects, those lyric Is or novel protagonists whose individuality and social existence converge in their typicality: the work and its form alike stand for a universality that transcends division and contradiction.

This conception of art as representative, in the rich, layered sense that the concept took on, determined the political and pedagogical function with which it was tasked as a free-standing institution, despite or even because of the claim to autonomy and its detachment from "the praxis of life," as Peter Bürger puts it.[30] However much individual artworks might challenge the specific injustices or forms of alienation that capitalist society spawned, they rendered the image of the formal representative subject that transcended the manifold divisions with which the social was riven. This fundamentally Schillerian project continues, even in the wake of twentieth-century challenges to aesthetic institutions, to inform at the most banal levels the pedagogy of the aesthetic: terms like representation and representativeness, identification, development, and universality remain the seemingly inexpungible vocabulary of the literary classroom and the museum catalog, betraying the continuing "common sense" of aesthetic institutions.[31]

Following hard on the normalization and institutionalization of this initially insurgent aesthetic regime, modernism seeks not to overthrow, but to intensify it. Modernism's break with Romanticism and realism takes the form of pushing aesthetic autonomy further, emancipating the artwork from the demands of representation, not only in the form of the burden of mimetic depiction and narrative development, but also with regard to the category of representativeness: alienation and social disintegration rather than reconciliation are the hallmarks of modernism. And yet, as Alex Davis puts it, "modernism, for all its apparent rupture with the past, preserves and, indeed, intensifies the primary function of art within Western society."[32] Modernism carries forward the specialization of art and of the artist that was always the contradiction in the Romantic conception of the genius—at once inimitable and representative. The artist becomes a practitioner of a specific mode and means of production and produces artworks to be enjoyed or appreciated according to a correspondingly specific mode of consumption. Paradoxically, the alienation of the artist is absorbed into a social function that requires the institutionalization of the work; within the institution, the consumer sees their own alienation reflected back as a confirmation of their unique and special individuality, along with everyone else. Where the Romantic artist could still aspire to speak to and for the masses or humanity in general, the modernist artist speaks to a public at once gathered and atomized within the museum or the cinema, or to the classroom of obedient exegetes. In continuity with the Schillerian project, art continues to produce the spaces in which a compensatory aesthetic experience of freedom and spontaneity furnishes momentary relief from the relentless heteronomy of social life. At the same time, those spaces reproduce heteronomy in their standardization of the conditions and the responses to aesthetic work. The special feeling of aesthetic uplift is all too reproducible.

Thus the enduring complaint of aesthetic populists, that the abstraction or obscurity of modernist work repels the "common man," grasps the phenomenon in reverse: the trajectory of art's emancipation from prescribed social functions and its corresponding confinement in institutions dedicated to a specialized, pedagogically reproducible mode of consumption entails art's self-reflexive problematization of itself and of its conditions in what Bürger calls "the ever-increasing concentration the makers of art bring to the medium itself."[33] As the painting is gradually freed to be what painting essentially is, a flat surface covered in colors, as the novel increasingly narrates its own narration and foregrounds its stylistic performances, that effect of specialization is at once the cost of emancipation and the rationale for art's institutionalization:

> At the moment it has shed all that is alien to it, art necessarily becomes problematic for itself. As institution and content coincide, social ineffectuality stands revealed as the essence of art in bourgeois society, and thus provokes the self-criticism of art.[34]

Bürger goes on to argue that the avant-garde is defined not as a form of advanced modernism, for all that modernism is driven by its own conditions to ceaseless innovation, but over against modernism, as a radical critique of the institutions of art that its actual practices seek to overthrow in the name of dissolving the boundaries that have come to separate art and "the praxis of life." For all the contradictions of the avant-garde—not least that its rationale depended on the institutionalization of art under modernism—and its eventual failure "to organize a new life praxis from a basis in art," the avant-garde's attack on art "did make art recognizable as an institution" and did so irrevocably: "All art more recent than the historical avant-garde movements must come to terms with this fact in bourgeois society."[35] This is a point to which we will return.

Canonical as it may seem, however, this more or less accepted account of the characteristics and conditions of modernism demands to be reconsidered in the "semi-colonial" context of Ireland. The forms of modernism against which post-independence Irish writers react, with consequences that continue to reverberate down to the present, do not correspond in the main to those that emerged in London or Paris, Berlin or New York. On the contrary, Irish modernism manifested in what we still know as "The Revival," though what precisely was being revived remains in question. As Terence Brown has noted, "the Revival's distinguishing literary forms in its nationalist context were those which in several respects anticipated and paralleled what commentators have isolated as the nexus of features which allow the term modernism such critical valency as it possesses."[36] To be sure, the work of the Revival was intensely aware of and open to the multiple strands of artistic practice and intellectual experiment that composed the complex international movement that was Modernism: Yeats absorbed in his fashion the doctrines of symbolism as much as those of Madame Blavatsky and later took what he needed from Pound and the Imagists. At the same time, a key volume that encapsulated the Revival's counter-modern principles, a collection of essays by Irish cultural nationalists from D. P. Moran to AE and Yeats himself and edited by Lady Gregory, *Ideals in Ireland*, could be prefaced by an epigraph that places Walt Whitman and Turgenev alongside Douglas Hyde.[37] Both Yeats and Synge, as Gregory Castle has shown, absorbed the methods of current French ethnography and were at the same time attuned to developments in European theatre from Ibsen to Strindberg to Chekov.[38] For all the pastel mysticism of his poetry and painting, AE drew the other side of his cultural practice, the co-operative movement, from advanced European models. The rejection of English colonial experiments on Irish society was not the rejection of modernity in its entirety. But the openness of the Revival to the diverse currents of international modernism does not alter the fact that the conditions out of which Irish modernism and its specific institutions emerged differed radically from those of their Western European or US counterparts. Ireland's colonial status changed everything. What the Revival represented was a modernism seeking to counter a modernizing process "compromised by its colonial source," rather than "a modernity of which the Irish have been the agents."[39]

Irish aesthetic modernism was, unlike those of metropolitan and mostly colonial powers, embedded in the larger context of a nationalist anti-colonial struggle for which emancipation was a collective rather than an individual project and the emancipation of art subordinated to that political project. Under colonial conditions, the colonized lack those institutions of art that correspond to the autonomy of the artist, whether one thinks of the art colleges and museums whose absence Thomas

Davis lamented in the 1840s, or of the cultural pedagogy undertaken by schools, or of institutions like the theatre or concert hall in which the performance of the autonomous work found its proper element. Even the publishing industry and the literary marketplace fret in the shadow of their imperial counterparts. The practical work of the cultural nationalist movement, from the Irish Literary Theatre to the Language League or the Gaelic Athletic Association, was devoted to constituting "nation-forming" para-state institutions that could displace those that had been introduced by the colonial regime and that the colonized populace did not control. Of necessity, these were not institutions that sought to furnish ideal conditions for aesthetic contemplation. On the contrary, they were designed to effect a counter-hegemonic mobilization of the populace through forming its consciousness and directing its desire in the service of the nation. Yeats among others was vividly aware of this function of art as "praxis of life" that was in actual fact intended both to shape and to "send out certain men" (and women) to take up arms against the British Empire, as he would put it in the late poem "Man and the Echo." Under such conditions, the formation of aesthetic institutions participates in an insurgent institutionalization of art quite at odds with the state-oriented academic or cultural institutions that modernism and the avant-garde successively required and contested elsewhere in Europe.[40]

The specifically colonial situation of the aesthetic, in Ireland and elsewhere, does not fail to produce contradictions, but they are different ones that produce a distinctly colonial mode of modernism. The autonomy of art finds itself in contradiction not only with its status as commodity, as post-Romantic writers from Charles Baudelaire to George Eliot keenly apprehended, but with the demands of nationalism that were at one and the same time the condition of the colonial artist's independence. At least until 1916, Yeats was preoccupied with the effort to establish his work as at once modernist in its autotelic forms and yet the expression of a distinct Irish culture that the poems and plays were devoted to forging.[41] Joyce's post-Revivalist *Portrait of the Artist* plays the extreme Satanic antagonism and alienation of the artist against the nets of "nationality, language, religion" that appear to define that distinctive culture, but still in the name of forging "the uncreated conscience" of his race.[42] For all each writer's convergence with and appropriation into international modernism, their work remains at some distance in its aims and effects from the modernist consummation of an artistic autonomy emblematic of human freedom in general.

The institutionalization of modernism within the insurgent cultural formations of a nationalist movement did not spare Irish writers from the epochal contradictions of aesthetic work. But it did inflect further Irish developments in both literature and criticism quite differently than in Western Europe. For one thing, nationalist cultural organizations had sought to take the place of the academic and pedagogical institutions that Ireland still lacked, as the Hugh Lane gallery controversy discussed in Chapter 3 dramatized, and thus could scarcely generate an avant-gardist reaction to modernism as Bürger theorizes it. The tendencies that would have "called art into question" in the post-Revival period were at best scarce and marked by a derivativeness that could find little purchase in the culture to sustain them. The handful of efforts in this direction, from the single-issue journal *Klaxon* in the 1920s to Beckett's parodic scholarly essays and performances of the early 1930s, or the experiments of the Dublin Drama League with international theatrical work, could have limited resonance in a post-independence state notoriously uninterested in funding the arts and whose institutional weakness was inversely proportional to the proliferation of its draconian censorship laws. Institutionally, the Northern statelet that developed alongside the Free State was no less inhospitable to the arts, for their own sake or any other.[43] Besides, as Lionel Pilkington has persuasively shown, especially in relation to the theatre, the actual critique of the institutions of art took a quite different form in a "regular recourse to a kind of theatricality, manifested in the riot and in labor militancy" and in protests whose performative conventions had deep roots in other areas of Irish popular culture and scandalized polite aesthetic taste.[44]

It was not that efforts to advance the aesthetic innovations of modernism were foreclosed: the exceptional artistic careers of Beckett and—perhaps more surprisingly, given his early association with the Revival and lifelong residence in Ireland—the painter Jack B. Yeats prove otherwise. Thomas MacGreevy astutely noted the ways in which the collapse of political and cultural representation in colonial Ireland created the conditions for the painter's radical formal departures in his later work and related it to his ongoing republicanism.[45] By and large, however, the postcolonial moment saw a reaction against Revival modernism that took the paradoxical form of a weak assertion of aesthetic autonomy against the Free State's counter-revolutionary reaction and a desire to bridge the antagonism between art and life in a manner as far removed from avant-gardism as could be. The autonomy of art takes the weak form of its withdrawal from the sphere of cultural politics that its earlier association with an insurgent nationalism had entailed. The defense of artistic freedom against state censorship posed art against the post-independence state and its conservative nationalism rather than against cultural institutions that remained in any case underdeveloped. In consequence, as Gerry Smyth has argued, by the 1950s, "there were thus fewer spaces in civil society where the relationship between literature and nation could be analyzed" while the "nationalist establishment" denied to "intellectual discourse the space for intervention it had enjoyed during the revolutionary period, and by means of which it had played so important a part in the anti-colonial struggle."[46]

Despite the fact that many of those who dominated Irish writing in the 1930s and 1940s—Seán Ó Faoláin, Liam O'Flaherty, Frank O'Connor, Ernie O'Malley, Peadar O'Donnell—were former Republicans who had opposed the Treaty and criticized the Free State, that opposition left unchallenged and even promoted the formal conservatism that Joe Cleary identifies as the dominant mode in which Irish anti-modernism was cast. The adherence to established formal conventions and the rejection of the "self-problematization of art" barred precisely the manifestations of "difficulty" through which modernist artists had found the means to resist their work's complete absorption into the institutions of art. In a manner remarkably in tune with the appeal to "common sense" that Beckett observed to be the foundation of the censor's discriminating judgments, Irish anti-modernism finds its means to dissolve the separation of art and life in a plain style that places none of the demands on active reading that modernism required.[47] The steady lapse of Kavanagh in poetry and Flann O'Brien in his novels from modernist experiment to aggressively conventional forms and sentimental moralism is emblematic of the limits of the Irish reaction against its own modernism.[48] As Seamus Deane remarked, "the attraction of the Free State world, in its ready-made language, cliché, consensus, is that it is a shared world, that it observes, even relishes limitation."[49] The caustic protest against his most transformative work that O'Brien puts into the mouth of his aging James Joyce in *The Dalkey Archive* seems only to predict the vituperations of contemporary critics against modernism and experiment even as it expresses the antagonism of Dublin's bar-room bohemia of the 1940s and 1950s against the figure of the artist.

O'Brien's flight into domestic values and his revisionary repudiation of his early formal inventions is symptomatic of a larger tendency in Irish writing to withdraw from social critique in the name of a depoliticization of art whose alibi in anti-nationalism could only resort to a dull, common-sensical version of art's representative and universal claims. To cite Deane's remarks on O'Brien again, "it had given up a system of representation, whose literary expression was modernism, for a representative system, whose literary expression was anti-modernist bureaucratese."[50] An abstract notion of the common man as public— the very object and addressee of a bureaucratic language—replaces the engaged and mobilizing force of Revival modernism. But the conditions of an Irish anti-modernism, which perforce framed its reaction in the context of the political and cultural failures of the post-partition states and as a universalizing transcendence of nationalist insularity, foreclosed the vantage point that might have registered that the Revival's version of modernism had been neither insular nor backward, but part of a wider social movement that sought to trace in all that the damage of Ireland's colonial modernization has let survive the possibilities of an alternative path within modernity. Indeed, a collection like *Ideals in Ireland* was eloquent testimony to that effort, including the contradictions and divergent approaches it entailed. The difficulty of Revival modernism lay, if anywhere, in its defiance of the "progressive" common sense of colonial modernity.

What I have mapped here in the initial anti-modernist reaction against Revival—or anti-colonial—Irish modernism was staged and articulated mostly by the writers themselves. Their reaction took place—as Gerry Smyth has shown in great detail—in the absence of any native version of the strong or "professional" literary critical institutions that were developing elsewhere in the anglophone world, in large part on the basis of precisely the modes of difficulty that modernist work embodied.[51] As Joyce himself had predicted, modernism gave rise to the scholarly investment in what are not unaptly known as the Yeats, Joyce, and, latterly, Beckett "industries."[52] Literary criticism in the academy to a great extent legitimated itself and its institutional growth through the endorsement of the confrontation with aesthetic difficulty as a mode of moral pedagogy, training the student in the virtues of "critical thinking" and an aesthetic discrimination that overlapped with ethical judgment.

The *difficulty* of the modernist work, despite its exemplification by internationally acknowledged Irish writers, became a principal target of the anti-modernist reaction from the 1930s through the 1960s—and even down to the present. It is the early work of Yeats, with its more accessible, late-Romantic textures, that furnished the model for those poets whom the young modernist Beckett dismisses in his caustic review, "Recent Irish Poetry," as the "antiquarians" or "thermolaters": whatever difficulty they may cause the reader lies rather in their arcane thematic material than in the formal qualities of the work. The later Yeats presented a more rebarbative—and largely neglected—set of possibilities that were easy to reject on the grounds of his eccentric patrician social fantasies, but at the cost of ignoring the radical and iconoclastic engagement with the founding violence of modernity and the state that lurks beneath his apparently traditionalist forms.[53] And if, as Cleary suggests, the Joyce of *Dubliners* and *A Portrait* remained palatable, *Ulysses* had to be reduced to its realistic renderings of Dublin locutions or locations and its formal energies ignored. Anti-intellectualism, paired with an aggressive disdain for the "artist," reproduces in the literary sphere the very insularity and conservative anti-modernity of the Free State against which naturalism directs its discontent. To contemporaneous social and literary critics as different as F. R. Leavis and Theodor Adorno, it was apparent that the difficulty of modernism in general derived not from the willful esotericism of the soi-disant artist, but from the effort to register the contradictions of modernity and the obstacle that its multiple and ever more complex divisions of language, labor, and social spheres posed to the legibility of the text and the social totality alike.[54]

Thus the urge, so clearly expressed by Ó Faoláin, for art to be "a vital part of common life" necessarily entails his aversion from the institutional professionalism of "the New Criticism" even though his adherence to the autonomy and universality of the literary sphere accords very well with its founding principles. Such unresolved contradictions, serenely held in what persisted of a literary public sphere through the 1950s, consorted with the philological bent of the academic study of Irish language literature and the residual English literature curricula of the major Irish universities, as Smyth has exhaustively documented.[55] This arrested the emergence of an indigenous Irish critical discourse even as the works it rejected were becoming the privileged matter of the post-war critical industries of an increasingly specialized, professional, and international criticism. Faced with the domination of the study of Irish literature by an "international scholarly élite," Ireland saw the belated emergence of a more specialized academic literary criticism in the shadow of and beholden to global developments. Much as the Irish modernization process that got under way in the 1960s manifested all the symptoms and vulnerabilities of dependency, Irish literary criticism gradually absorbed international models and methods while at the same time losing purchase on the specificity of Irish historical experience and the peculiar vantage point it had to offer to the developing colonial capitalist world of the post-war era.[56] The flight into things like regionalism or "parochialism" offered a short-circuit from the particular to the universal that secured Irish writing a niche in the global literary market, but it also served to suppress the critical insights that Ireland's own colonial history could have brought to bear on contemporary global developments.

We still lack any study of the institutionalization of international literary critical models in Ireland in the wake of Lemassian modernization or around Northern Ireland's brief period of liberalization under Terence O'Neill equivalent to Gerry Smyth's empirically detailed and theoretically sophisticated account of the previous decade. In a larger sense, we have yet to exhaust, particularly in the domain of poetry and poetics, the opportunities to produce, in Mark Quigley's words, "a more sustained longitudinal analysis that can allow us to discern discrete moments and aesthetic impulses arising within postcoloniality over time."[57] In particular, we need a full account of the ways in which critical institutions in the later postcolonial period shaped the reception and expectations of literary work in relation to the waning of the decolonizing project. Accordingly, the following effort at mapping the rise of an Irish academic literary criticism and its shaping of the parameters for the reception of poetic work must remain somewhat speculative. What can be seen, however, is that together with international methods, Irish literary criticism by and large adopted the militantly apolitical and effectively ahistorical stance that was intrinsic to the hegemonic function of departments of literature across the anglophone world. However much that academic critical discourse shaped itself around the challenging and unabashedly political work of modernist writers, right and left, from Yeats and Joyce to T. S. Eliot and Ezra Pound, its approach, with few exceptions, maintained a dehistoricized commitment to aesthetic autonomy and to a universalism for which the specific geographical and cultural conditions that inflected the work were matters of indifference or, at most, local color—a color readily enough supplied in the engaging anecdotes of Irish critics and poets alike.[58] The role of native informant is a tempting enough ticket to a footstool at the banquet.

Any challenge that radical modernism might have posed to the institutions and ideologies that it critiqued was defused by the very criticism that canonized and promoted it. The latter thus reduced modernism to performing what Bürger describes as "a specific function of art in bourgeois society: the neutralization of critique."[59] The emancipation of art from any programmatic social function then becomes its functionlessness, divorced from political engagement and subsumed into a generalized and civil stance of critical contemplation that displaces the commitments of critique. That was to be its function: deriving its tenets uncritically from those of an academic literary establishment housed in the more powerful institutions of Britain and North America, Irish literary criticism was thus perfectly placed to reproduce within a local academy that was growing apace with the new developmentalism's need for a well-educated population the depoliticizing anti-modernism that had circulated informally among the writers and in the non-academic periodicals of a previous generation. Literary pedagogy routinized the procedures of Practical Criticism, devoted to the "close reading" of well-made poems in order to descry in them the capacity to reconcile contradiction and ambivalence and to balance antagonisms in a manner conducive to the moral development of a subject schooled in liberal equivocation and averse to "one-sided" political or social commitments. In a world where all ambiguities resolve to gray, undecidability was reduced to indecision and critical intelligence to ever-suspended acts of "discrimination" modeled on the artist's supposed distantiation from the world. If the figure of the "common man" in pub or marketplace had become—with no less contradiction—the ideal of the "common reader," the well-schooled student of literature was the academic humanist equivalent of the apolitical technocrat of developmentalism.

Of course such ahistorical precepts have their histories, and where the anti-modernist reaction of the previous generation was coupled with an antagonism to the conservative nationalism that had institutionalized itself in the Free State in the wake of the historic defeat—and extra-judicial murder—of the main proponents of left Republicanism, the apolitical precepts of the new Irish criticism aligned perfectly with the post-nationalism of the new regimes on either side of the border. What began as the supercession of nationalist concerns in the name of a new—and uncritical—developmentalism was rapidly overtaken by events. In the face of the Northern Irish civil rights movement and the subsequent anti-colonial insurgency against the Northern settler state and its institutionalized discrimination, the literary critical establishment manifested the affinity of its "empiricist technocracy" with historical revisionism's academic reworking of anti-nationalism as anti-Republicanism.[60] In their methodological positivism and uncritical relation to the state institutions that housed them—and whose historical imposition under the auspices of colonial governance revisionism regards as the index of Britain's "improvement" of Ireland—the historian and the critic became the specialists of a counter-insurgency discourse that I have described at greater length elsewhere.[61]

In this discourse, the norms of "civility," with their deep colonial roots in Elizabethan racial discourse, and the institutions of a civil society that all too often furnished the ceremonial robes of Protestant supremacy, found their counterpart in the projection of an imagined atavism and entrapment in myth onto a criminalized insurgent population. This critical rhetoric of civilization vs. barbarity or, as it rapidly became, terror, which an anti-modernist and eagerly depoliticized poetry served all too well, could maintain its own apolitical pretensions and the autonomy of its objects only on the scarcely tenable assumption of the political neutrality of the states that were at once its condition and the end it served.[62] Nor was this a symptom only of the rearguard immune-response of an embattled Northern intelligentsia. Joe Cleary argues that both the UK and the Republic of Ireland state governments gradually evolved strategies and ideologies of containment designed to downplay as much as possible their own involvement in the struggle and to suggest that its roots lay exclusively in the intractable sectarianism of Northern Ireland's hostile communities.[63]

In this context, as Conor McCarthy emphasizes, intellectuals in the Republic "increasingly felt the need to mount a struggle in the ideological realm to prevent the spread of subversive ideas."[64] Ironically, perhaps, or logically, the exacerbation of the question of partition and its production of a discriminatory settler state north of the border led to an unprecedented convergence of the Northern and Southern cultural elites, whose specific class fraction committed them to a state-mediated project of modernization that simultaneously served the interests of pacification, not of any form of institutional or cultural decolonization. In the "intellectually impoverished" and externally driven climate of Irish modernization, there was no place for the disruptive force of new forms of critical modernism and little appreciation for the few avant-garde artistic practices that manifested mainly in theatrical street protests and in relation to social movements to which official cultural institutions were largely irrelevant.[65] If, as Desmond Bell and others have argued, Ireland seems to have lacked an avant-garde, and even a fully-fledged modernism, that has not been on account of its failure to modernize but because of the peculiar forms that both its colonial and postcolonial state-driven modernizations did take and because of the consequent misrecognition of what are characteristic conditions and forms of aesthetic modernism in decolonizing cultures.[66] Nonetheless, as McCarthy goes on to argue:

> The irony of the situation is that the reaction of the Southern state to the Northern violence was to shut out critical discourses—Marxist and neo-Marxist theories of economics, dependency and culture—that would have helped to explain the crisis *in the Republic*.[67]

The problem, however, was not the lack of "universalizing . . . public intellectuals," but a failure to understand Ireland's differential relation both to the networks of a burgeoning neoliberal capitalism and to a postcolonial world on which the new regimes of accumulation were being imposed.[68] What did emerge eventually and in a sustained way in the 1980s, and for the first time since the Revival, was a formation of literary and cultural critics whose work sought to reconsider Ireland's by then disavowed colonial past not simply in the framework of a binary nationalism discredited by its own withdrawal from the task of decolonization, but in relation to histories of colonialism and decolonization elsewhere. Doubtless this new investigation, whose motivations clearly exceeded individual curiosity, was impelled by the Troubles and by the urgency of reconsidering the theory and history of nationalism. Several decades of critical work on nationalism by political theorists had enabled a more dispassionate analysis; at the same time, the latent Eurocentrism and modernizing perspectives that hampered most scholars of nationalism, from Ernest Gellner or Elie Kedourie to Eric Hobsbawm and Tom Nairn, left the ongoing dynamics and contradictions of nationalist anti-colonial movements insufficiently explained. The theoretical and historical prejudice whose ideological function was all too clear in the Irish context, that nationalism mobilized the atavistic affects of the populace, was often hard to square with the rationalities of anti-colonial struggle and its knowing adaptations of contemporary technologies, from media to armaments, or with nationalism's generally modernizing programs and impacts, or with the constant invention of new cultural forms that thinkers like Frantz Fanon or Amílcar Cabral identified in the dynamics of liberation movements.

This approach to the legacies of both colonialism and nationalism, pioneered by the intellectuals and artists of the Field Day collective, especially under the directorship of Seamus Deane, opened the way for a more critical address to the legacies of colonialism and the anti-nationalist reaction. In turn, postcolonial theory, emerging as it did simultaneously out of other post-independence states that had suffered British rule—India, Pakistan, Palestine, Kenya, and Nigeria—offered a comparative—or, rather, differential—framework within which the peculiarities of Ireland's historical and cultural developments might be thrown into relief.[69] It offered a critical perspective on nationalism that did not abandon the decolonizing project. Rather than subsuming Ireland into the empty formal universality of aesthetic criticism, or lamenting its failure to pursue a normative path of capitalist industrial and technological development, postcolonial thought and the archival research it inspired allowed critics to rethink Ireland's specific histories as offering a singular vantage point on global processes of modernization, differentiated as those were by geographical and historical factors. Those processes were not ones behind which Ireland lagged, or with which it was boldly catching up. They were colonial interventions whose destructive impact had been felt in comparable ways in other sites. The recalcitrance of elements of Irish culture to a colonially imposed course of "improvement" was not an irrational adherence to backwardness, but embodied the potential, held in common with other colonized cultures, to realize alternative and more ecologically and socially rational sets of possibilities than those the colonial power sought to inculcate in the name of progress and development. Both the forms of modernization that Ireland underwent and the modes of its collective cultural, political, and economic resistance to them form part of the larger global history of modernity and of colonial capitalism and offer a quite specific coign of vantage from which their effects can be registered and theorized.

It is not, then, that Ireland failed to undergo the full panoply of modernizing processes and therefore failed to produce a fully-fledged modernity or its own aesthetic modernism, or that its various forms of nationalist experiment were shelters from the experience of dislocation that is supposedly one of the signatures of modernist alienation. Like historical and cultural discontinuity, dislocation was fundamental to the Irish experience, in the displacement from the land and the emigrants' consequent circulation through all the circuits of capital and empire. Nationalism itself is one of the effects of modernization, and can at times be highly innovative of cultural forms and practices wherever its emancipatory ends impel it to imagine otherwise. Likewise, Irish modernism registered the experience and the potential of modernity in ways that reflect not so much the alienation of the modern individual as a collective history of dispossession and displacement. The migrant laborer or tramp in flight from the law or the poetic-critic turned armed insurgent are not less figures of modernity than are the flaneur or the bank official. Nor is anti-colonial cultural mobilization necessarily any less formally innovative than urban life with its shocks and crowds: colonialism, as Luke Gibbons so eloquently showed, has its own modalities of "*external shocks*" and its own capacity to move the masses.[70] They may just be haunted by different ghosts made restless by modernity's ceaselessly destructive energies and in pursuit of alternative means by which to realize the potentials that live on through destruction.

It is with this sense of the complex and contradictory currents that relate the aesthetic formations of modernity to the violent processes of modernization that I have opted not to offer another account of the lineages of Irish innovative or experimental poetry that descend from its forebears in the 1930s, or to furnish one more study of the vicissitudes of the Irish poetic tradition, whether since Yeats or after Joyce. Rather, I conceive of the condition of modernity as it has been experienced in Ireland as one of the discontinuities occasioned by the external shocks and inner ruptures that a colonial and post-colonial society continually confronts. These conditions produce in those who, refusing either to adapt or to lament with consoling nostalgia the losses modernization everywhere inflicts, find poetic means to register and contest its prescriptions, in innovative forms that constitute what I am calling here, after Glissant, a counterpoetics of modernity. This counterpoetics, unlike the anti-modernism that has dominated criticism since partition and partial independence, is marked by its deep skepticism with regard to the association of a protected aesthetic realm with a freedom compensating for the constraint that prevails in every domain of modern life. Such a counterpoetics is committed to the reinvention of means to negotiate rather than to disavow those constraints and to draw them into both the matter and the form of the writing itself. That commitment is not the consequence of affiliating with any particular lineage, troubled as such formations are in the Irish context. It comes from a willingness, that I explore most fully in Chapter 5, to allow poetic form to emerge dialectically from its immersion in and transmutation by its material. This dialectic offers little space for the autonomous poet whose contemplative and observant gaze plays freely across the surface of the world; rather, the material, historical and determined through and through, changes both the subject and the form.

Notes

1. For Renan's remark on the nation and forgetting, see Ernest Renan, "What is a Nation?," translated by Martin Thom. *Nation and Narration*, edited by Homi Bhabha. Routledge, 1990, p. 11.
2. Charles Gavan Duffy, *Young Ireland: A Fragment of Irish History, 1840–1850.* Cassell, Petter, Calpin and Co., 1880, p. 297.
3. "The Individuality of a Native Literature." *The Nation*, August 21, 1847, p. 731. I discussed the Young Ireland anxiety to create a continuous and unifying "common story" by way of literary production at greater length in *Nationalism and Minor Literature: James Clarence Mangan and the Emergence of Irish Cultural Nationalism.* University of California Press, 1987, ch. 2.
4. Tom Nairn, "The Modern Janus." *The Break-Up of Britain: Crisis and Neo-Nationalism.* New Left Books, 1977, pp. 331-50.
5. Ernie O'Malley, *On Another Man's Wound*, edited by Cormac O'Malley, revised edition. Mercier Press, 2002, p. 163.
6. W. B. Yeats, "Coole Park and Ballylee, 1931" in *The Winding Stair. The Poems: A New Edition*, edited by Richard J. Finneran. Macmillan, 1983, p. 243.
7. Thomas Davis, "Irish Songs." *The Nation*, January 4, 1845, p. 314; Thomas Kinsella, "The Irish Writer." *Davis, Mangan Ferguson: Tradition and The Irish Writer.* Dolmen Press, 1970, p. 59.
8. Kinsella, "Irish Writer," pp. 65–6.
9. Sean Golden, "Post-Traditional English Literature: A Polemic." *The Crane Bag*, vol. 3, no. 2, 1979, pp. 7–8. "Constable background" is a phrase borrowed from Stanislaus Joyce's *My Brother's Keeper.* Viking Press, 1985, pp. 185–6. Jed Esty's *A Shrinking Island: Modernism and National Culture in England.* Princeton University Press, 2004, is an impressive

and extended demonstration of this turn to cultural insularity in English modernism.

10. Conor McCarthy, *Modernisation: Crisis and Culture in Ireland, 1969–1992*. Four Courts Press, 2000, p. 215. I have discussed this history of state-driven modernization at length in *Irish Culture and Colonial Modernity, 1800–2000: The Transformation of Oral Space*. Cambridge University Press, 2011.

11. See Aimé Césaire, "Lay of Errantry." *Corps Perdu/Lost Body: The Collected Poetry*, translated by Clayton Eshleman and Annette Smith. University of California Press, 1983, p. 255; Declan Kiberd, *Irish Classics*. Harvard University Press, 2001, pp. xiii and 21.

12. Kenneth Keating's introduction to his *Contemporary Irish Poetry and the Canon: Critical Limitations and Textual Liberations*. Palgrave Macmillan, 2017, "Spectres of Irish Poetry," is a witty and exhaustive study of this repetitive effort both to establish lines of continuity and to escape the "great progenitors," Yeats and Joyce. My own sense of haunting that frames Part I of this book is in tune with his sense of the spectral in Irish poetry, but more concerned with hauntings from Ireland's colonial culture than its critical and poetic tradition. I refer the reader to this introduction for an overview of the critical works that have perpetuated the "after Yeats or since Joyce syndrome" (p. 1). Trevor Joyce is an interesting exception to this pattern. In an interview with Marthine Satris, he comments that "Yeats is one of the main people I like to argue with, sometimes with particular lines or ideas in specific poems. He's a major figure for me, worth arguing with." For this and his comments on Yeats's and Joyce's own structuring of his poetry as "single works . . . deliberately balanced," see Marthine Satris, *Journal of British and Irish Innovative Poetry*, vol. 5, no. 1, 2013, p. 19.

13. Thomas Kinsella, *The Dual Tradition: An Essay on Poetry and Politics in Ireland*. Carcanet Press, 1995, p. 100.

14. Samuel Taylor Coleridge, *Biographia Literaria, or Biographical Sketches of My Literary Life and Opinions*, edited by George Watson. J. M. Dent and E. P. Dutton, 1975, pp. 188–200.

15. Kinsella, "The Irish Writer," p. 65.

16. Joe Cleary, "Capital and Culture in Twentieth-Century Ireland: Changing Configurations." *Outrageous Fortune: Capital and Culture in Modern Ireland*, 2nd edition. Field Day, 2007, p. 97.

17. Cleary, "Capital and Culture in Twentieth-Century Ireland," p. 98.

18. Flann O'Brien, "A Bash in the Tunnel." *Stories and Plays*. Penguin Books, 1977, p. 206. As Seamus Deane has pointed out, "O'Brien's battle with Joyce duplicates the Free State's battle with the Irish Renaissance. O'Brien's rebuke to Joyce is of a piece with Patrick Kavanagh's rebuke to Yeats and the Revival." Seamus Deane, *Strange Country: Modernity and Nationhood in Irish Writing Since 1790*. Oxford University Press, 1997, p. 158.

19. Harold Bloom, *The Anxiety of Influence*. Oxford University Press, 1973. Keating's "Spectres of Irish Poetry" is in many ways a subversive and anti-Oedipal rewriting of Bloom's argument, replacing the "anxiety of influence" with anxious haunting by literary forebears.

20. Kinsella, "Irish Writer," p. 59.

21. On Kinsella's loss of a specifically English readership, see Dillon Johnston, *The Poetic Economies of England and Ireland, 1912–2000*. Palgrave, 2001, p. 136. In a footnote, p. 219, n. 8, Johnson refers to Kinsella's "Butcher's Dozen," his ballad-form satire on British judicial whitewashing of the Bloody Sunday massacre in Derry, 1972, as having alienated his English public. It seems equally likely that the poem alienated an Irish literary culture that, as I explore further below, was largely allied with establishment counter-insurgency discourses by that time. On Clarke's neglect, see W. J. McCormack, "Austin Clarke: The Poet as Scapegoat of Modernism." *Modernism and Ireland: The Poetry of the 1930s*, edited by Patricia Coughlan and Alex Davis. Cork University Press, 1995, pp. 75–102.

22. See Alex Davis, *A Broken Line: Denis Devlin and Irish Poetic Modernism*. University College Dublin Press, 2000, pp. 55–73 on Devlin's reception by New Critics. Davis also discusses Devlin's relation to and difference from MacNeice, pp. 35–6.

23. Patrick Kavanagh, "The Same Again." *Collected Poems*. Martin Brian and O'Keeffe, 1972, p. 191. For Seamus Heaney's account of the "revelation and confirmation of reading Kavanagh" and how "Kavanagh gave you permission to dwell without cultural anxiety among the usual landmarks of your life," see "The Placeless Heaven: Another Look at Kavanagh." *The Government of the Tongue: Selected Prose, 1978–1987*. Farrar, Straus and Giroux, 1989, pp. 7–10.

24. On this phenomenon of distinct cultural developments north and south of the border, see Joe Cleary, *Literature, Partition and the Nation State: Culture and Conflict in Ireland, Israel and Palestine*. Cambridge University Press, 2002, p. 77–8. Of course, where the rural–urban divide may have left less of a mark on Northern poetry, the sectarian divide was all the more prominent, even in its disavowal.

25. See Dillon Johnston, *The Poetic Economies of England and Ireland, 1912–2000*. Palgrave, 2001, pp. 129–46.

26. Edna Longley, *The Living Stream: Literature and Revisionism in Ireland*. Bloodaxe Books, 1994, pp. 18–20 sheds light and cold water on the inflation of the influence of Philip Hobsbaum on the Belfast "Group" of poets of the 1960s, but suggests that "he helped to create a recognizable and recognized focus for poetry in the North"—a crucial contribution to publication by major British publishers.

27. Frank Hutton-Williams, "Against Irish Modernism." *Irish University Review*, special issue on "Irish Experimental Poetry," vol. 46, no. 1, Spring/ Summer 2016, p. 26.

28. See Peter Bürger, *Theory of the Avant-Garde*, translated by Michael Shaw, foreword by Jochen Schulte-Sasse. University of Minnesota Press, 1984, p. 26: "As regards the difficult question concerning the historical crystallization of art as an institution, it suffices if we observe in this context that this process came to conclusion about the same time as the struggle of the bourgeoisie for its emancipation." On the circum-Atlantic revolutionary upsurge and Ireland's place in it, see Peter Linebaugh, *Red Round Globe Hot Burning: A Tale at the Crossroads of Commons and Closure, of Love and Terror, of Race and Class, and of Kate and Ned Despard*. University of California Press, 2019.

29. Georg Lukács, *The Theory of the Novel: A Historico-Philosophical Essay on the Forms of Great Epic Literature*, translated by Anna Bostock. MIT Press, 1983, pp. 62–3.

30. Bürger, *Theory of the Avant-Garde*, p. 26.

31. For a fuller account of the "regime of representation," see David Lloyd and Paul Thomas, *Culture and the State*. Routledge, 1997 and David Lloyd, *Under Representation: The Racial Regime of Aesthetics*. Fordham University Press, 2019.

32. Davis, *Broken Line*, p. 29.

33. Bürger, *Theory of the Avant-Garde*, p. 27.

34. Bürger, *Theory of the Avant-Garde*, p. 27. Davis cites this passage also in *A Broken Line*, p. 30, and my own account of Modernism is greatly indebted to him, even if I take it in a somewhat different direction in what follows.

35. Bürger, *Theory of the Avant-Garde*, pp. 49–50 and 57.

36. Terence Brown, "Ireland, Modernism and the 1930s." *Modernism and Ireland: The Poetry of the 1930s*, edited by Patricia Coughlan and Alex Davis. Cork University Press, 1995, p. 34. Following Brown, my own argument runs against Desmond Bell's argument that "Ireland ... was largely untouched by the high tide of European modernism and cultural internationalism." See his "Ireland without Frontiers? The Challenge of the Communications Revolution." *Across the Frontiers: Ireland in the 1990s*, edited by Richard Kearney. Wolfhound Press, 1988, p. 228.

37. Lady Gregory, editor, *Ideals in Ireland*. Unicorn Press, 1901.

38. Gregory Castle, *Modernism and the Celtic Revival*. Cambridge University Press, 2001.

39. McCarthy, *Modernisation*, p. 215. The interest in Irish modernism shown by African American, Caribbean, and African writers, from Claude McKay to Chinua Achebe and Amiri Baraka, doubtless signals their recognition of their shared counter-modernity. Derek Walcott's *Omeros* may be the most well-known instance of that phenomenon. For some of the work that has begun to explore those corrections—still insufficiently reciprocated by Irish writers, it must be said—see Alison Donnell, Maria McGarrity, and Evelyn O'Callaghan, editors, *Caribbean Irish Connections: Interdisciplinary Perspectives*. University of the West Indies Press, 2015 and Peter D. O'Neill and David Lloyd, *The Black and Green Atlantic: Cross-Currents of the African and Irish Diasporas*. Palgrave Macmillan, 2009. The notion of a colonial "counter-modernity" is indebted to Paul Gilroy's phrase "countercultures of modernity" in *The Black Atlantic: Modernity and Double Consciousness*. Harvard University Press, 1993, ch. 1.

40. Terry Eagleton's inflection of this point reinforces it: "To take the Revival as a whole project ... is to observe a quite astonishing transgression of the frontiers between the aesthetic and the social, of a distinctively avant-gardist kind." *Heathcliff and the Great Hunger: Studies in Irish Culture*. Verso, 1995, p. 303.

41. On this and on Yeats's commitment to "deepen the political passion of the nation," see David Lloyd, "Nationalism and Postcolonialism." *W. B. Yeats in Context*, edited by David Holdeman and Ben Levitas. Cambridge University Press, 2010, pp. 180–2.

42. James Joyce, *A Portrait of the Artist as a Young Man*, edited by Seamus Deane. Penguin, 1992, pp. 220 and 276.

43. On *Klaxon* and the larger context for Irish poetic modernism in the early years of the Free State, see Tim Armstrong, "Muting the Klaxon: Poetry, History and Irish Modernism." *Modernism and Ireland: The Poetry of the 1930s*, edited by Patricia Coughlan and Alex Davis. Cork University Press, 1995, pp. 43–74. Armstrong argues that "the linguistic difficulty of Coffey and Devlin serves not to break a language (the original intention of the avant-garde) but to conserve it in a space beyond the always compromised world of social action" (p. 70). On Beckett's ambivalent involvement with the parody of Corneille, *Le Kid*, and his own spoof academic lecture, "Le Concentrisme," see James Knowlson, *Damned to Fame: the Life of Samuel Beckett*. Simon and Schuster, 1996, pp. 124–8. On the Dublin Drama League and its theatrical experiments, see Elaine Sisson, "'A Note on What Happened': Experimental Influences on the Irish Stage, 1919–1929." "Forum Kritika: Radical Theatre and Ireland (Part 2)." *Kritika Kultura*, vol. 15, 2010, pp. 132–48. Admittedly, it is a stretch to see even in the performances of international theatre or Irish experiments with expressionism a fully avant-garde counter-culture. On the lack of funding for the arts in the Free State and on "the general downgrading of cultural activity" North and South, see Gerry Smyth, *Decolonisation and Criticism: The Construction of Irish Literature*. Pluto Press, 1998, pp. 94–5 and 143.

44. Lionel Pilkington, *Theatre and the State in Twentieth-Century Ireland: Cultivating the People*. Routledge, 2001, pp. 86–111.

45. On the anti-representational nature of J. B. Yeats's later painting and its relation to a republican ethic, see David Lloyd, "Republics of Difference: Yeats, MacGreevy, Beckett." *Beckett's Thing: Painting and Theatre*. Edinburgh University Press, 2016, pp. 27–84.

46. Smyth, *Decolonisation and Criticism*, p. 162.

47. Samuel Beckett, *Disjecta: Miscellaneous Writings and a Dramatic Fragment*, edited with a foreword by Ruby Cohn. Grove Press, 1984, pp. 85–6.

48. As Smyth points out, this withdrawal from modernism by the writers had its counterpart in academic criticism across the same period: "The place where questions of national identity had, relatively recently, been raised with most force and insight—in Yeats's poetry and Joyce's fiction—is noticeably absent from all the research materials of this period. Perhaps more than any other factor, this lack of institutional engagement with the work of the two seminal figures in modern Irish intellectual history indicates the regressive modes of national consciousness in which Ireland was stuck at this time." See Smyth, *Decolonisation and Criticism*, p. 162.

49. Deane, *Strange Country*, p. 162.

50. Deane, *Strange Country*, p. 162. As Joe Cleary has pointed out to me (personal communication, May 1, 2021), Irish anti-modernism had as little in common with the leftist rejection of modernism by writers associated with the Popular Front, from Arthur Miller to Dashiell Hammett, as it did with writers who maintained "both modernist and communist commitments," such as George Oppen, Lorine Niedecker, or Muriel Rukeyser. For a study of poetic work outside the traditions of High Modernism, see

Joseph Harrington, *Poetry and the Public: The Social Form of Modern U.S. Poetics.* Wesleyan University Press, 2002.

51. On modernism, difficulty and the critical industry see, among many works, Leonard Diepeveen, *The Difficulties of Modernism.* Routledge, 2013, who traces the relation between the gradual specialization of the artist and the professionalization of the critic: see pp. 96–7 and passim.

52. On the emerging critical industry and the "international scholarly élite which began to dominate the study of Irish literature at this time," see Smyth, *Decolonisation and Criticism*, pp. 178–9.

53. Samuel Beckett, "Recent Irish Poetry." *Disjecta*, p. 70. Deane, *Strange Country*, p. 171, has commented on how for Yeats's occultism, "Violence is its foundational moment—therefore a constructive violence—and destructive violence is the terminal moment of modern rationality's history." However, I would say that Yeats's later poetry is actually attuned to and obsessed with the violence that underpins the rationality of the State. See David Lloyd, "The Poetics of Decision: Yeats, Benjamin and Schmitt." *Études Anglaises*, vol. 68, no. 4, October–December 2015, pp. 468–82.

54. See, for example, F. R. Leavis, *New Bearings in English Poetry.* Faber and Faber, 1932, and the full range of Adorno's work from *Dialectic of Enlightenment* (written with Max Horkheimer in 1944 and published in 1947) to *Negative Dialectics* (1966) and *Aesthetic Theory* (drafted 1956–69 and published in 1970). W. J. McCormack has remarked on the fact that "the impact of *Scrutiny* and *Horizon*, even of T.S. Eliot's *Criterion*, is nowhere evident" in Ireland through the 1950s. Cited in Smyth, *Decolonisation and Criticism*, p. 97.

55. On these developments, see Smyth, *Decolonisation and Criticism*, pp. 123–31, 149–62, and 178.

56. See Smyth, *Decolonisation and Criticism*, p. 199.

57. Mark Quigley, *Empire's Wake: Postcolonial Irish Writing and the Politics of Modern Literary Form.* Fordham University Press, 2013, p. 15. My account of Irish counter-modernism, which Quigley regards as a "postcolonial late modernism," is somewhat at odds with his challenging reading of both the postcolonial situation of the 1930s through the 1950s and of the politics of form that it entailed. Quigley argues that Irish late modernists "actually *make use* of their significant formal or stylistic departures from conventional modernism to pursue a critique of its shortcomings" (p. 6). Our different perspectives may have to do with his focus on prose rather than poetry, though that would open questions beyond the scope of this book.

58. Luke Gibbons, "Montage, Modernism and the City." *Transformations in Irish Culture.* Cork University Press, 1996, pp. 165–6, points to the fact that this divorce of the work from the specificities of Irish colonial history extends equally to "perceptive critics" like Franco Moretti for whom the politics of the work is of great import: "indeed, the more avant-garde the idiom, the less it has to do with what is perceived as the backward state of Irish culture." I discuss other manifestations of this critical prejudice in Chapter 4.

59. Bürger, *Theory of the Avant-Garde*, p. 13.

60. The term is Conor McCarthy's: see his *Modernisation*, p. 199. For a nuanced account of the mutual antagonism of nationalism and historical revisionism in Ireland and the affinity between historical and literary revisionism, see Deane, *Strange Country*, pp. 181–97.

61. On "counter-insurgency discourse" and its relation to counter-insurgency practices and techniques, see in particular David Lloyd, "Regarding Ireland in a Postcolonial Frame" and "True Stories: Cinema, History and Gender." *Ireland After History*. Cork University Press, 1999, pp. 37–52 and 53–76.

62. On the opposition of English civility to Irish barbarity, see Seamus Deane, "Civilians and Barbarians." *Ireland's Field Day*. University of Notre Dame Press, 1986, pp. 33–42. In *Strange Country*, p. 193, Deane remarks that revisionism "is an institution that denies the atrocities of colonialism in order to defend the state as an outgrowth of colonialism rather than the achievement—however flawed—of nationalism."

63. Cleary, *Literature, Partition and the Nation State*, p. 100.

64. McCarthy, *Modernisation*, p. 31.

65. For lively accounts of such protests and cultural events in Ireland since the 1960s, in West Belfast and in Dublin, see Robert Ballagh, *A Reluctant Memoir*. Head of Zeus, 2018.

66. Bell, "Ireland without Frontiers?," pp. 227–30. The phrase "intellectually impoverished" is McCarthy's: see *Modernisation*, p. 30. Quigley's *Empire's Wake* sees in Ireland's postcolonial late modernism "some of the earliest examples of postcolonial modernism . . . on the geopolitical or aesthetic peripheries" (p. 8).

67. McCarthy, *Modernisation*, p. 198.

68. McCarthy, *Modernisation*, p. 198.

69. On the necessity for a "differential" rather than comparative approach to the study of colonialism, see David Lloyd, "Introduction." *Ireland After History*, pp. 14–16.

70. Gibbons, "Montage, Modernism and the City," pp. 166–7. The cited phrase is taken by Gibbons from James Wills and Freeman Wills, *The Irish Nation: Its History and Its Biography*, vol. I. A. Fullerton and Co., 1876, p. 3. The cited passage insists again that Irish history "presents a dream-like succession of capricious and seemingly unconnected changes, without order or progress."

Chapter 2

Crossing Over:
On James Clarence Mangan's
"Spirits Everywhere"

A transition between the two moments of spirit, the ghost is just passing through.

Jacques Derrida[1]

Writing on James Clarence Mangan in the late 1970s and early 1980s, I was often overtaken by a sense of haunting, of possession, perhaps. Despite my frequent misgivings about the achievement of the poetry I was reading, misgivings amplified by the widespread assumption that few of Mangan's poems were worth critical consideration any more, the work refused to let me go. It was as if, from beyond the grave, the poet compelled attention. Fantastical as this confession may sound, and I do not know if the sensation is one shared by other readers of Mangan, it remains the case that in a very precise sense, Mangan's work is itself the scene of hauntings, and by no means unaware of itself as such. I think not only of the poet's lifelong interest in ghosts and ghost-seers, manifest most notably in his essay "Chapters on Ghostcraft," based extensively on the work of the German poet and spiritualist Justinus Kerner,[2] but also of the ways in which Mangan's work—as, indeed, I came to argue in my book on him—is itself a tissue of hauntings of various kinds. It constantly invokes the ghosts of other works, reminding us of the close relation between the work of citation and the force of the summons: to quote another work always risks summoning up not merely a brief and aphoristic fragment whose meaning is absorbed into the text that cites it, but the shadow of the whole other text whose appropriate limits as context can never finally be established. There lies always "within the lowest deep a lower deep," as Mangan reminds us in his autobiography, citing Milton's *Paradise Lost*, a work whose narrative of satanic rebellion haunted his own Gothic self-presentation as a kind of *poète maudit avant la lettre*.[3]

Above all, however, it is the practice of translation—the mode in which the vast majority of Mangan's writing appeared—that invokes the presence of haunting in the very structure of the work. Certainly any translation must be haunted by the specter of the original whose place it seeks to take, haunted both by a sense of inevitable inadequacy or failure with regard to its transmission of its urtext—a kind of debt or guilt (*Schuld*) towards it—and by a sense of betrayal that may amount to a killing of the spirit of the original. Translation theory itself, and particularly in Mangan's own time, is possessed by this metaphor of spirit, by the notion that in some sense the translation must transmit the "spirit of the original" if that work is to live again, be resurrected, or have an afterlife in the language of the translation. This was peculiarly so for nationalist traditions of translation, for which the pure transmission of the "spirit of the nation" through translation was an essential concern, but the metaphor of the spirit of a work, not unlike the spirit or "genius" of a place, pervades Romantic notions of creativity and interpretation, making of each work the body in which the spirit has its life or afterlife. For Walter Benjamin, working much later in the German tradition that produced so much of nineteenth-century translation theory, it is largely in translation that a work has its afterlife:

> Just as the manifestations of life are intimately connected with the phenomenon of life without being of importance to it, a translation issues from the original— not so much from its life as from its afterlife. For a translation comes later than the original, and since the important works of world literature never find their chosen translator at the time of their origin, their translation marks their stage of continued life. The idea of life and afterlife in works of art should be regarded with an entirely unmetaphorical objectivity.[4]

The notion of the afterlife of the work slips almost unobtrusively here from being a property of the original work to being an effect of translation. Benjamin's remark suggests to us, then, that it is not only that the work haunts the translation, but also that the work itself is no less haunted by its translations, by the various afterlives in which its spirit lives on, fragmentary or mutilated as it may be, occupying the material form of another language than its own.

It is perhaps for this reason that I have been haunted again, and for some time now, by a seemingly insignificant poem of Mangan's, entitled "Spirits Everywhere." The poem was published initially in the *Dublin University Magazine* series "Anthologia Germanica" that was for many years Mangan's staple mode of publication, along with the "Literae Orientales" in the same journal, the translations that he claimed to make from various West Asian languages. It was reprinted in John Mitchel's New York edition of the poems, but not in D. J. O'Donoghue's canon-establishing centenary edition of the Poems

(1903). Nor is it included in Sean Ryder's excellent *James Clarence Mangan: Selected Writings* (2004). The poem is a translation of one by the German poet Ludwig Uhland, entitled "Auf der Überfahrt," which could be literally translated as "On the Crossing Over" or, more loosely, "On the Ferry."[5] Uhland was in Mangan's time a still highly respected German writer of ballads and songs, compared by some even to Goethe and Schiller, though the former expressed some notorious contempt for the putative school of Schwabian poets of which Uhland was the major representative. Having been appropriated, despite his avowed and oppositional liberalism, and on account of a handful of nationalist ballads, by conservative and even Nazi critics, Uhland's reputation declined in the post-war period.[6] For Mangan, writing in Ireland in the 1840s, he may have represented an important figure on account of his engagement with politics, as a liberal nationalist and, briefly, political representative, as well as a scholar of German medieval literature. Now, however, the poems both seem like minor productions of minor poets. Be that as it may, "Spirits Everywhere" could still have something to tell us about the post-Romantic, even proto-modernist characteristics of Mangan's work as a translator, and perhaps about translation in general.

Mangan's title already signals the fact that this is by no means a literal translation, even if his version follows more or less accurately the development of the situation in Uhland's poem: the phrase "Spirits Everywhere" is certainly far from a literal translation of "Auf der Überfahrt." Indeed, the "unforced error" of this translation, its gratuitousness, where a more literal translation would have been both adequate and colloquial, is what continues to perplex and to haunt me. How does one get from "Auf der Überfahrt" to "Spirits Everywhere"? By what logic can the substitution of a general dissemination of spirit for an actual voyage across seem appropriate as an act of translation? This question becomes all the more pertinent in the light of Mangan's often-stressed awareness of the German term for translation, *Übersetzung*, which he frequently invokes in his denomination of his German translations as "Oversettings from the German." With an ironic gesture typical of Mangan's hints to the reader, the apparent felicity of his interlingual neologism actually disguises a misalignment. Where *Übersetzung* is the standard German term for translation, and nicely renders the primary meaning in the Latin root of a lateral movement (as in the translation of a bishop), its (mis)translation into a somewhat uncolloquial English as "oversetting" introduces to the field of its possible meanings the specter of an *overlay*, even as it retains the sense of movement, of movement from one side, or shore, to another. In the latter case, it activates the deep connection between translation and *transferre*, transfer or ferrying across, or, one might say, between translation and metaphor, *metaphorein*, the Greek term that also means to carry something across. Translation, like metaphor, establishes an identity across differences, if only by laying in abeyance the non-identical elements that it cannot subsume. At the same time, however, "oversetting" conveys—to remain with the connotations of transport— the sense of an elaboration, of an accretion of ornament or superfluous decoration that gilds or drapes the literal meaning of the original. Its ambiguity in this respect is like that of the German word that Mangan occasionally adopted as a pen-name, *Drechsler*, turner (in the sense of a wood-turner), but also elaborator, ornamenter.

As I have argued before, it is often the case in Mangan's translations that we are dealing with a very deliberate elaboration, one close to the etymological sense of that word as a "working out": even where they are in one or other sense parodic of their originals, his translations deliberately extend or project the logic of their originals in such a way as to draw out their inner logic, often in order to overturn (or overset) it. In the case of "Spirits Everywhere," we are dealing with the translation of a poem whose original title denotes indeed a process of *Übersetzung*, the carrying across or transfer of passengers from one shore to another.[7] That is, of course, the situation of the original poem: Uhland returns to a river that he has crossed many years before in the company of two companions, since deceased, and is reminded of them in his crossing over for the second time. These two companions, who had crossed the Neckar together with Uhland near Münster, were his maternal uncle, the priest Christian Eberhard Hoser, and the friend of his youth, Friedrich Harprecht, whose poems Uhland published posthumously. Both died in 1813, ten years before the date of the poem.[8] Thus, even before we come to his reflections on the spiritual (*geistig*) meaning of that repetition, the situation is already of itself a repetition that is figurative: the second crossing provokes a reflection that allows for its relation to the first to become an allegory of the spirit. Or, one might say, the repetition allows for the spiritualization of the first instance. What was in that first instance a mere contingent event becomes in the second a sublimation into meaning, and a meaning that is the presence of the spirit:

Geistig waren jene Stunden,
Geistern bin ich noch verbunden.

For Uhland, the relation that persists between his present self and the now dead companions that once crossed the same river with him is thus purely spiritual, in the sense that their afterlife with him lies in the act of memorial that is the poem's own process of sublimation into meaning and remembrance. The spiritual is a function of a repetition that mobilizes a metaphor: the death of his friends effects the transformation of the quotidian ferryman into Charon and of the river into Lethe against whose work of oblivion the poem stands. In its final stanza, the poet makes this explicit in not only paying the ferryman his own fare, but offering two coins more for the spirits of the erstwhile companions whose physical absence is converted by memory into spiritual presence:

> Nimm nur, Fährmann, nimm die Miete
> Die ich gerne dreifach biete!
> Zween, die mit mir überfuhren,
> Waren geistige Naturen.

Playing on the complex set of meanings that the German *Geist* retains, which embraces a range of shades from simply mind or wit to spirit, both in the sense of expressions like *esprit de corps* or spirit of the nation and in that of ghost, or evil spirit, Uhland transforms spirited companions into metaphorical ghostly presences. Having recalled the one as a quietly working "father figure" (*vatergleicher*) and the other as a young and stormy (*brausend*) warrior, as if they represented two tendencies of his own spiritual being, Uhland nonetheless affirms their pastness: "Zween, die mit mir überfuhren, / Waren geistige Naturen." The poem reckons the cost of its own sublimating metaphor in the deaths that made it possible.

Mangan's translation, in a fashion not unfamiliar to attentive readers of his work, elaborates the moment of wish-fulfillment that persists even in Uhland's self-conscious metaphor of spiritual bonds, and does so through a kind of mischievous literalization. Uhland's two *geistige Naturen* become suddenly present in the ferry, not as metaphors but as phantoms:

> For though thou seest them not, there stand
> Anear me two from the Phantomland!

The appearance of these phantoms—a term whose root is simply that, appearance, *phantasma*—is prepared for by Mangan's translation of Uhland's quite sober fourth stanza into a scenario of magic and fanciful dream, a Gothicizing movement that is common to his renderings of German romantic verse and part of a pattern of deliberate derealization that is sufficiently consistent to suggest critique rather than personal idiosyncrasy.[9] The stanza reads:

> Yet still, when Memory's necromancy
> Robes the Past in the hues of Fancy,
> Medreameth I hear and see the Twain
> With talk and smiles at my side again.

Necromancy, that art of summoning dead spirits, creates the illusion of an actual restoration to presence of the dear companions whom, as a more literal rendering of Uhland would have put it, Death had torn or snatched away (*Teure, die der Tod entrissen [hat]*).

The act of necromancy, as Mangan here represents it, succeeds in bringing phantoms to life precisely through its work of elaboration, "rob[ing] the Past with the hues of Fancy." It functions in this respect as a kind of allegory for the work of translation, not only as Mangan performs it, but also as Benjamin later comes to theorize it. If we take seriously Benjamin's contention that the work lives its afterlife in translation, translation becomes a form of possession or of necromancy: the original parasitically inhabits the translation or the translator summons the spirit of the work from the shell of its decayed self to live again in another body. Furthermore, the test of good or "genuine" translation is not, for Benjamin, its capacity for the accurate or even approximate transmission of some content, but, rather, a process that compensates for the ill-fit between the spirit of the original and the language of the translation by a kind of enrobing:

> In translation, the original rises into a higher and purer linguistic air, as it were. . . . The transfer can never be total, but what reaches this region is that element in a translation which goes beyond transmittal of subject matter. This nucleus is best defined as the element that does not lend itself to translation. Even when all the surface content has been extracted and transmitted, the primary concern of the genuine translator remains elusive. Unlike the words of the original, it is not translatable, because the relationship between content and language is quite different in the original and the translation. While content and language form a certain unity in the original, like a fruit and its skin, the language of the translation envelops its content like a royal robe with ample folds.[10]

Translation is, paradoxically, both sublimation "into a higher and purer linguistic air" and a form of elaborate overlay. We could think of Mangan's translation of Uhland as performing both movements simultaneously: its somewhat baroque elaboration of Uhland's dry and sober language, signaled self-reflexively in Mangan's characteristic adoption of a language of allegory that was already anachronistic in his own time, is crucial to his derealizing projection of a poem that was already a meditation on metaphorical sublimation.[11]

In doing so, Mangan's translation at once figures and enacts its distance from that dominant ideal conception of translation of his moment, which effectively prescribed the transfer of the "spirit" of the original into the translation's language. Such theories, which understood translation as a kind of resurrection of the spirit in a new body, were continuous with Romantic theories of poetic composition in general as a constant return to the inspirational sources of human creativity.[12] They are correspondingly remote both from Mangan's allegorical "robing" of the original and from Benjamin's similar later theorization of translation that emphasizes the necessity for the translation *not* to reproduce the original. For Benjamin, it is the very condition of a living language that meaning alters and decays and that this process of transformation, "one of the most fruitful historical processes," in turn means that "the tenor and significance of the great works of literature undergo a complete transformation over the centuries."[13] Accordingly, if paradoxically, the afterlife of the work lies in the death of its original spirit, not in its reproduction either in later reading or in translation,

> no translation would be possible if in its ultimate essence it strove for likeness to the original. For in its afterlife—which could not be called that if it were not a transformation and a renewal of something living—the original undergoes a change.[14]

Accordingly, the proper metaphor for translation is neither the organic one of recreating the work from its creative seed nor the theological one of resurrecting its self-identical spirit in a new body, but rather that of the proximity of two distinct entities:

> What remains for sense, in its importance for the relationship between translation and original, may be expressed in the following simile. Just as a tangent touches a circle lightly and at but one point—establishing, with this touch rather than with the point, the law according to which it is to continue on its straight path to infinity—a translation touches the original lightly and only at the infinitely small point of the sense, thereupon pursuing its own course according to the laws of fidelity in the freedom of linguistic flux.[15]

Translation, like the practice of necromancy that also operates according to the laws of similitude and contiguity, brings two languages into proximity by aligning two works in such a way that what takes place is not the reproduction of the one in another but a kind of deflection of meaning.[16] This simile of Benjamin's is mathematical, but by the same token, the "ample folds" of a robe equally take shape by their contact with the body they envelope but are not entirely changed or solely informed by it, in so far as they continue to obey the laws of their own fabric and textures. The approximation of the translation to the original is rather one of juxtaposition and divergence than of an asymptotic approach to identity. Translation is as much a departure, a setting off on its own way, as it is an attempt at equivalence. It exists in proximity to its original, following its own path, a "parallel text" rather than a convergent one.

These reflections allow us to pursue yet further the ways in which Mangan's translation may also stand as a reflection upon translation itself. His version of Uhland is peculiarly seeded with metaphors of proximity or adjacency that have no equivalent in the original, which emphasizes rather the irredeemable separation of death: *so ist er auch geschieden; Teure, die der Tod entrissen*. Mangan introduces the notion of "nearness" early in the poem and reiterates it several times:

> Beside me then in this bark sat *nearest*
> Two companions the best and dearest;
>
> Medreameth I hear and see the Twain
> With talk and smile *at my side* again!
>
> For, though thou seest them not, there stand
> *Anear me* two from the Phantomland.

We have seen how that final couplet transforms Uhland's stoical acknowledgment of the pastness of his friends into an assertion of the ghostly reappearance of their spirits in a paradoxical spectral presence—one whose paradoxes, indeed, we have yet to exhaust. Mangan's transformation of Uhland is justified by a previous line that boldly asserts the relation between death and nearness: "It is *after* Life they are truly nigh!" By permission, as it were, of Benjamin's essay, we may see this line not only as a somewhat heretical theological assertion regarding survival after death, one that affirms the *greater* reality of the dead spirit than of the corporeal existent, but also as a kind of theology of translation: in the afterlife that is the poem's translation, it most nearly approximates to the meaning that was produced in its prior movement from material actuality to sublimated or spiritual (*geistig*) sense. That is, Uhland's poem is already a translation of the material fact of death and loss into the recuperative claim of persisting spiritual bonds. It is perhaps precisely his point, even if it conflicts with his wishful sentiment, that the actual appearance of these friends as ghostly presences would undercut the compensatory sense of the continuity of his spiritual bond with them.

Mangan's translation of this poetic movement effects a kind of hypertrophy of its sense: the companions are more real in their appearance as phantoms, as the movement of the translation doubles that of its original, transforming the metaphor of spiritual presence into the phantom appearance of the spirit as ghost. Mangan's phrasing is peculiar in several senses: "there stand / Anear me two from the Phantomland." The assertion is not quite that they are phantoms, but that they come from a land of Phantoms: their identity is a function of metonymy, thus rhetorically implying a kind of perpetual recession of contiguity that defines the relation of presence to signification and of original to translation. This is, indeed, the paradox of their appearance as phantoms. Finding its remote etymology, via the French *fantôme* and the Latin *phantasma*, in the Greek *phanein*, to appear, the phantom embodies the ambiguity of appearance itself: appearance is at once the coming-into-presence of an entity *and* a mere semblance, *Schein*. Are these presences "truly nigh," or merely deceptive projections, what we might call phantasms, that only seem to wear the features of their corporeal originals? Mangan does not decide this question for us, nor does he resolve the paradoxes his poem raises, but leaves us suspended between the presence of phantoms that are more real than the material beings of which they are the representations and appearances that deceive by assuming the likeness of those whose place they have taken.

This is no less than the paradox of the work that dies in order to find its afterlife in a translation, of the translation that, in rendering it, displaces its original. In a very mundane sense, of course, Mangan's translation did take the place of Uhland's poem for its readers. Indeed, with a certain impudence, he makes his translation of this quite straightforward poem stand as exemplary of Uhland's superior gift of Fancy, comparing the poet's gifts in this respect to Schiller.[17] In this regard, Mangan's translation not only takes the place of Uhland's poem, but also stands for and displaces Uhland in a larger sense. On the other hand, no translation can ever quite displace what it translates, but remains bound in relation to it as one shore of a river always assumes the other. The lateral movement of *Übersetzung* always remains possible and can flow in either direction, as the translation interprets the original but can always in turn be checked against it. Every translation is always implicitly a parallel text: even in the case of as parodic a translation as Mangan's, where the point of the poem lies in its critical departure from the original, its meaning can be established only in its difference from an original with which it is compared. Indeed, the more "original" the translation, the more it needs to be compared with the source poem in order for the significance of its departure to become manifest. As a mode, parody is always in a relation of dependence to that which it opposes, and this constitutive relation of debt and displacement it shares with translation.

The work of translation thus never quite arrives at its other shore, its movement across always counterpointed by a necessary move back, a return that resurrects precisely what the ideal version would have laid to rest. As earlier noted, Uhland's poem is already structured by the occasion of a return, his return to the river he had previously crossed with his two companions. Its status as a poem of anniversary is marked by the date that follows the title: *9. Oktober 1823*, a date that we know to signal the conventionally significant tenth year since his companions' deaths. Mangan's translation makes the structure of the anniversary all the more emphatic in its opening verse, and in doing so slips in another of his peculiar and apparently unmotivated mistranslations or deviations. Uhland's first two lines read, in more or less word for word translation, "Over this river, years ago, have I once already crossed." Repetition is limited by his emphatic "once," *einmal*. Mangan, on the contrary, emphasizes the continuing series of repetitions or returns that mark the passing of the years:

> A many a summer is dead and buried
> Since over this flood I last was ferried.

And not only does the phrase "dead and buried" foreshadow the fate of the two friends; in rhyming on "ferried" it also evokes the peculiar oscillating movement of this poem and of translation itself between interment and transfer. If the burial of the year, like the burial of the corpse, ritually confirms the passage of time and the event of death, the anniversary resurrects them, transferring both to the realm of spiritual reflection. Yet each such return is itself a moment of passage, a midnight or a noon that comes and goes in the same instant. Noon, as Derrida has remarked in another context, though also writing of the anniversary,

> n'est pas un lieu, il n'a pas lieu. Et ce n'est pas un moment, par cela même, seulement une limite aussitôt disparaissante. Et puis ça revient tous les jours, toujours, chaque jour, à chaque tour d'anneau. Toujours avant-midi, après-midi.[18]

> But the noon of life is not a place and it does not take place. For that very reason, it is not a moment but only an instantly vanishing limit. What is more, it returns every day, always, each day, with every turn of the annulus. Always before noon, after noon.[19]

There and not there in the same instant, a kind of spectral moment whose appearance is its disappearance, the anniversary comes and goes, even as the movement of translation produces that "infinitely small point" of sense or meaning that emerges only in the back and forth of its returns between an original and what, as if recognizing its provisionality as well as its circulating movement, we habitually call a *version*. Is this, then, the logic that brings Mangan almost ostentatiously to render

Uhland's *Abendschimmer* (evening glimmer, twilight) as Noon, and to replace the here and there (*Hier* and *Drüben*) with a then and now that Noon joins and divides?

> And then, as now, the Noon lay bright
> On strand, and water, and castled height.

Rather than a fading, a dissolution into the identity of the undifferentiated, shadowless Noon brings to light distinction and difference, the non-identity of the shores between which the ferry moves.

The ferry, indeed, as a vessel defined precisely by the back and forth motion of its outward and return voyages, becomes the fitting emblem of the process of translation. Such considerations may well remind us, especially in the context of a poem one of whose quietly masterful spirits is a "father figure," of the repetitive structure of another mode of transference, that of psychoanalysis. The point here is not to seek to establish an absolute correlation or analogy between translation and transference (*Übertragung*), but rather to identify another mode of interpretive movement than that of a lateral transfer of content or that of a tangential or parallel departure from the point of origin, an other movement, that is, which multiplies the effects of translation. Transference in psychoanalysis, if we follow Jacques Lacan, is not simply the act of repeating within the analytic situation, but the repetition of a constitutively *missed* encounter.[20] Set in motion by the presence of the analyst, the subject who is "supposed to know," or to be in possession of the truth or meaning that might be revealed by interpretation,[21] transference necessarily repeats a structure formed in the past as an "effect of deception in so far as it is repeated in the here and now."[22] It constitutes a realm of betrayal (*trahison* or *Betrug*) rather than a space for the transmission or communication (*Übertragung*) of the truth.

It may be tempting, and translation theory is always at least implicitly caught up in this temptation, to consider the original work as in possession of its truth, as utterly identified with its own meaning, and to lament that the translation always misses that meaning and is therefore never possessed of it. Uhland's poem, in our instance, would then bear its meaning in the double sense of being its originator, as a mother bears her child, and its vehicle, as a ferry bears its freight. We recognize in these very metaphors, however, that slippage whereby the meaning ineluctably splits from the signifiers that communicate it and the impossibility of ever establishing the identity of the text and its truth. *Auf der Überfahrt* already lends itself to being read as an allegory of this process. The crossing in the poem is a repetition that already doubles the single (*einmal*) prior crossing, but only after having been crossed by another event, or couple of events, the deaths of his companions. It is the death of the other that endows the event of crossing with a meaning that in the first place was merely latent in it, that which is conveyed by the metaphor of Charon and his ferry—a metaphor almost necessarily latent in any representation of such a crossing, given the cultural dissemination of the image. And yet the truth of this meaning, whose work of displacement is perhaps marked by the representation of the dead companions in the form of an exchange of coins, is at the same time a deception, one that seeks to overcome the splitting or parting (*scheiden*) that death imposes by sublimating that knowledge, or repressing it, in the appeal to spirit. We know that for Freud, the template of all repression lay in the primal murder of the father, whose tale he tells in *Totem and Taboo*. The historical truth of that bizarre narrative need not concern us here. What counts is the structure Freud identifies, whereby that event is repeated in a double form: in the internalization of the figure of the father in the form of the superego, a movement repeated in the dissolution of every individual's Oedipal complex, and in the ritual sacrifice of a human or animal in whom the spirit of that father is thought to reside. In both cases, the material death is displaced symbolically into the form of the spirit, *Geist*, which takes its place.

Uhland's poem, with its *vatergleicher* paired with a fallen youth, and with its displacement of death into spirit, seems to embody precisely such a structure, a structure that I have suggested Mangan's translation draws out and elaborates. At the same time, original and translation form a further double, one that repeats the Twain or *Zween* that both poems turn around, and between which the play of meaning and interpretation passes or transfers. In this movement between the two, what is accomplished is not so much the bearing across or transmission (*Übertragung*) of a determinate content that would be the portable meaning of the poem, as a ferrying back and forth of meanings realized only in a movement in which now the one and now the other work takes priority—much, indeed, as a ferry originates alternately on either shore and finds its destination on the other, turn by turn. This movement, which is a movement of multiplication rather than of determination, constitutes the third term through which alone the couple of original and translation are related. Being embodied in neither work, but operating the sublimation of the one into the "higher and purer linguistic air" of the other, the transformation of some matter into a sphere of pure signification, this ferrying is perhaps identifiable as "that element in a translation which goes beyond transmittal of subject matter." It is what remains, after the passage of the matter of one poem into its translation, as the sheer movement of language itself. But in that case, it is hard to tell whether this movement of language bears the spirit of the original, or whether it is no more than its ghost, its apparition in another body. This uncertainty hovers about any invocation of the spirit whose equivocal meaning we have already noted, as it hovers about language itself, composed always at once of material and sense, in ways which every poem exploits. Translation, in detaching sense from word and reincorporating it in other words, multiplies an effect that is already in play in the poem. Derrida's remarks are again pertinent:

> Once ideas or thoughts (*Gedanke*) are detached from their substratum, one engenders some ghost by giving them a body. Not by returning to the living body from which ideas and thoughts have been torn loose, but by incarnating the latter in another artifactual body, a prosthetic body, a ghost of spirit, one might say a ghost of the ghost . . .[23]

Translation, as the ghostly vehicle of the spirit of the poem, functions as its prosthesis, extending it into another material, enabling its passage into another state.

In both Uhland and Mangan, the name of this figure of passage and prosthesis is the *Fährmann*, ferryman, the one element that seems to undergo no change either in the poems or between them. And yet that appearance of changelessness in fact conceals a continual and instantaneous oscillation between actuality and figure, reality and myth, ferryman and Charon, which is what crosses or passes through the poet's repeated journeys. The ferryman is the figure of death and the figure of figuration, *metaphorein*, itself. To Mangan's two phantoms, a third at least must then be added: at once body—or letter—and spirit, matter and meaning, this operator of transfer is also "the apparition form, the phenomenon of spirit," as Derrida puts it of the phantom or ghost.[24] The ferryman, indeed, is the very type of the *revenant*, the one whose task it is always to return. As such, the ferryman also describes the locus of endless repetitions: committed, or summoned as he is by vocation to the work of exchange, of continual transfer, his labors cannot be redeemed by simple payment, much as the poet wishes to do so. Translation produces no equivalent: rather, like Derrida's spirit, or because it seeks to capture and transfer the spirit into a new form or appearance, it *proliferates*, disseminating "spirits everywhere."[25]

Mangan's translation of *Auf der Überfahrt* as "Spirits Everywhere" thus finds its justification as a kind of metacommentary on the practice of translation as oversetting, *Übersetzung*. It is not an equivalent, if by that term be meant a transposition of the words of one language into those that correspond semantically to them. It is, however, a reflection on the process and effect of translation understood as a crossing over, a crossing that proliferates meaning rather than seeking to be definitive and that, in doing so, holds out the prospect of innumerable possible versions, in each and none of which the spirit of the original would be reflected back as yet another. Every translation, we might say, is the apparition of the poem, and as such a secondary form that owes its life to another. The translator's is the restless spirit who finds a home only in others' words, who resorts, as Mangan famously commented, to "fathering upon other writers the offspring of his own brain."[26] Secreted in these reflections, and in Mangan's translation of Uhland, is the further knowledge that the translator, who conveys the spirit of the poem into the body of the language of translation, is no less a ghost than the ferryman that is his metaphor. That both the ferryman and the translator are paid for their conveyancing, sustaining their lives though another form of spectral equivalence, is an aspect of the analogy unlikely to have escaped Mangan's morbid wit.

It would be right, then, to intuit a relation between haunting and Mangan's translations. And, once again, it may be necessary to insist on the levels of sustained reflection on his practice, as poet and translator, that often appear cloaked in the voluminous robes of his playful indirection and dissembling. Minor or anachronistic as his practice might seem, Mangan's work continues to foreshadow insights whose pertinence only becomes apparent many decades after he wrote. Lodged in a space and a time where the question as to what languages could authentically bear, of spirit or of cultural material, was of increasing political urgency, and writing at a moment in which it was possible to witness the fading of one language into the shadow of another that was being transformed by the evolving of the capitalist marketplace into an overwhelming means of exchange, Mangan's peripheral and minor location may have given him a peculiarly privileged vantage point. From there he elaborated, through translation as practice and medium for reflection, an allegory of the ways in which a culture lives on, in debt and in an alienation that, while it cannot be redeemed, continues to transmit its effects. Already in the mid-nineteenth century his work— for which translation was always the metaphor as well as a favored practice—stood as a counterpoetics of modernity, questioning and parodying the Romantic and nationalist insistence on spirit and origin, and interrogating translation as the means through which, across the political spectrum, fragments of a culture destroyed by colonial power could be carried across into modernity. Inhabiting, like a phantom cloaked in others' words, the interstices of his own time, he remains of our time, out of time, "in the transition between the two moments of spirit, a ghost just passing through."

Notes

1. Jacques Derrida, *Specters of Marx: The State of the Debt, the Work of Mourning and the New International,* translated by Peggy Kamuf. Routledge, 1994, p. 136.
2. See James Clarence Mangan, "Chapters on Ghostcraft." *Prose Writings,* centenary edition, edited by D. J. O'Donoghue. M. H. Gill, 1904, pp. 160–98.
3. For my discussion of this passage and Mangan's use of citation, see David Lloyd, *Nationalism and Minor Literature: James Clarence Mangan and the Emergence of Irish Cultural Nationalism.* University of California Press, 1987, pp. 182–7.
4. Walter Benjamin, "The Task of the Translator," translated by Harry Zohn. *Selected Writings: Volume 1: 1913–1926,* edited by Marcus Bullock and Michael W. Jennings. Belknap Press, 1996, p. 254.
5. For Mangan's translation, see James Clarence Mangan, "Anthologia Germanica, No. XVI: Ballads and Miscellaneous Poems." *Dublin University Magazine,* vol. 18, no. 103, July 1841, p. 24 and John Mitchel, editor, *Poems of James Clarence Mangan.* P. M. Haverty, 1859, pp. 94–5. For Ludwig Uhland's "Auf der Überfahrt," see Ludwig Uhland, *Dichtungen, Briefe, Reden: Eine Auswahl,* edited by Walter P. H. Scheffler. J. F. Steinkopf, 1963, pp. 216–17. Both poems are reproduced in the Appendix.
6. For a brief but useful account of Uhland's career and reception over a century and a half, see Victor G. Doerksen, *Ludwig Uhland and the Critics.* Camden House, 1994.
7. This is, of course, one literal and even primary meaning of the German verb (*von einem Ufer zum andern fahren*), reminding us that translation is always in the first instance a matter of metaphor.
8. See Scheffler's note to the poem in Uhland, *Dichtungen,* p. 482. Waterman T. Hewett, in his edition of *Poems of Ludwig Uhland.* Macmillan, 1904, p. 243, gives these details: "The elder of the two companions was his favorite uncle, Pastor Hoser, the brother of his mother, the minister of the church in the neighboring village of Schmieden." The other, "in Kampf und Sturm gefallen," "refers to Uhland's friend, the young poet Friedrich von Harprecht (1788–1813), who was a fellow-student of law with Uhland at Tübingen in 1805. His military spirit led him in 1807, in his nineteenth year, to enlist as a cavalry officer in the army of Würtemberg against Austria. Later, he was an officer of ordnance under General Berthier. At the bloody battle of Wagram he was on the staff of the emperor Napoleon. With the army of this country he marched to Russia, where he distinguished himself at the battle of Smolensk, when his bravery won for him the Order of Military Merit of Würtemberg and the French cross of the Legion of Honor. At the battle of the Borodino, he fought desperately and lost his leg by a cannon shot. He suffered great hardships on the way to Wilna, where he died from the effect of his injury, and the terrible sufferings of the retreat." See online at: https://archive.org/details/3358018 (last accessed July 29, 2021).
9. On this tendency of Mangan's translation practice, see my discussion of his versions of Friedrich Rückert and Ludwig Tieck in Lloyd, *Nationalism and Minor Literature,* pp. 136–45.

10. Benjamin, "Task of the Translator," pp. 257–8.
11. This allegorical tendency in Mangan's work forges another link with Benjamin, in that the latter's *Origin of German Tragic Drama* is an extended examination of the baroque use of allegory as the index of a fallen and dead nature. The affinity is striking between the poet who proclaimed in his autobiography that he could see "nothing in creation but what is fallen and ruined" and allegories, which are "in the realm of thoughts, what ruins are in the realm of things." See James Clarence Mangan, *James Clarence Mangan: Autobiography*. Dolmen Press, 1968, p. 33 and Walter Benjamin, *The Origin of German Tragic Drama*, translated by John Osborne, introduction by George Steiner. Verso, 1985, p. 178. For further on the baroque, see Chapter 7, "*Rome's Wreck*: Joyce's Baroque."
12. For a discussion of Romantic translation theory, see Lloyd, *Nationalism and Minor Literature*, pp. 103–17.
13. Benjamin, "Task of the Translator," p. 256.
14. Benjamin, "Task of the Translator," p. 256.
15. Benjamin, "Task of the Translator," p. 261.
16. On the "laws of contiguity, similarity and opposition" that inform magical practices, see Marcel Mauss, *A General Theory of Magic*, 1950 edition, translated by Robert Brain. Routledge and Kegan Paul, 1972, p. 64.
17. See Mangan's introduction to this poem in "Anthologia Germanica, XVI," p. 24.
18. Jacques Derrida, *Otobiographies: l'enseignement de Nietzsche et la politique du nom propre*. Éditions Galilée, 1984, p. 59.
19. Jacques Derrida, *Otobiographies: The Teaching of Nietzsche and the Politics of the Proper Name*, translated by Avital Ronell. University of Nebraska Press, 1985, p. 14.
20. Jacques Lacan, *The Four Fundamental Concepts of Psychoanalysis: Book XI of The Seminar of Jacques Lacan*, edited by Jacques-Alain Miller and translated by Alan Sheridan. W. W. Norton, 1981, p. 143.
21. Lacan, *Four Fundamental Concepts*, p. 253.
22. Lacan, *Four Fundamental Concepts*, p. 254.
23. Derrida, *Specters of Marx*, p. 126.
24. Derrida, *Specters of Marx*, p. 135.
25. See Derrida, *Specters of Marx*, p. 135: "Since this spirit 'is' everywhere, since it comes from everywhere (*aus Allem*), it proliferates *a priori*, it puts in place, while depriving them of any place, a mob of specters to which one can no longer even assign a *point of view*: they invade all of space."
26. See "Sketches of Modern Irish Writers: James Clarence Mangan." *Irishman*, August 17, 1850, p. 28. The text, written by Mangan, is signed "E. W." [Edward Walsh] and is therefore an instance of the process it describes, the poet's attributing to others his own writings. It is also, as chance would have it, a posthumous text in which Mangan returns to haunt the reader in a body other than his own.

Chapter 3

1913–1916–1919: Yeats's Dates

Ten years of centenary commemorations of the events from 1913 to 1922 that led to Ireland's very partial decolonization have highlighted the importance of memory and historical record to the politics of the present. Commemoration, generally an institutional practice of the state, has the capacity to awaken memories at odds with the official narrative or to generate counter-histories that summon up occluded events that contained the potential for other futures. The contested space that arises calls into question the intent of commemoration, asking both what drives commemoration and in what direction it tends as an act of historicization as well as one of remembrance. Self-evidently, the period of 1913–16 is commemorated as a kind of historical watershed. From the singular cluster of events that occurred in those years—the passing of the Home Rule Bill, the Dublin Lockout of 1913, the slaughters on the battlefields of the Great War, and the Easter Rising—can be traced the turbulent dynamics that shaped the Anglo-Irish war and the founding of both the independent Free State and the devolved parliament of Northern Ireland. This is without doubt a history that has marked us all down to the present, one hundred years later—if only in so far as it has shaped the unchosen conditions in which we make or remake our own history. To this series of events, my own title adds another set, one whose significance was more immediately determined by 1913 and 1916, that of the year 1919: the year of the commencement of the Irish war of decolonization that seemed to stem with virtual inevitability from the events of Easter 1916 and even from those of 1913. I list this series of dates partly in the spirit of Ciaran Carson's remark in *Belfast Confetti*, that in Irish history "there's any God's amount / Of Nines and Sixes,"[1] but no less in the interest of denoting another trajectory and sketching another, counter-commemorative constellation. That ideal constellation marks unrealized possibilities and potentials through which Irish events and debates resonate with a wider frame, that of Europe at least, if not also of the global scene that by 1913 had already emerged as the sphere of operations of a fully imperial capitalism.

A constellation is, as Walter Benjamin reminds us, a different relation to the past than that of historicism. A constellation, in its assemblages and in the gaps and breaks between the elements that compose it, assures a resonance among events that is not exhausted by causality or determination. Unlike the historicist dogma of progress and development that foregrounds those events and tendencies whose actualization seems to underwrite the mere factuality of that which has come to be the case, the construction of the constellation produces an arrest of thought "in a configuration saturated with tensions."[2] It can include not only those events whose significance lies in their effects as causes, in their consequentiality, but also those events and possibilities whose potentialities have not been exhausted or subsumed in cause and effect or in their consequence for the future—those, in short, that do not make part of a historicist narrative of progress and modernity. The constellation is fundamentally antagonistic to historical thinking: in defiance of the Aristotelian conditions for verisimilitude, it embraces not the probable, the event that can be inscribed within a universal history, but the *possible*. The constellation of past events includes within it those possibilities unrealized in historical time, for, as Benjamin puts it, "nothing that has ever happened should be regarded as lost for history."[3] As Theodor Adorno later put it, reflecting on this passage,

> knowledge must indeed present the fatally rectilinear succession of victory and defeat, but should also address itself to those things which were not embraced by this dynamic, which fell by the wayside—what might be called the waste products and blind spots that have escaped the dialectic.[4]

This dictum must also embrace what might have happened, the possibilities embedded in time which mere contingency may have forestalled.

Commemoration is always suspended between a historicist desire to read in the past its consequences for the present—requiring a future perfect tense—and the formation of a constellation between the past and the present in which possibilities in the past that remain unrealized might become readable again, suggesting a future conditional. Ours has certainly been a time of commemoration and if the prior commemorations of the Great Hunger in conjunction with the first celebrations of Ireland's "Celtic Tiger" taught us anything, it was not only to beware of premature celebrations of progress and development, but also to interrogate the tendency of commemoration to lay the past to rest. To do the latter is to embrace historical violence—a violence which exceeds the gross brutality of military conquest or dispossession and would include the extinction of forms of living, the daily round of exploitation and reification, the consignment of beings to disposability or redundancy—and to accede not only to the extermination of natural life but also to the extinction of those possible futures projected in the hopes and imaginaries of the victims. For what violence takes from the living is not merely their lives, maybe not their biological lives at all, but their futures, futures that may be the most mundane or quite epochal in their force. Commemoration cannot restore those futures, futures not in any case ours to restore, given that we dwell in the legacy of their destruction. At best, it can seek to forge a constellation of our present and its own spectrum of violence and resistance with those of the past, not to secure redress, but to wrench both times out of joint with any meliorative concept of history that would make of commemoration that premature reconciliation with past violence that justifies the violence of the present.

In that spirit, I want to commence with an encounter that—for purely contingent reasons—never did take place, a might-have-been whose theoretical force has real resonance for 1913 and 1916 and perhaps for our present. The encounter that ought to have been would have been between the Irish Marxist and syndicalist organizer, James Connolly, and his counterpart, Rosa Luxemburg, the Jewish Polish socialist who had moved to Germany and would eventually become, with Karl Liebknecht, a founder and leader of the Spartacist movement that spearheaded the German revolution of 1919. Their encounter might have taken place as early as 1900 at the Socialist International in Paris where Luxemburg launched her critique of Karl Kautsky and the Social Democratic reformists and which was attended by the first Irish Socialist Republican Party (ISRP) delegation. According to Desmond Greaves, the ISRP was represented by E. W. Stewart and Tom Lyng, Connolly being unable to attend for "economic reasons."[5] Nonetheless, this encounter was imagined as taking place at least virtually by Margaretta D'Arcy and John Arden in *The Non-Stop Connolly Show*, produced at Liberty Hall in 1975, where Connolly comments from the wings on the action and debates at the Congress.[6] At the conference, the Irish delegation were aligned on the left with Luxemburg's critique of reformism, as Connolly would have been, even though Luxemburg simultaneously launched a critique of the "dangerous utopia" of the "nationalist heresy."[7] D'Arcy and Arden imagine Connolly's response to Luxemburg in the form of an appeal to specific Irish conditions, different from those prevailing in Poland, and with an acknowledgement of Luxemburg's alienation from Polish and German nationalism as a Jewish intellectual facing the histories of anti-Semitism in both countries.

But a more compelling theoretical configuration would emerge within the constellation of 1913. As we know, 1913 was the year of the Dublin Lockout, the first major, nationally resonant trial of the syndicalist labor organizing of Connolly and Jim Larkin. But 1913 was also the year in which Luxemburg wrote and published her major work, *The Accumulation of Capital*, a critique of Marx's theory of accumulation that aimed to designate the historical limits of capitalist growth. There, Luxemburg argues that capitalist accumulation cannot be understood either within the static national economic framework within which Marx theorized it, or solely as the inaugural moment of colonial conquest and of enclosure that he termed "primitive accumulation." Rather, she argues:

> From the very beginning, the forms and laws of capitalist production aim to comprise the entire globe as a store of productive forces. Capital, impelled to appropriate productive forces for purposes of exploitation, ransacks the whole world, it procures its means of production from all corners of the earth, seizing them, if necessary by force, from all levels of civilisation and from all forms of society. . . . It becomes necessary for capital progressively to dispose ever more fully of the whole globe, to acquire an unlimited choice of means of production with regard to both quality and quantity, so as to find productive employment for the surplus value it has realised.[8]

The colonial form of capitalism is thus not merely the condition Marx identified as "the travails by which the capitalist mode of production emerges from a feudal society": accumulation is ongoing, no less violent and destructive for not being "primitive," while "capitalism in its full maturity also depends in all respects on non-capitalist strata and social organisations existing side by side with it."[9] These non-capitalist strata, however, do not simply persist coevally with capitalism: they are targeted for eventual liquidation:

> Since the primitive associations of the natives are the strongest protection for their social organisations and for their material bases of existence, capital must begin by planning for the systematic destruction and annihilation of all the non-capitalist social units that obstruct its development. With that we have passed beyond the stage of primitive accumulation; this process is still going on. Each new colonial expansion is accompanied, as a matter of course, by a relentless battle of capital against the social and economic ties of the natives, who are also forcibly robbed of their means of production and labour power.[10]

In thus theorizing accumulation and the global development of capitalism, Luxemburg wittingly or unwittingly furnishes the theoretical bases for the conjunction of socialism with nationalism that was crucial to the simultaneous struggle in which workers in Dublin were engaged during the Lockout. Indeed, her theoretical argument coincides with the more occasional and empirical observations Connolly had composed over the same period in grasping the historical conjunction of labor radicalism and anti-colonial organizing in Ireland—a foundation for what he considered the more radical tendencies of Irish than British labor and a crucial aspect of the ways in which the Irish workers' struggle unfolded during the Lockout.[11]

Let me proceed by sketching briefly three points about the Lockout. The Dublin Lockout initially emerged from a dispute about union representation, as William Murphy and his fellow employers sought to prevent the Irish Transport and General Workers Union (ITGWU) from expanding its organizing within the transport and other sectors by "locking out" workers who refused to renounce the Union. But, as Emmet O'Connor points out, Murphy's antagonism was to "general" unionism: the dispute was not only about the right to organize but about the inroads of syndicalism itself and the right to the sympathetic strike within the context of the "one big union."[12] Secondly, it needs also to be emphasized that syndicalism was a social or cultural as well as labor movement. As O'Connor puts it:

> Larkin [and Connolly] had always been attracted to the syndicalist idea of underpinning the socialist struggle with a working-class counter-culture based on collectivist values like sharing and solidarity, and standing in opposition to the bourgeois ethic of possessive individualism.[13]

The Lockout has thus to be seen also as a cultural struggle that opened onto the question of the nature and tendency of nationalism itself, especially where Connolly was concerned, with his theorization of the ways in which colonialism, by deflecting in Ireland the normative European development from feudalism to capitalism, had succeeded in preserving the vestiges of Celtic Communism in the form of an adherence to ideas of common property. This cultural claim underlay the division between, on the one hand, the employers, represented by the former Nationalist MP Murphy, together with the nationalist press and an element of Sinn Féin, led by Arthur Griffith, and, on the other, the syndicalist labor movement joined, increasingly, by the "advanced nationalists," together with, for a brief moment, the artists, poets, and intellectuals of the middle classes. It is for this reason, thirdly, that 1913 represented, in Desmond Greaves's words, "a climacteric as fateful as 1916" and may, perhaps, have determined the specific forms of the Irish decolonization struggle that played out between Easter 1916 and 1924.[14] The Lockout seems one of those brief if decisive divisions of time, a tympanum dividing before and after, and determining the future direction and meaning of events. Did the defeat of the workers in the Lockout exacerbate the differences between advanced nationalists and the Home Rule party that, having been clarified by John Redmond's commitment of constitutional nationalists to the British war effort in 1914, led to the precipitation of military nationalism in 1916? Was it that defeat that increasingly impelled Connolly to ally with Pearse and the Irish Republican Brotherhood (IRB), with the "advanced nationalists," culminating in the joint uprising of 1916? If so, to commemorate the Lockout is to commemorate equally that which it seems, with a certain inevitability, to have determined: both the Rising and the political violence of the following years and also the growing eclipse or occlusion of syndicalism in Ireland by nationalism.

The question then arises as to the form in which we commemorate: does the form of commemoration that reads in the event an outcome apparently determined by that event not itself consolidate and confirm the defeat that the event necessarily represents for those who did not emerge from it victorious, as active precursors of the future? Is there a form of commemoration that might grasp in the defeat, even in the death of the defeated, not the extinction but the preservation of a possibility? A possibility preserved in potential precisely by its defeat, as a refusal of what is merely the case and encrypted in failure, is one that can only be revealed or de-cyphered by "brushing history against the grain."[15] Such a counter-commemoration, which resists the forward-moving progress of historical verisimilitude, I would designate "poetic."

To invoke the relation of poetry to commemoration is immediately to evoke the problem of the relation of the poem to its occasion, to the events that date it. We could propose that it is the work of the poem to gather the contingent moments of its occasions—and there may be more than one occasion for any single poem—into a single, significant constellation. In the poem, as Jacques Derrida puts it, "A discontinuous swarm of events may be commemorated all at once, *at the same date*, which consequently takes on the strange, coincident, *unheimlich* dimensions of a cryptic predestination."[16] The date, *datum*, is here the merely given, in all its singularity and contingency, transformed into significance by what is willfully, intentionally, gathered under its sign. But the date is also that which returns, in order to be commemorated. It signifies the time whose rhythm is one of returns: as Benjamin reminds us, revolutionaries destroy the clocks that measure the mechanical passage of time, but they establish new calendars and with calendars, the recurring "days [or dates] of remembrance."[17] But in returning, the date annuls the singularity of the events that it marked:

A date marks itself and becomes readable only in freeing itself from the singularity that it nonetheless recalls . . . It belongs to the always eventful and damaged essence of the date to become readable and commemorative only in effacing what it will have designated, in becoming each time no one's date.[18]

Commemoration that dates from the event the "cryptic predestination" it entails annuls at once the contingency and the possibility that the given secretes.[19] That which constellates the datum of the past with the present may, however, enable the disencryption of what was occluded in it. It gives back to the event not so much its singularity as its potentiality, its capacity to differ from what is the case. It offers a reading that produces not so much the sense *of* the moment as sense *from* the moment, precisely by detaching sense from what dates it.

In what follows, I will be reading W. B. Yeats against his own grain and, perhaps, against the grain of the readings he has invited and to which he has been subjected. We know that Yeats insisted on the absolute division between the poem and the contingencies from which the poem is forged. As he famously remarked in "A General Introduction for My Work":

A poet writes always of his personal life, in his finest work out of its tragedy, whatever it be, remorse, lost love, or mere loneliness; he never speaks directly as to someone at the breakfast table, there is always a phantasmagoria. . . . he is never the bundle of accident and incoherence that sits down to breakfast; he has been reborn as an idea, something intended, complete.[20]

Be that as it may, there is perhaps no anglophone poet more alert to the occasions of his work than Yeats, no poet whose poems are more fully given to interpreting their times or to interpretation through their times, even to the extent that any periodization of his work would almost inevitably be at the same time a periodization of Irish history or of the nationalist movements and state formation that shaped it. His is a work saturated with the tensions of his moment and of his responses to the moment, a work—to borrow a phrase of Paul Celan's—marked by "a kind of concentration mindful of all our dates."[21] Yet there are, however much almost every poem of Yeats's could be tied to its date, only three poems in his collected oeuvre that are titled with a date: "September 1913," "Easter 1916," and "Nineteen Hundred and Nineteen." Here I will try to read again these dated poems, dated perhaps as much by their familiarity as by their titles, each one of which is clearly germane to this moment of commemorations, and to what it summons us to consider.

Each of these poems is tied to a date that names a moment of violence, of change: the quiet, erasing violence of accumulation by which the past and present are changed and memory itself impaired; the violence of revolutionary insurrection; the violence of war, decolonization, and counter-insurgency. They are no less tied to one another, both formally and thematically and by the subterranean connections among them that mark the shifts in the poet's own relation to his occasions. It is evident that the interval between these dates and the time of our own commemoration of them changes too what they designate: we do not share the uncertainty that faced Yeats and his contemporaries in 1913, 1916, or 1919, their inevitable ignorance as to what the meaning and outcome of the events of these years might be. Nonetheless, we confront another uncertainty, certainly, that of not knowing what we may miss in the relation of occasion to event, what among its multiple determinants may yet be at work or ready to return out of the molework of occluded histories, even as we do not know and cannot know into what unexpected constellations these poems, all too familiar to us, may yet enter. I am thus trying to perform a double constellation, that of the poems with their own moment and with ours, as well as to see what specific constellations of the contingent the poet performs in them.

"September 1913"

The initial occasion of Yeats's "September 1913" was the Hugh Lane controversy rather than the Dublin Lockout at the beginning of which it was published in the *Irish Times*. The villain of both pieces was William Martin Murphy, who as a leading member of the Dublin Corporation had opposed furnishing the funds for the building of the gallery that Lane had made a condition of fulfilling the bequest of his paintings to the city. The controversy became for Yeats what Pádraig Yeates, in his monumental work on the Lockout, has called an "intellectual duel" with Murphy and with those nationalists who, in what the poet regarded as the philistinism of "minds without culture," had voted down funding the gallery.[22] Yet "September 1913" makes no direct mention of the controversy, standing instead as a lament for the debasement of an insurrectionary tradition of nationalism that Yeats, through John O'Leary, former Fenian and lover of literature, connected with a certain kind of cultural nationalism. Nor was it, in the first place, a poem related to the Lockout, even though it was published in the *Irish Times* on September 8, and dated September 7, 1913, four days after the Lockout of the workers by four hundred members of the Employers' Federation had begun. Though initially entitled "Romance in Ireland / (On reading much of the correspondence against the Art Gallery)," its gradual renaming as "September 1913" [23] inevitably configures it with the larger context of the moment, not least in that Yeats's antipathy to Murphy was notorious or that majority Labour support for the gallery, including Larkin's, may have impelled Yeats's increasingly vocal support for the striking workers. In this, he was joined by other leading intellectuals and artists, including AE (most famously), Padraic Colum, Susan Mitchell, and James Stephens, as well as Pearse, McDonagh, and Plunkett, advanced nationalists who would become leaders of the 1916 Rising.

The poem's opening lines are a direct attack on Ireland's capitalist classes, even if, in Yeats's romantic anti-capitalist imagination, they appear as the epitomes of vulgar petty capitalists, rather than as international transport and press barons like Murphy:

> What need you, being come to sense,
> But fumble in a greasy till
> And add the halfpence to the pence
> And prayer to shivering prayer, until
> You have dried the marrow from the bone;
> For men were born to pray and save;
> Romantic Ireland's dead and gone,
> It's with O'Leary in the grave.[24]

The poem thus opens abruptly with an image of the disenchantment of a debased Enlightenment—"being come to sense"—that anticipates in some ways the fate of bourgeois society depicted in Horkheimer and Adorno's *Dialectic of Enlightenment*, sharing their vision of that dialectical "declension of the soul" and of social function, from slaveholder to free entrepreneur to administrator, that makes the burgher "the logical subject of the Enlightenment."[25] That debased enlightenment goes hand in hand with the debasement of sense from both universal reason and sensuousness to mere self-preservative common sense. The cumulative rhythms of petty accumulation, "adding the halfpence to the pence" (a rhyme that makes "cents" of "sense"), and of mere repetitive religious duty counterpoint the figures he will evoke and that will provoke a numeration of a very different kind, an enumeration of the singular and no longer repeatable in which the unique name displaces the number:

> Was it for this the wild geese spread
> The grey wing upon every tide;
> For this that all that blood was shed,
> For this Edward Fitzgerald died,
> And Robert Emmet and Wolfe Tone,
> All that delirium of the brave? (108)

The citation of the names of past heroes whose insurrections came to naught seeks to overcome the spectacle of discontinuity that haunts Irish culture in the wake of the nineteenth century and to assert the subterranean continuity of a tradition. I need not belabor the obvious point that Yeats asserts here an openly romantic nationalism (and one might simply recall that in any case nationalism is a romanticism even as it is a modernism), one that conforms to his long-standing project to unify the desire of the people into a common design through the analogy between political and erotic desire:

> You'd cry 'Some woman's yellow hair
> Has maddened every mother's son':
> They weighed so lightly what they gave. (109)

Defeat and failure are not obstacles, but rather stimuli, to that project of open-ended desire.[26]

Thus the gesture Yeats makes in "September 1913" is flauntingly double-edged: that project of his cultural nationalism is affirmed, even as he declares its redundancy. He rhetorically seeks to resurrect the dead and exiled precisely by proclaiming their second death, that of their memory, even as, in constellating them together, the events he commemorates "in a fantastic constellation" are to be "transfigured by an incantation."[27] Precisely the moment that threatens to be that of their final forgetting, "in the grave" along with the last of their kind, O'Leary, is the moment of their invocation as a kind of collective talisman against that other magic of transformation, of change, the small change of the daily rituals of exchange and monetization, that threatens to banish them for good and all. Counting cannot account for all that counts. The very refrain, "But let them be, they're dead and gone, / They're with O'Leary in the grave" (109), seeks to transform the logic of commemoration— its secular "let it be"—into the occasion of a last, somewhat ghoulish return, through its own cycle of returns in the performative "let there be . . ." Even the antiquated form Yeats adopts, that of the popular ballad, a dated form in the time of mass circulation newspapers and the advent of the silent film and newsreel, embodies as a "distressed" artifact, in Susan Stewart's sense of the belated literary ballad, his commitment to a resurrection of the past.[28] This capacity to dwell on if not in the past— and its uncanny potentials—was peculiarly well captured in Murphy's *Sunday Independent*'s cartoon of Yeats as spook, mourning over "the dead past" (Figure 3.1)—yet, precisely as "spook," threatening to resurrect that past and its resonances, in a "turning of the years."

But if we can say that the poem always exceeds its occasion, is it not true also that the occasion may exceed the poem? "September 1913," with its

Figure 3.1   Yeats as Spook, from *Sunday Independent*, 1913.

query as to whether it was "For this that all that blood was shed," takes on a new and less controlled set of resonances when published in the immediate aftermath of the "Bloody Sunday" of August 31, 1913, when a police riot killed two and injured some four hundred peacefully demonstrating strikers. If the poem marks a watershed, a bloodshed, indeed, in Irish history, its depiction of it as a division of times between a dead romantic past of memory and resistance and a debased and acquiescent present may have missed its mark or at least been overtaken by events. Certainly, Connolly's understanding of the afterlives of the heroes Yeats invokes and of their active significance for Irish workers was quite different. None understood better Benjamin's dictum that "*even the dead* will not be safe from the enemy if he is victorious."[29] To take only Robert Emmet, the subterranean tradition that his memory embodied was tied for Connolly in *Labour and Irish History* to the "domestic materials" with which his abortive insurrection worked, that is, "working class elements fired with the hope of political and social emancipation."[30] Precisely what, "on every recurring Emmet anniversary," those nationalist commemorators occlude, "who know all about Emmet's martyrdom but nothing about his principles," is his incipient socialism: that the national will was superior to property rights and that revolution must promise "freedom from social as well as political bondage."[31] These are the two principles that Connolly will infuse into Ireland's proclamation of independence in 1916. In the meantime, as if in recognition of his audience's continuing familiarity with the name and its resonance, and as the Lockout entered its final stages, he will joke in a January 1914 article of John Scully, High Sheriff of Dublin and candidate for the Municipal elections, that "If Robert Emmet was to be hanged tomorrow, and the professional hangman went on strike, Mr. Scully is bound by the oath of his office to do the job and hang the patriot."[32] For Connolly, the names that Yeats recites are by no means forgotten, but active referents of an ongoing working-class struggle with which their nationalist rebellions intersected. "September

1913" is thus changed by its configuration with its time, its own epochal sense of history and commemoration crossed both by the contingencies of events playing out even as it was published and by a counter-memory that belies its claims. In that configuration, more spooks return, slipping up from the cellarage, than the poem allows for.

"Easter 1916"

If, as Benjamin claimed, it is in its afterlife that the work truly lives, perhaps "September 1913" lives fully not only in the configuration it makes with its own time, but also in Yeats's bitter recall of it in "Easter 1916."[33] It is hard not to catch Yeats posturing a little in "September 1913," though in a posture somewhat different than that of the mourning aesthete of the *Sunday Independent*—already a dated image of an earlier Yeats. The posture is that of the radical nationalist, laid bare in Connolly's image of the "crop of orators," scarcely Croppies, who celebrate Emmet but not his principles. But for poet and historian alike, it is always "violence yesterday, violence tomorrow, but never violence today," as one might say after the White Queen. The quite explicit celebration of revolutionary violence that the earlier poem's acts of commemoration perform finds its check in the later one. For if "September 1913" casts forward an unexpected set of resonances when placed in conjunction with the Lockout, "Easter 1916"—long recognized to be its palinode—offers it the tribute of an afterlife that speaks back to it.[34] Formally, the relation and the difference is marked in the balladic octosyllables that furnish the basic meter of each and in the substitution of the regular eight-line stanzas of "September 1913" for the peculiar but regular alternation of "Easter 1916" between sixteen-line and twenty-four-line stanzas—a regularity clearly based on the octets characteristic of the ballad but dissolving them into another, more elegiac framework. So too the regular iamb of "September 1913"'s refrain falters in the stress patterns of "Easter 1916"'s almost recurrent burden (it disappears in stanza three):

> Romantic Ireland's dead and gone,
> It's with O'Leary in the grave.

> All changed, changed utterly:
> A terrible beauty is born.[35]

If "Easter 1916"'s burden (and its most famous lines) reject "September 1913"'s peculiarly jaunty despair and refrain, inverting its meaning in recognition of the fierce and unexpected creativity of violence, the rhythmic faltering of that burden marks Yeats's own uncertainties, the ambivalent hindsight with which he "comes to sense" in relation to his own advocacy of political violence.

"Hindsight is"—as Anne Enright's Gina Moynihan remarks in a novel about another moment of crisis and realization, *The Forgotten Waltz*—"a wonderful thing."[36] But it always comes too late. I have written elsewhere of Yeats's sense that the insurrection in 1916 had made his own poetic nationalist project redundant:[37] as he was to put it in the "General Introduction," "my movement perished under the firing squads of 1916."[38] Here, what I want to note is that no poem of Yeats's is more concerned with the gap between the contingent or quotidian and the ideal or symbolical, and that this gap undoes the distinction between "accident and incoherence" and the "intended or complete," troubling the transformation or sublimation of the former into the latter. We could say that the poem opens with a misrecognized, if not a missed, encounter:

> I have met them at close of day
> Coming with vivid faces
> From counter or desk among grey
> Eighteenth-century houses.
> I have passed with a nod of the head
> Or polite meaningless words,
> Or have lingered awhile and said
> Polite meaningless words,
> And thought before I had done
> Of a mocking tale or a gibe
> To please a companion
> Around the fire at the club,
> Being certain that they and I
> But lived where motley is worn. (180)

The speaker fails to see in the quotidian appearance of his contemporaries the possibility of their assuming the very roles that, in "September 1913," he had at once assigned and denied them. Accordingly, the transformation, the change, of that "motley crew" from the contingencies of daily encounter into the "terrible beauty" that supplants it takes place, not by poetic "incantation," by the power of rhythmic naming, but by the force of violence. It is a political violence that, in provoking what Yeats would later come to endorse, the right of the state to take life, drew into sharp relief what he would engage with for the rest of his poetic career, down to the late, great poem, "The Statues," that in certain ways resumes the concern of all three poems on which I dwell here: the *performative* violence of foundation and its all-changing "let there be."

"Easter 1916," then, is not so much an act of commemoration as an interrogation of the act of commemoration as a constitutive or foundational moment in itself. That performativity, which is at once theatrical and linguistic, about performance and the declarative performativity of any act of constitution, is most acute where most violent and counter-intuitive in the transformation enacted on the vulgar contingency of the everyday: where it is, we may say, most improbable, contrary to verisimilitude, and does violence to some moral sense.

> This other man I had dreamed
> A drunken, vainglorious lout.
> He had done most bitter wrong
> To some who are near my heart,
> Yet I number him in the song;
> He, too, has resigned his part
> In the casual comedy;
> He, too, has been changed in his turn,
> Transformed utterly:
> A terrible beauty is born. (181)

The lines refer evidently to John MacBride, Maud Gonne's estranged and abusive husband, executed along with the other leaders of the Rising. It is perhaps no accident then that a tautology haunts that line, "He, too, has been changed in his turn," confusing the distinction between quotidian and transformed appearances: the "turn," the troping that changes the quotidian into the symbolic, remains tainted by the "vainglorious" role, the banal "turn" of the "casual comedy." And yet whatever the valence of the performance, it is performative in its effect, an utter and transformational act of foundation, the declarative forging of a new state, an act before which the performative and commemorative capacities of poetry in its turn are fundamentally challenged. That act of sacrifice, one inevitably haunted by the symbolic and foundational sacrifice that was Easter, whose force was to universalize a specific form of teleological time and make it available for secular appropriation, appears to give a determinate sense (with all the doubleness of the French *sens*, both meaning and direction) to the event of "Easter 1916."

> Too long a sacrifice
> Can make a stone of the heart. (181)

On first reading, the stone appears to oppose the contingency of the merely living being:

Hearts with one purpose alone
Through summer and winter seem
Enchanted to a stone
To trouble the living stream.
The horse that comes from the road,
The rider, the birds that range
From cloud to tumbling cloud,
Minute by minute they change;
A shadow of cloud on the stream
Changes minute by minute;
. . .
Minute by minute they live:
The stone's in the midst of all. (181)

But that stone: is it the indispensable condition of life, "troubling" the stream to life, or that which, like Medusa's gaze, petrifies the living? Yeats's ambiguity is the index of his ambivalence, an ambivalence that transforms the apparently honorific act of commemoration into a merely redundant act of enumeration or naming:

> . . .   our part
> To murmur name upon name,
> As a mother names her child
> When sleep at last has come
> On limbs that had run wild. (181)

The role, the "part" of the poet may be reduced to the performance of what Homi Bhabha has designated the function of a "pedagogical" nationalism: the repetition time and again, "wherever green is worn," of the names of the heroes, to perform repeatedly, winding and unwinding in a virtual purgatory, exactly what "September 1913" had prescribed: acts of commemoration whose function is to consolidate and legitimate acts of foundation that constitute the state and its monopoly of violence.[39] The commemorative poetic act can no longer forge the living continuity of a tradition; it is obliged to recite the names and the event that mark an absolute division, a temporal cesura, that divides the before and after of the new state and the new law with the simultaneous singularity and recurrence that marks any memorable date.

"Nineteen Hundred and Nineteen"

"Easter 1916," then, envisages the reduced role of the poet as being that of the terrible repetition of acts of interminable commemoration, acts that endorse utterly that which is the case or has become so through the performative violence of foundation. It represents, we might say, the closing of a trap set for the poet by his own political program, one that envisaged a process by which the mere citation or invocation of the past dead or the dead past might provoke the desire that would unify a people. When the living die that death, and in dying find themselves transformed, the invocations of the poet become redundant. But if "Easter 1916" was such a chastened palinode of "September 1913," "Nineteen Hundred and Nineteen" abolishes their teleology. It envisages neither the epochal division of times between the Romantic and the cumulative temporality of capital, nor the transformative time of foundational violence that changes the merely contingent motley of the present into the symbolic vector of performativity. In it, time becomes devoid of any redemptive capacity at all. In *Yeats and Violence*, Michael Wood has read this poem so exhaustively, and with such unwavering attention to its relentlessly disconsolate gaze, that it would be superfluous to recapitulate his invaluable work.[40] Let me just remark, then, that "Nineteen Hundred and Nineteen" in its opening section evokes the terrible contingency that is the mark of a pre-Enlightenment human condition of heteronomy, or subjection to external forces, that Benjamin denominates *fate*, "the natural condition of the living."[41] It eclipses the almost universally accepted historicism that saw in the present the culmination of a quasi-Hegelian development from the primitive sphere of blood and kinship to the institutions of civil society and the state:

> We too had many pretty toys when young:
> A law indifferent to blame or praise,
> To bribe or threat; habits that made old wrong
> Melt down, as it were wax in the sun's rays;
> Public opinion ripening for so long
> We thought it would outlive all future days.[42]

The disenchantment of this assumption of an irreversible progress and development toward civil society in light of the extreme violence, not only of the Irish war of decolonization, but also of the First World War and of the revolutionary upheavals that accompanied and succeeded it, gives way to the spectacle of mere contingency, the dissolution of sense rather than the subsumption of the contingent into symbol:

> Now days are dragon-ridden, the nightmare
> Rides upon sleep: a drunken soldiery
> Can leave the mother, murdered at her door,
> To crawl in her own blood, and go scot-free. (207)

This mother, the Ellen Quinn whose unmotivated death at the hands of the Black and Tans was reported to Yeats by Lady Gregory, however associated with kinship and blood, is not Hegel's Antigone any more than she is a nationalist martyr.[43] Her bloody death leads to no resolution in the establishment of civil society or state: rather, "Mere anarchy is loosed upon the world." Her death is a *casual* tragedy that furnishes the occasion of the poem, as the shrugging indifference registered in the phrase "a drunken soldiery" seems to emphasize. In allowing his own rhetoric to become saturated with the indifference of motiveless violence, Yeats performs here an act of commemoration that is radically, desolately, unhistoricist, one that confronts directly the possibility that desire in the end leads to no formation, no unification, but only to the uncomfortable formulation that:

> Man is in love and loves what vanishes,
> What more is there to say? (208)

The only antidote to this disconsolate formulation appears to be the obstinate and counter-factual force of denial of the radically destructive possibilities of human violence:

> That country round
> None dared admit, if such a thought were his,
> Incendiary or bigot could be found
> To burn that stump on the Acropolis. (208)

The spectacle of constitutive violence and the anxiety it provoked as to the redundancy of poetry itself would lead Yeats, on the one hand, to that radical interrogation of acts of foundation in which the richest of his mature poetry is based, and, on the other, to an expressly authoritarian politics that draws its sustenance from an unshirking recognition of the violent artifice that grounds all institutions. Foundation and commemoration are one another's counterparts, each demanding acquiescence to the performative violence of what has been declared to be the case; their mutual motto is: It is what it is. Let it be. If anything saves Yeats's poetry from its politics, and from the latter's swaggering postures, it is surely the relentlessness of its interrogation of violence, its refusal of the consolatory denial of the intimacy of the state with the state of force, and the depth with which his very language registers and bends to the savagery of what it commemorates in its witnessing.[44]

Eden

Let me conclude, arbitrarily and by way of an abrupt shift of focus, by returning to my starting point, the missed encounter between Connolly and Luxemburg. Connolly died, we know all too well, before a firing squad in 1916. The configuration that he envisaged, of nationalism with socialism, of a cultural resistance inseparable from the economic resistance to capitalist accumulation, ran its course in the war of decolonization that began in 1919 and culminated in the Irish Civil War. His was a theoretical and historical intervention that succumbed to apparently total defeat in the acquiescence of Irish labor to the superordination of nationalism and in the violent eradication of the left republican leadership by both the British colonial state and by the Free State, in large part by the man Yeats dubbed the "Irish Mussolini," his much admired friend, the Free State's Minister of Justice, Kevin O'Higgins.

Rosa Luxemburg, too, died violently and prematurely, before her work was done, in 1919. Like Ellen Quinn, and alike perhaps in this respect alone, she died at the hands of auxiliaries, killed by the Freikorps, the German equivalent of the Black and Tans, composed, like them, of the brutalized and brutal veterans of the trenches of the First World War.

Only with hindsight, and through an arbitrary constellation, can we align their deaths in the commemoration of 1919.[45] Almost fifty years later, a very different poet than Yeats, Paul Celan, traveled to Berlin where, in January 1919, Rosa Luxemburg met her end, shot and then drowned in the Landwehrkanal. The poem that he wrote on or out of the occasion of his unique visit to Berlin, "Du liegst im großen Gelausche," is by no means a commemoration of Luxemburg's death in any simple sense. It is, rather, a poem that embraces the sheer contingencies of an occasion together with the de-cypherment, the disencryption, of the material spaces of any site that retains the memory of violence, of any time that re-enacts unwittingly the conjunction of violence with the quotidian.

As Celan's friend and critic Peter Szondi, who accompanied him for much of this visit, remarks: "The poem appears to exist in the charged space between the half-random assortment of images and events marking Celan's stay in Berlin and the artful constellation that is the poem."[46] The poem opens with the addressee, "Du," lying listening *in* (*lauschen*) to the random sounds of the night: *Du liegst im großen Gelausche.*[47] *Lauschen* is stronger than *hören* or *anhören*, signifying a listening in, even an eavesdropping or surveillance, that demands a peculiar degree of attention, one that perhaps seeks sense in the random sounds it apprehends. What follows are, according to Szondi, allusions to Celan's visits during his stay: to the cell in Plötzensee where the July 20 conspirators against Hitler had been executed in 1944—hence the meathooks, *Fleischerhaken* of line 4—and to the Christmas market where, among other ornaments, the "roten Äppelstaken / aus Schweden" (red apple-stakes from Sweden) were sold. The rhyme of *Fleischerhaken* with *Äppelstaken* betrays the secret affinity or convergence between the instruments of torture and execution and the seemingly innocent "apple stakes" that secrete the violence of the Christian sacrifice—their conjunction perhaps invoking the *Hakenkreuz* of the Nazi swastika.

This elaboration of a subterranean connection opens onto a further elaboration of coincidence. Celan had been reading an account of the murder of Rosa Luxemburg and Karl Liebknecht lent to him by Szondi during his visit, and been shown the location of their murder—the site of the former Hotel Eden, in 1919 the quarters of the proto-fascist Freikorps, mobilized by the Social Democratic Party (SPD) in defense of the new Weimar Republic. In 1967, it was the site of an apartment complex still insouciantly named the Eden. The irony of these conjunctions—of Eden with Christmas, of the site of a far from innocent and brutal assassination with the indifferently retained name "Eden," of the sacrifice of victims whom the poem ineffectually resurrects—conjoins to produce what is, as Szondi suggests, a profound meditation on contingency and historical indifference. The Christmas offering—*der Tisch mit den Gaben* (the gift-laden table)—thus bends around or is warped by the invocation of Eden as the occluded and bitterly ironic associations of that term continue to effect a troping or turning of the present, even where that present remains indifferent to them. The force of the occluded remains even where it is unregistered.

But this is not a poem of commemoration, even if it recalls explicitly the deaths of Luxemburg and Liebknecht. Both Jewish revolutionaries are invoked, not by name or by deed, but by the casual language of the assassins as recorded in the inquest into their deaths:

Der Mann ward zum Sieb, die Frau
mußte schwimmen, die Sau

(The man became a sieve, the woman
Had to swim, the sow)

Commemoration is performed, if at all, in Celan's citation here of the very damaged, brutalized language of the assassins that reduces both Luxemburg and Liebknecht to things, to the thingliness in which they resemble ourselves, reified if indifferent victims of the ongoing processes of accumulation:

für sich, für keinen, für jeden

The caustic, mocking injunction to swim, to survive, for herself and for no one, to no end, is finally hedged with the ambiguous "für jeden," where *jeden* may signify both each alone and everyone together. *Jeden* picks up the rhyme with *Eden*, first anticipated in *Schweden*, only to be contaminated now by the association of the Hotel Eden with brutality and murder. Yet at the same time it preserves, if only as a faded or distorted echo, the "edenic" desire of the Spartacist revolution, not as a promise in the future but as a hope located in the past.

The poem performs, then, no identification with any teleology: it leads to no universality, no inevitable commonality, though that too may be descried even in the terrible violence of a political murder. It bespeaks a commonality that counts the cost of the contamination and damage through which it must pass, warped, bent, into any possible future. And it goes on:

> *Nichts*
> > *stockt.*

Nothing stops. Or nothing falters, or stalls. It is impossible to tell whether this is a privative or a substantive nothing. Does nothing stop? Or is it that nothingness itself stops, falters, or stalls? But in any case, it is in the ongoing process of dehumanization that such a constellation becomes possible, the constellation, through sheer contingency, of the past with the present, of the casual with the predestined, the occasion with its signification. Here, in the poem where nothing stops, is spelt out the in/difference of the past and the present: the resonances of Luxemburg's death, of Connolly's death, of Ellen Quinn's mundane, forgotten death, do not cease, but continue into our own time. If they do so, it is not because, like some sacrificed god, they represent the eternal incarnated in the present, but because the damaged lives they incarnate are ineluctably contemporaneous with our own, in that we inhabit the future that was blocked for them, even as we are disjoined from them by the very violence that has historically constituted and shaped our present: *für sich, für keinen, für jeden.*

Slight as it may seem at first glance, this brief poem sustains a profound meditation on the afterlife of violence and its secretion in the present, before or beneath any act of commemoration. It reflects on the contamination of the present by a past violence that is constitutive of a present given by the very violence it ignores. In particular, it is a poem that inhabits the contamination of ordinary language by associations it hardly registers even as it invokes an Eden whose innocence already contained the means of its corruption into evil, the no engrained in the yes. In certain respects, "Du liegst" is a thoroughly traditional lyric in the resources it commands but holds modestly in reserve: the fractured sonnet form underlying its fourteen broken lines, the insistent rhymes, emphatic in their simplicity, that weave through the whole poem and, together with the pattern of consonance and half-rhyme, demand an attentive listening in, *Gelausche*. The declension of *Eden*, the rhyme that picks up those syllables in *Schweden* and echoes in *jeden*, the full rhymes of *–haken* and *–staken*, register almost beneath the threshold a kind of toxic seepage in the language that language in everyday use hardly registers, so indifferent, as Szondi remarks, has it become to the violence it carries forward. Only the slightest hint connects that contamination with the processes of commodification that cluster round the commemoration of religious sacrifice: the table bearing Christmas gifts perhaps softens or blunts the sound of *haken* into that of *Gaben*, *staken* into mere decor.

But the fullest register of violence is in those citations of the language of the witnesses, doctor and soldiers, to Liebknecht's and Luxemburg's deaths. The brutality of the language is entirely casual, unmarked hearsay. Its counterpoetic force cuts abruptly, with a fierce ugliness akin to that of Yeats's "Nineteen Hundred and Nineteen," against the incompletely sensed undercurrents of the previous lines, surfacing their submerged potential for menace. Undoubtedly, *für jeden* picks up the jarring resonances of the Nazi motto "Jedem das Seine," inscribed above the gate of Buchenwald, that utterly contaminated the old bourgeois saw, "to each his own," and the utopian Marxist variant, "to each according to his needs," into a nightmarish "abandon hope all ye who enter here": "everyone gets what they deserve." The notion of the gift, *Gabe*, that is at once talent or skill and whatever is gratuitously rendered, declines into the brute givenness, the *es gibt*, of the actual, the meting of reward and punishment on the basis of mere existence, even as the gift of sacrifice is reduced to the cheap commodified gifts strewn on a market-table.

And so it goes on, *Nichts stockt.*

It is all too easy to forget, as we recall what 1913 means to us now, that the volume of world trade had "reached a share of global output in 1913 that it was not to surpass until the 1970s," and that globalization was already considered—in the words of J. M. Keynes—"normal, certain, and permanent, except in the direction of general improvement."[48] The eve of the First World War was a high point in imperial globalization, a moment, as Luxemburg knew, of accelerating accumulation on a world scale. The labor struggles around the Dublin Lockout and the formations of Irish syndicalism were one site of resistance, economic and cultural, and no less significant for all their apparent marginality, to what Luxemburg named "the systematic destruction and annihilation of all the non-capitalist social units that obstruct capital's development." One hundred years later, it may be that we confront what Luxemburg foresaw, a crisis in global capitalism generated by its approach to a limit on its capacity to accumulate. We inhabit a moment of change, one possibly as critical as that of the period the passing centenary recalls, another moment of restructuring that signifies a shift in the regime of accumulation. What Marx designated, erroneously according to Luxemburg, "primitive accumulation" targeted raw materials, land, resources. The new mode of accumulation targets what we may call the "second commons," those institutions wrested from capital historically by social struggles for the collective means to life that were expropriated in the process of accumulation by dispossession that enclosed the "first commons." These institutions of the second commons include social welfare, public health, transportation, water, and education. *All* these institutions are subject now to an increasingly systematic and violent effort of effective enclosure that goes by the new name of privatization, which seeks to take back the forms of the second commons that have been the means both to biological life and to life-in-common and to subject them to monetization.[49] This seizure is proclaimed in the name of a "crisis" that is really, as we well know, a crisis of distribution of abundant wealth in a time when increasingly large portions of the population have been consigned to permanent redundancy, to disposability. It is my hope that in recalling the events of 1913 and 1916, the Lockout and the Rising, and in reflecting not only on the names but on the thought and the work of those like Connolly and Luxemburg, that we do not engage in merely pious acts of commemoration, but will commit ourselves to shaping the spaces in which our resistance to this new regime of accumulation, one that targets for destruction every value that is not subject to monetization and exchange, can be affirmed and articulated, thought anew. For it is only in our resistance to the violence of the present that the afterlives of futures imagined in the past, futures violently denied, can find a way to speak to us of other possible modes of living in common, of living abundantly.

Notes

1. Ciaran Carson, "Queen's Gambit." *Belfast Confetti*. Wake Forest University Press, 1989, p. 35.
2. Walter Benjamin, "On the Concept of History." *Selected Writings: Volume 4: 1938–1940*, edited by Howard Eiland and Michael W. Jennings and translated by Edmund Jephcott and others. Belknap Press, 2003, p. 396.
3. Benjamin, "On the Concept of History," p. 390.
4. Theodor Adorno, *Minima Moralia: Reflections from Damaged Life*, translated by E. F. N. Jephcott. Verso, 1978, p. 151.

5. C. Desmond Greaves, *The Life and Times of James Connolly*. International Publishers, 1971, p. 127.
6. See Margaretta D'Arcy and John Arden, *The Non-Stop Connolly Show: A Dramatic Cycle of Continuous Struggle in Six Parts*. Pluto Plays, 1977–8, Part 3, III. 4–5, pp. 129–34. I am grateful to Alexandra Poulain for calling my attention to this moment in the play.
7. Greaves, *James Connolly*, p. 128.
8. Rosa Luxemburg, *The Accumulation of Capital*, translated by Agnes Schwarzschild, introduction by Tadeusz Kowalik. Routledge, 2003, p. 338.
9. Luxemburg, *Accumulation of Capital*, p. 345.
10. Luxemburg, *Accumulation of Capital*, p. 350.
11. On Connolly's theorization of the relationship between labor and nationalism, and on his account of the greater radicalism of Irish workers, see David Lloyd, "Rethinking National Marxism: James Connolly and 'Celtic Communism.'" *Irish Times: Temporalities of Modernity*. Field Day, 2008, pp. 101–26. See also Gregory Dobbins, "Whenever Green is Red: James Connolly and Postcolonial Theory." *Nepantla: Views from the South*, vol. 1, no. 3, 2000, pp. 605–48, which similarly argues that Connolly produced "a new understanding of how the Marxist theoretical category of dialectical contradiction could be articulated within the colonized world" (p. 623).
12. Emmet O'Connor, *A Labour History of Ireland, 1824–1960*. Gill and Macmillan, 1992, p. 85.
13. O'Connor, *Labour History of Ireland*, p. 88.
14. Greaves, *James Connolly*, p. 305.
15. Benjamin, "Concept of History," p. 392.
16. Jacques Derrida, "Shibboleth: For Paul Celan." *Sovereignties in Question: The Poetics of Paul Celan*, edited by Thomas Dutoit and Outi Pasanen. Fordham University Press, 2005, p. 24.
17. Benjamin, "Concept of History," p. 395.
18. Derrida, "Shibboleth," pp. 35–6.
19. Derrida, "Shibboleth," p. 24.
20. W. B. Yeats, "A General Introduction for My Work." *Essays and Introductions*. Gill and Macmillan, 1961, p. 509.
21. Paul Celan, "The Meridian." *Collected Prose*, translated by Rosemary Waldrop. Carcanet Press, 1986, p. 50.
22. Pádraig Yeates, *Lockout: Dublin 1913*. Gill and Macmillan, 2000, pp. 143–4.
23. See *The Variorum Edition of the Poems of W. B. Yeats*, edited by Peter Allt and Russell K. Alspach. Macmillan, 1973, pp. 289–90 and A. Norman Jeffares, *A Commentary on the Collected Poems of W. B. Yeats*. Stanford University Press, 1968, p. 129.
24. W. B. Yeats, "September 1913." *The Poems: A New Edition*, ed. Richard J. Finneran. Macmillan, 1983, pp. 108–9 (p. 108); hereafter, page numbers are given in the text.
25. Max Horkheimer and Theodor W. Adorno, "Juliette, or Enlightenment and Morality." *Dialectic of Enlightenment*, translated by John Cumming. Continuum, 1972, p. 83.
26. On that project of unification, see W. B. Yeats, "Four Years: 1887–1891." *The Autobiography of W. B. Yeats*. Macmillan, 1953, p.119 and my

comments on this and related passages in David Lloyd, "Nationalism and Postcolonialism." *W. B. Yeats in Context*, edited by David Holdeman and Ben Levitas. Cambridge University Press, 2010, pp. 180–2.

27. Derrida, "Shibboleth," pp. 25–6.
28. Susan Stewart, "Notes on Distressed Genres." *Crimes of Writing: Problems in the Containment of Representation.* Duke University Press, 1994, pp. 66–101.
29. Benjamin, "Concept of History," p. 391.
30. James Connolly, *Labour in Irish History. Collected Works*, 2 vols, introduction by Michael O'Riordan. New Books, 1987, vol. I, p. 101.
31. Connolly, *Labour in Irish History*, vol. I, pp. 102–3.
32. Connolly, *Labour in Irish History*, vol. II, p. 287.
33. Walter Benjamin, "The Task of the Translator," translated by Harry Zohn. *Selected Writings: Volume 1: 1913–1926*, edited by Marcus Bullock and Michael W. Jennings. Belknap Press, 1996, pp. 254–5. See Chapter 2 for a full discussion of this remark.
34. The term is V. K. Menon's, cited in Jeffares, *Commentary*, p. 225.
35. W. B. Yeats, "Easter 1916." *Poems*, pp. 180–2 (p. 180); hereafter, page numbers are given in the text.
36. Anne Enright, *The Forgotten Waltz*. McLelland and Stewart, 2011, p. 38.
37. David Lloyd, "The Poetics of Politics: Yeats and the Founding of the State." *Anomalous States: Irish Writing and the Post-Colonial Moment.* Lilliput Press, 1993, pp. 59–87.
38. Yeats, "General Introduction," p. 515.
39. On the pedagogical and the performative modes of nationness, see Homi Bhabha, "DissemiNation." *The Location of Culture.* Routledge, 1994, p. 145.
40. Michael Wood, *Yeats and Violence*. Oxford University Press, 2010.
41. Walter Benjamin, "Fate and Character." *Selected Writings: Volume 1: 1913–1926*, edited by Marcus Bullock and Michael W. Jennings. Belknap Press, 1996, p. 204.
42. W. B. Yeats, "Nineteen Hundred and Nineteen." *Poems*, pp. 206–10 (p. 207); hereafter, page numbers are given in the text.
43. Despite the date of the poem, Ellen Quinn was in fact murdered on November 1, 1920. My thanks to Timothy G. McMahon for reminding me of this.
44. I have discussed Yeats's virtual obsession with the founding and legitimating violence of the state, and its relation to contemporaneous discussion of that topic in the work of Walter Benjamin and Carl Schmitt that is inseparable from the revolutionary moment in Germany in 1919 to which Rosa Luxemburg was key, in "The Poetics of Decision: Yeats, Benjamin and Schmitt." *Études Anglaises*, vol. 68, no. 4, October–December 2015, pp. 468–82.
45. The association between Celan and Yeats is made somewhat less arbitrary by Celan's own acknowledgment of what he owed to Yeats. See Pierre Joris's note to Paul Celan, "In Gestalt eines Ebers"/"In the Shape of a Boar." *Memory Rose into Threshold Speech: The Collected Earlier Poetry*, translated by Pierre Joris, bilingual edition. Farrar, Straus and Giroux, 2020, pp. 402–3.

46. Peter Szondi, "Eden." *Celan Studies*, edited by Jean Bollack and translated by Susan Bernofsky and Harvey Mendelsohn. Stanford University Press, 2003, p. 85.

47. Paul Celan, "Du liegst." *Gedichte*, vol. I. Suhrkamp, 1975, p. 334.

48. Charles Emmerson, *1913: In Search of the World Before the Great War.* Public Affairs, 2013, cited in Mark Archer, "The Year of Globalization." *Wall Street Journal*, June 15, 2013, p. C5. http://online.wsj.com/article/SB 10001424127887324299104578527420006048876.html (last accessed July 29, 2021).

49. See further on the second commons in David Lloyd, "Countering Legitimacy: Prison Protest and the Colonial Welfare State." *States of Welfare*, special issue of *Occasion*, vol. 2, December 2010. http://arcade.stanford.edu/journ als/occasion/articles/countering-legitimacy-prison-protest-and-colonial-wel fare-state-by-david-lloyd (last accessed July 29, 2021).

Chapter 4

"To Live Surrounded by a White Song," or, The Sublimation of Race in Experiment: On the Margins of Susan Howe

The various terms that have been applied, with whatever hesitation, to the alternative strain of Irish poetry on which this book focuses—experimental, modernist, late modernist, neo-avant-garde, avant-garde—might each seem to be qualified, if not directly contradicted by the appendage of the modifier "Irish." We are accustomed to consider "modernism" a cosmopolitan or international venture, to the extent that to speak of "international style" almost immediately suggests that the style in question is modernist. The noun seems then to negate what the modifier "Irish" implies, a specific location or a sense of national identity that inflects modernism in ways that counteract its associations with territorial deracination, global flows of form as well as capital, and abstraction from the particularities of geography or culture. Franco Moretti's by now notorious, and certainly ill-timed comment that "*Ulysses* fully belongs to a critical turning point of international bourgeois culture—a status it would not have achieved in the investigation of Ireland's peripheral and backward form of capitalism" nicely encapsulated that critical prejudice.[1] Though a generation of postcolonial Irish studies has challenged such judgments, emphasizing the precocious ways in which Ireland was drawn violently into colonial modernity and questioning the attribute of "peripherality" to any location in the system of capitalist relations, the critical assumption persists: the addition of the qualifier "Irish" (as with any other such adjective, whether "Indian," "Brazilian," or "African American") inevitably suggests a qualified modernism, one whose relatively conservative, derivative, or "backward" forms fail to register the full impact of global modernity. The rubric "Irish Modernism" implies likewise the specific and local emplacement of a poetry while appealing to precisely what might be thought to *displace* and undo attachment to the local, that is, innovation or aesthetic experiment. Is it the case, then, that the poetic experiments of modernist form negate their identification as Irish? Such a question forces the further question as to how culture, local knowledge, or historical influences play into or against the constitutive autonomy of aesthetic form, or to what degree identity or place are constitutive of culture in ways that bar the universal reach of the aesthetic. It also opens the possibility that poetic forms dedicated to a scrupulous undoing of any predetermining cultural inflection may be more or less inevitably punctuated by the other rhythms of what is occluded, unseen, erased in its displacement and which yet returns or, in the sense in which Jacques Lacan defined the real, "always come back to the same place," haunting the very scene from which it is displaced.[2]

The question of "Irish modernism" thus allows us to bring together two distinct registers of critical inquiry. The first is the place of what one might call identity and its associated rubrics— nationality, coloniality, and, finally, race—in the context, again with a hardly innocent adjective, of *Irish* circuits of migration or circulation. For what "Irish" might refer to is interrupted and troubled by all those ambiguities and points of mixing that stem from Ireland's long experience of crossing and of crossing over, determined by its historical location in the networks of colonial capitalism that are relentlessly transnational in tendency. Indeed, the definitions of nationality and race are, given the potentially transatlantic or even global extension of what constitutes Irish poetry in the context of migration and displacement, peculiarly troubled by the ambiguous, double place occupied by the Irish, violently racialized on one shore, whitening no less violently on the other of what we have lately begun to call the "Black and Green Atlantic."[3]

The second register has indirectly to do with the first, having to do with poetics, and the place of poetry in the articulation of Irishness, whether we speak of a long tradition of poetry, from Thomas Moore to Seamus Heaney, that expressly raises the question of Irishness, or that modernist vein of Irish poetry that *Counterpoetics of Modernity* foregrounds, from Denis Devlin and Brian Coffey to Maurice Scully, Trevor Joyce, or Catherine Walsh, that we might call modernist, innovative or experimental and, as by default and almost in the same breath, *international*. What circuits define, link, and divide an Irish poetry circulating across the space of what Ed Dorn once dubbed "the North Atlantic turbine"?[4] If we assume that what defines any poetry as "Irish" may lie either in the ostensible point of origin of its writer or in the consistency of its concerns with a certain "matter of Ireland," what interruptions and hauntings are governed by the specific matter with which poetry engages, or by the matter which, in its disavowal or erasure, imposes its own pressures, the pressures of the "real," on every *poiesis*, leaving its mark on the *form* even where it is suppressed as *content*? In that case, the question of innovation itself returns, of what it means to renew, do anew. Has innovation to do primarily with *formal* matters, or rather with *matter* itself, with the matter of poetry, for example, the matter of Ireland? Is renewal or experiment driven by the pressure of the material with which it engages as much as from any immanent formal dialectics within the medium itself? The latter supposition would again trouble the dichotomy of innovation and identity, suggesting that the formations of race or identity, so often regarded as the mere material embarrassment of poetic work, are never so easily extricated either from matter or from form, but insist in ways that cannot help but impact form in the aesthetic domain, including the forms of those most innovative poetries that might seem to have nothing to do with race, or even with experience or identity.

My title is drawn from a peculiarly haunting and poetic phrase in a chapter of Frantz Fanon's *Black Skin, White Masks*, "The Fact of Blackness":

> All round me the white man, above the sky tears at its navel, the earth rasps under my feet, and there is a white song, a white song. All this whiteness that burns me . . .[5]

> Alentour le Blanc, en haut le ciel s'arrache le nombril, la terre crisse sous mes pieds et un chant blanc, blanc. Toute cette blancheur qui me calcine . . .[6]

Apart from its haunting resonances, Fanon's phrasing here condenses poetically two distinct modalities of race: the first involving the idea of *race as erasure*, or as a lived invisibility—race bleached out in a too white light; the second suggesting that *race appears as matter*, as a recalcitrant material, as the ash or cinders that remain, as opposed to the universal position of the *formal* subject that is occupied by the White with its abstract song. These two modalities appear to be opposed, even contradictory. In one, the racialized subject is erased from humanity and occupies the very threshold of the human at and as its vanishing point. The racial subject—or object—is obliterated by the crushing power of what Fanon elsewhere calls a "unilateral declaration of universality."[7] In the other, the racialized object persists, obdurately, as the very figure of materiality, or as an insistent corporeality, recalcitrant in its refusal to be erased, to go away: here it is the earth that rasps its coarse noise against the pure white song.

These contradictory modalities are mediated by the force of *abstraction* that secretly underpins the constitution of race. Abstraction is the process in which identity as the negation of difference meets with the indifference of identity as formal equivalence in its sheer fungibility. For abstraction performs the double function of erasing difference in the process of positing an undifferentiated human subject that occupies the place of the universal and of posing itself against the particularity and concreteness of the material that is the irreducible remainder of any act of formalization.[8] The human is defined against the particularities of what, by virtue of its very materiality, must become the non-, or in the terms Fanon everywhere suggests, not-yet human. And it is the sheer, formal abstractness of identity that constitutes whiteness, for whiteness is in the first place not a "racial" position, an ethnic identity among others, but is the formal subject that lays claim to a universally representative position: that of the human as identical to itself. What Fanon so poetically identifies can be understood, then, as a poetics of race, a relation of form to matter, a principle of selection and omission, a whiteness that is both a margin that surrounds, and confines, and defines, and a song whose ubiquity and saturation of the field of representation drowns out and erases that which is not identical with it.

Fanon's perception is in accord with the recognition that race is, as much as anything, an instance and a product of the aesthetic. We can trace this aesthetic back to Kant's *Third Critique*, *Of Judgement*, where the moment of judgment is one in which, in the act of judging, "we let go as far as possible the element of matter in our representation" and focus instead on the formal qualities of the mode of our representative activity.[9] For only in the *form* of the representation, in the form of disinterested contemplation unaffected by the material or sensuous qualities of the phenomenon, do we rise, by way of abstraction from those properties, to the formal identity of sheer human subjectivity. For Kant, those who are unable to do so, those who are *not yet* human subjects, are represented by the Caribs and the Iroquois, the savage "raw men" (*die rohe Menschen*) detained still at the threshold of humanity by the seductions of the sensuous. In Fanon's terms, the black man "represented a stage in development."[10] Accordingly, these savage subjects are, as Kant puts it in the *Second Critique*, still at the level of the "pathological," subject to the impulses of need and desire, pleasure and pain, and as such incapable of rising to the disinterested disposition of the representative human subject. Trapped in their corporeal particularity, they cannot yet assume the categorical status of ethical subjects.[11] Immersed in the immediacy of a pleasure and pain that are all too visceral, physiological, or pathological, they cannot attain to the level of the formal and universal subject of judgment freed both of its contingent particularity and, as far as possible, from materiality.

Of course, this pure formalism of the aesthetic judgment always and inevitably stumbles, caught on the constitutive contradiction that the object of aesthetic judgment must be some particular thing, not a rule or a concept or a principle, but a material entity, an example: it cannot finally be reduced to the pure formality of a representative instance, but retains something of the resistant particularity of the unsubsumable. Form can never entirely shuffle off the burden of materiality.[12]

These considerations bring us back to the question of poetry as a particular instance of the aesthetic. For we may say that a similar structure informs both the aesthetic judgment according to Kant and experimental poetry. Critics are by now alert to the recurrently posed dichotomy between poetries that deal with race or identity and the innovative or experimental, between a poetry all too often read for its quasi-sociological interest or for an affirmation or exposition of identity, and an experimental or avant-garde poetry rigorously critical of identity formation, suspicious of groundings in experience or of representation, understood in the restricted but connected forms of the presentation of personal experience or of "speaking for" a community. As Dorothy Wang expresses it in *Thinking Its Presence: Form, Race and Subjectivity in Contemporary Asian American Poetry*:

> The double standard extends to how we read works of poetry closely. Critics are more likely to think about formal questions—say, poetic tone and syntax—when speaking about Ashbery's poems but almost certainly to focus on political or black "content" when examining the work of Amiri Baraka, a poet who has pushed the limits of formal invention for over half a century—certainly as long as Ashbery has.[13]

Wang notes further that critics of poetry

> overwhelmingly tend to ignore race by focusing exclusively on formal properties or other themes in the writing . . .; to explicitly oppose political and social "content" (including racial identity) against formal literary concerns; or to distinguish between "bad" ethnic poetry (autobiographical, identity-based) and "good" poetry (formally experimental) that just happens to be written by a person of color.[14]

There is, as Wang notes, something almost self-evident in the dichotomy, one that seems to suggest the alignment of racial concerns with a poetry of *experience* and formal concerns with a poetics of *experiment*. Indeed, we recognize in the suspicion of experimental poetry toward the sensuous—its reserve with regard to certain forms of rhythmic recurrence and verbal music, toward rhetorical voicing and metaphoric webs—a relation to its anxious dismantling of seductive ideological investments, its subordination of the material, of the racialized matter of corporeal pleasures. We can recast these very schematic attributes otherwise, in terms of experimental writing's suspicion of reference, its distaste for anecdote or fable, or for mimesis, that we might refer to as its anti-narrative taboo. It is no less subject to an anti-imagistic taboo: experimental writing tends to be obedient to the iconoclastic tradition, to honor the commandment against representation. In the Irish context, Beckett is perhaps the crucial figure here, as attempts, including my own, to recruit Beckett to postcolonial or political readings have tended to founder in the writing's resolute refusal to denote, to represent unequivocally. Such readings might be saved by arguing that it is Beckett's *form* that is political, performing a continuous deconstruction of representation. Or, to put it another way, is Beckett's very Irishness precisely to be read off his corrosive suspicion of mimesis, his dismantling of the structures of representation? Yet this surely is to return Beckett to an identity formation, and indeed, to a rendering of "experience" that he rejected in the most uncompromising of terms, insisting as he did that "the material of experience is not the material of expression."[15]

But is the alternative then to abstract the writer entirely from the pressures of history and culture that manifestly formed him or her? The dilemma is not easily resolved and has its analogies. Take, for example, the instance of Theresa Hak-Kyung Cha's *Dictée*: critical objection to her treatment as among a group of US avant-garde writers to the disregard of her deep concern with the history and culture of Korea and with the experience of the Korean diaspora led to crucial rereadings of her work that reinstated the constitutive importance of Korean and Korean American histories to her writing. Yet such readings also produced the effect, as Naoki Sakai has argued, of transforming form into the trace or representation of historical trauma or racial alienation:

> To say that the text has to be read as a typical reaction to a foreign environment by the Korean is to insulate the reader from the questioning power of the text and thereby to distance the reader from the text by means of the imagined and somewhat invisible screen that warrants the eternalized and, therefore, separatist *distinction* between "us" and "them." It is, consequently, to refuse to read the text itself insofar as the text is a work or a working.[16]

Dictée's formal fragmentation, we might say, becomes thus reduced to the correlative of empirical experience, the adequate representation of fragmented, postcolonial life, non-identity merely a mode of identity. The distinctive formal qualities of both Beckett's and Cha's work seem to resist, in their experimental or innovative drive, attempts to return them to the material or biographical foundations from which one might claim them to emerge, and critical work that endeavors so to return them risks seeming reductive in the last instance. Not to do so, however, is to ignore the degree to which the innovative forms of their work may yet be impelled by material pressures and to risk another mode of reduction, that of reading them as formal instances of aesthetic universality. In what follows, I will propose that we need a rethinking of the virtually aporetic terms that establish a generally hierarchical dichotomy between the formal and the material that underwrites the specific dichotomy between the experimental and the experiential, between formal universality and the condition of racialization or the exploration of identity.

Let me turn then, by way of example, to one of the finest instances of experimental poetry of the last couple of decades, Susan Howe's "Melville's Marginalia," a poem that makes explicit the links between its transatlantic Irish points of departure. Although, as Howe puts it in her classic *My Emily Dickinson*, "the facts of an artist's life will never explain that particular artist's truth," I will indulge for a moment in biography, biography that in the course of the work she herself invokes.[17] Susan Howe is an American Irish poet, daughter of playwright Mary Manning, Beckett's lifelong friend, sister of poet Fanny Howe, raised in Boston, and deeply interested in the cultural history and formations of white and Puritan New England. She might be, in other words, the consummate instance of "Irish crossings." She is at the same time an avant-garde poet thoroughly in the American grain. As John Wilkinson writes:

> Susan Howe is a poet whose writing is revered for its spareness, its scholarship, its implicit feminist politics, and its exploration of what it is to be American. It draws for its prime example on Charles Olson's *Maximus Poems*, an epic of migration and American colonisation making much use of documentary materials, a debt which Susan Howe generously affirms. Her book-length projects of reading and recovery, starting with *My Emily Dickinson*, substitute for Olson's vitalism an attachment to the tradition of American transcendentalism.[18]

At the same time, and despite these apparently traditional resources, "Imminent transcendence and aching postponement, erasure and reframing characterise Susan Howe's poetry," and in ways that have proven "central to contemporary poetic theory."[19]

"Melville's Marginalia" indeed works by a *method* that seems to emulate the Emily Dickinson of her earlier *My Emily Dickinson*: "Forcing, abbreviating, pushing, padding, subtracting, riddling, interrogating, re-writing, she pulled text from text."[20] In many respects it is a "found poem" that "pulls" the elements of its own text primarily from the eponymous 1965 PhD thesis by Wilson Walker Cowen that compiled the marginalia and annotations of every text marked up in Melville's library. It is thus a text concerned from the outset with poetic material, with margins and marginality, and with erasure. I refer not only to the construction of the text around Melville's marginalia to a number of works, most notably for Howe the poems of the nineteenth-century Irish poet James Clarence Mangan,[21] but also to erasure and margin as principles of construction and figures for the relation of form to material in both the lyric and prose segments of the text, segments that are often generically mixed:

> Round about the margin or edge of anything in a way that is close to the limit. A narrow margin. Slightly.
>   If water is margined-imagined by the tender grass.
>   Marginal. Belonging to the brink or margent.
>   The brink or brim of anything from telepathy to poetry. . . .' (MM 92)

> The pale bright margins . . . . (MM 109)

>   In those places think him to be

>   In those breaks and pauses

>   Turned to the boats

>   that landscape meets the air

>   I could only plan

>   All other simulacra

>   marked then ERASED

>   Some green forest annotation

>   failed have forgotten

>   Between two negations (MM 111)

Melville's marginalia, and the associations they throw up, are the matter of the text, a matter that draws the marginal into its material as a matter of form. We are allowed to observe the maker in the act of mining her materials, the mode of her making exposed like some postmodern kitchen:

> I began to write *Melville's Marginalia* by pulling a phrase, sometimes just a word or a name, at random from Cowen's alphabetically arranged *Melville's Marginalia* and letting that lead me by free association to each separate poem in the series.
>   Poetry is thought transference.
>   Free association isn't free. (MM 105)

For these are "bound margins," the poet bound by some ineluctable compulsion to return time and again to a singular figure, that of the poet Mangan.

> Names who are strangers out of bounds of the bound margin: I thought one way to write about a loved author would be to follow what trails he follows through words of others. (MM 92)

And the reader in turn is bound to ask what deep compulsion draws Howe to return from the author of the "white whale" to the blond poet of the ballad "Róisín Dubh," "O My Dark Rosaleen," possibly the most famous Irish nationalist ballad of the mid-nineteenth century? This ballad she recalls someone singing in her great-aunt's garden on Killiney Bay in her childhood, awakening a dim transatlantic memory at the edge of consciousness (MM 105):

> Margins speak of fringes of consciousness or marginal associations.
> What is the shadow reflex of art I am in the margins of doubt. (MM 91)

What is this "shadow reflex" that haunts the text in the figure of the "spectral-looking man," Mangan, with his "corpse like features / as still as marble" (MM 91, 99, and 126)? What frames the peculiar dialectic by which this pale poet appears as a dark shadow haunting the pale margins of the text? A pallor that becomes a shadow, we may observe, is a "negation of the negation."

Mangan, himself a denizen of the Dublin libraries, is a specter almost literally troubling the library, the archive of texts. Obsessed in his own turn with specters and haunting, he returns through Melville to Howe as another spectral and unexhausted potential. We have two clues as to the source of the haunting, one in what the text omits or erases, one in what it marginally declares. The flyleaf to Melville's copy of *The Poems of James Clarence Mangan* is dated February 16, 1862, toward the end of the first year of the Civil War (MM 106). It had been published in New York in 1859; its editor was John Mitchel, the radical Irish nationalist who had been transported to Tasmania for his involvement in the Young Ireland uprising of 1848 and later escaped and made his way to the United States. Mitchel notoriously cast Mangan as an inveterate rebel, in a passage heavily underscored by Melville, as "a rebel politically, and a rebel intellectually and spiritually,—a rebel with his whole heart and soul against the British spirit of the age" (MM 107). But we should also note that Mitchel's typology of Mangan is racial, not only in his characterization of the poet as "an Irish papist rebel," but in his deeper typology of Mangan as a two-fold being with a duality canonical for stereotypes of the Irish: "the one well known to the Muses, the other to the Police." [22] The Irishman appears as ever as criminal and bard, singer and drunk: that is, as angel and ape, in L. P. Curtis's well-known summary formulation.[23] In Thomas Carlyle's terms, this is the ineluctable duality of the "white negro"—a term whose origin in a chapter of *Sartor Resartus* that aligns the ragged Irish peasantry and the English dandy conveniently furnishes the link between Mangan's idiosyncratic dandyism and Mitchel's identification of his racial Irishness.[24]

But what Howe does *not* mention is that by 1859, Mitchel had undergone the sea-change of the transatlantic Irish: from being an Irish felon, a rebel against English Empire, he had become a supporter of slavery and one of the Confederacy's most vocal advocates in *The Citizen* and, later, *The Southern Citizen*. In this context, Mitchel's description of Mangan as a rebel against "the British spirit of the age" takes on a different complexion, making him not only a rebel against imperialism but also one against the spirit of industrial capitalism that defined both Britain *and* the Union, colonialism *and* the abolition of slavery. Mangan's racial Irishness in all its oppositional figuration marks the peculiar reversible margin where, as Mark Quigley has argued, the *Irish* themselves become white, but *Irishness* continues to occupy the oxymoronic status of the "white negro." But it now functions in a new fashion, distinguishing the ethnic group that continually marks the boundaries of race, highlighting its differential modality, its inessential positionalities. Above all, the invocation of Irishness performs "the dirty work of protecting and concealing the preserves of white racial privilege by way of its strategic management of difference."[25]

If, then, this "author-evacuated text" is haunted by the specter of the poet Mangan, "Ghost of one's own glory / into the subjectless abject" (MM 113), is not this figure of abjection also haunted, compulsively, compulsorily, by the peculiar racial conjunctions, those of his moment, those of our moment, which makes its shadowy outline somewhat clearer? But these are conjunctions that the text erases, rubbing them out into "<u>VERBAL PHANTOMS</u>" that overwrite, white on white, "the liquid clearness of an Ionian sky" (MM 100).

This other haunting is indeed summoned, if briefly, through the figure of Melville's Bartleby who appears for a moment, almost marginally, in Howe's text: "I saw the pencilled trace of Melville's passage through John Mitchel's introduction and knew by shock of poetry telepathy the real James Clarence Mangan is the progenitor of fictional Bartleby" (MM 106). "They are always masked" (MM 114): throughout "Melville's Marginalia," Mangan appears as the mask of Bartleby, Bartleby as the mask or avatar of Mangan. This chiasmatic figuration remains in the margins of the text and yet, as we shall see, opens onto the whole question of race and representation precisely in and through its momentary invocation and almost instantaneous marginalization or forgetting. There is, however, one problem with the self-evidence of the conjunction that strikes Howe so forcibly: as she notes, "the problem was chronology" (MM 106). The Haverty edition of *Poems by James Clarence Mangan, with Biographical Introduction by John Mitchel* that Melville bought in 1862 was only published in 1859; "Bartleby the Scrivener" was published in 1853. Howe endeavors to show that Melville may have known of Mangan's work as early as 1851, but ultimately hers is a "preposterous history," as Mieke Bal defines it in a work that is all about citation and repetition, *Quoting Caravaggio*: "This reversal, which puts what came chronologically first ('pre-') as an aftereffect behind ('post') its later recycling, is what I would like to call *preposterous history.*"[26] As Bal remarks, "Quoting Caravaggio changes his work forever."[27] Howe's text similarly changes both the text of Mangan and that of Melville's Bartleby. In her citing or summoning of the specters of Bartleby and Mangan, in her intertextual crossings, she abstracts them from history even as she deepens in other respects their historicity, precisely by setting into play through invocation the whole weave and texture of the historical moment from which they have been abstracted. Uprooted by citation, deterritorialized, they undergo a sea-change as radical as any that affected the Irish in their own material deterritorialization during the years that Melville wrote.

That deterritorialization is the effect of a doubleness that we could characterize as belonging to the operations of citation itself, belonging on the one hand to the domain of law and authority, on the other to the less canny world of the spirit where, as Mangan knew well, every deep sounded by a citation, every allusion that summons the text that lies beneath it, raises unruly spirits from the "lower deeps" that lurk unpredictably below it.[28] As an invocation of authority, citation calls the subject before the law in the vigorous movement of interpellation: it demands, in the form of the summons, recognition of the force or authority, the *Gewalt*, of the law. Or it calls upon precedent to establish the authority of the prior, the "progenitor" of the present case. Literary citation mimics these processes in invoking the authority of the text that is their source, the authority of precedence and of influence that shapes and constrains the "secondary" text within "bound margins." It establishes the "real progenitor" behind the succession of texts and, out of this ordered sequence, constitutes ultimately the authoritative canon of its legitimate members. Those that do not belong or fail to assimilate remain on the margins of the law and of literature.

Yet every citation summons more than it intends, bringing into play an indeterminate cascade of "free associations" in accord with the word's root meaning in exciting or calling into movement (*citere*). On the margin or in the obscure depths of any citation that intends to authorize or determine the bounds of meaning or lineage is secreted precisely that which the law would foreclose, the other text with its own associations, disseminations, and allusions. If a citation summons the subject before the law, it also acts to summons specters whose unruly manifestations may be less easily disciplined.[29] What seems peripheral, a marginal note, turns out to have a force that irrupts, opening in the text movements that exceed its bounds. This double effect of citation, binding and mobilizing at one and the same time, informs the procedures of "Melville's Marginalia," bringing into play potentials that lie in the very margins of the work.

If, then, Bartleby is the mask of Mangan, the representative who veils the "real progenitor," what does he represent? What networks of association does his invocation in the margins of the text, in the "fringes of [Howe's] consciousness," disseminate through the whole?

Is not Bartleby, this figure "Like a very ghost," whose pallor is stressed over and again throughout Melville's story, *prima facie* the figure of the writer, of an "author-evacuated" writing become automatic, mechanical, procedural, forever copying, reduced to a formal labor of repetition, invisible behind "a high green folding screen"—much indeed, as Mangan, who also worked as a scrivener in Dublin law offices, made a whole poetic out of translation, citation, disguised repetitions, and masked himself in others' work? Bartleby's fate, that of the first occupier of Wall Street, is the "passive resistance" of a writing become abject, just as his labors in turn have taken on the formal, abstract, alienated quality of capitalist labor, a labor and a fate that the story's narrator, his employer, futilely seeks to humanize by sentimental identification and compassion: "Ah, Bartleby! Ah, humanity!"[30] As Michael Rogin comments:

> Bartleby inhabits the mass society that Tocqueville feared would triumph in America if meaningful, free, political action decayed. The power of Melville's short story comes from its abstractness. By resituating *Bartleby* historically, we can see it as a comment on the historical triumph of abstraction.[31]

Through his "power of negativity" Bartleby "drains his surroundings of the humanity in which the lawyer would like to believe."[32] Yet in another sense, of course, the narrator is correct to associate the repetitive labor of copying with the abstract figure of humanity as it appears in "mass society," just as Bartleby's previous labors in the Dead Letter Office reduced the particularities of individual existences to mere waste to be eliminated.

Abstraction is the very condition of commodity production, the condition that transforms the particular concrete labor of production into mere quanta of labor power, itself capable of commodification and exchange. Abstraction is the necessary condition also of what became known as "free labor" as opposed to slave labor. The abstraction of *labor*, which produces labor as political economy's universal measure of value, is no less the counterpart to and condition for the abstraction of the subject on which ethical value is predicated, as we saw above, and which yet makes that subject's identity at once universal and indifferent, subjected to merely formal equivalence. It was also the condition that afflicted writing itself, as Melville already painfully knew, as a writer constrained to produce for exchange in forms reproducible and commodifiable.[33] In this respect, we may read Bartleby as the figure of the writer reduced to a kind of writing machine, pallid and bloodless, facing the indifferent walls of the lawyer's office, one black, one white, that, as the narrator insists, frame his labor.

But I want also to counterpoint this reading of the figure of Bartleby as standing for the abstract formal labor of which writing itself partakes, in all his attenuated pallor and contemplative abstraction, with a countersense. For all Bartleby moves like a pallid presence throughout the text, he is not only an abstract specter and not only writing. His "passive resistance" makes of him no less an obdurate physical presence: "*he was always there*" to the narrator's increasingly desperate frustration, like an inexpungible trace of recalcitrant matter that refuses to be "let go of" (B 15). What or who is this thing that declares, "I am not particular" (B 30) and though, accordingly, *is* indifferent, is *not—pace* the narrator—the universal human? What is this thing that in the all too evident particularity of its resistance to "working by itself" interrupts the drive of capitalist enterprise, the lawyer's business of property deeds and conveyancing that lubricates Wall Street, this thing that prefers not to perform, as the other clerks do, "with submission" (B 12 and 20–1)?

Indeed, we might say that Bartleby is indeed a *thing*, precisely in Heidegger's sense, one whose thingliness is presence and therefore resistance, the obdurate occupation of space:

> The thing in the sense of a natural body is, however, not only what is movable in space, what simply occupies space ... but what fills space, keeping it occupied, extending, dividing, and maintaining itself in this occupying: it is resistance, i.e., force.[34]

As "resistance, force," Bartleby's passivity registers contradictorily for the narrator and others as a mode of violence and has effects that are those of a violence that not merely resists but expels: it takes on all the ambiguity that Walter Benjamin explores in his "Critique of Violence," where the very exercise of a nonviolent right of resistance may be read by the state as violent once it appears to threaten that state's legitimacy.[35] Thus Bartleby's insistence on remaining in place even after he has ceased to write eventually drives the narrator away from his office to new quarters and to a peculiar form of vagrancy or peregrination as he revolves the suburbs in his rockaway, crossing over to Jersey City and Hoboken and paying "fugitive visits to Manhattanville and Astoria" (B 30–1). In return, Bartleby alternately evokes compassion and provokes "the old Adam of resentment" (B 25) in the narrator. Those contradictory responses will lead inexorably to the violence of the lawyer's willed erasure of his employee's "passive resistance." Ultimately, Bartleby must be incarcerated, "removed to the Tombs as a vagrant" (B 31) where, effectively on hunger strike, he starves to death. But it is not what he does or does not do, in the end, that provokes this violence of erasure, but the mere insistence of his presence, his being there, like a thing, like a piece of furnishing, "like the last column of some ruined temple" (B 23).

Perhaps "preposterously," I cannot help reading in this figure of "wasted Bartleby" a representation of redundant labor of a very specific kind. Redundancy here is the negative counterpart of what Giorgio Agamben thinks of as "potential" when he claims that Bartleby represents "pure absolute potentiality ... nothing other than his white sheet."[36] Indeed, such sheer potentiality, undetermined by any particularity, would be the figure of the abstract subject in its indifference and equivalence. It is, by the same token, the very figure of whiteness. But Bartleby's "redundancy," the unused and unusable capacity for labor, his being [there] without actualization, is not the as-yet unrealized or exploited potential for the realization of value, but its paradoxical negation in an excess of existence, an existence, as the narrator indeed registers it, that persists after it has become unnecessary. Bartleby represents not only the figure of the abstraction of labor, of the labor of writing, of free labor, that is, of *white* labor, but also, for all the insistence on Bartleby's pallor, and perhaps because of it, the counter-figure, perhaps a *pre*-figuration, legible *post*-hoc, of a *black* labor that will not go away. This insistent potential for remainder haunted the discourse on abolition and every other remedy for slavery, raising the more than spectral possibility that in the United States as in post-Emancipation West Indies, a population of redundant former slaves might overwhelm the economy with unemployed bodies that, it was assumed, would prefer not to work even if able to find it.[37]

Of course, the figure of the slave or of the black appears nowhere in the text, and yet the half-occluded signs of it are everywhere, metonymically, contrapuntally, traceable. They are there in the comparison of Bartleby to "Marius brooding among the ruins of Carthage" (B 17), referring to John Vanderlyn's 1807 painting, *Caius Marius Amidst the Ruins of Carthage*, which depicts an anything but pallid Marius, the Roman general who subdued Africa.

They are there in the very opposition of the black wall and the white wall that the narrator insistently describes as bracketing the ends of his office, those walls whose very indifferent blankness signals in this tale the interchangeability of black and white (B 5).[38] The specter of blackness, and of the racial riots that periodically convulsed New York, is there in the fears of mob violence that greet Bartleby's refusal to vacate the Wall Street premises (B 29). I would say that the shadow of blackness falls most tellingly of all in Bartleby's terse response to the narrator visiting him compassionately in the Tombs: "I know you" (B 32). Bartleby's gift, after all, is his singular capacity to read the narrator in his complacent white benevolence with the canny accuracy that is informed by the perspicacity of the oppressed.

But the figures of blackness are there not only in these metonymies, but more deeply in the very figure and tropes of opposition that structure the text throughout and that countermand the appeal to "common humanity" that seeks to annul these insistent dichotomies:

> The bond of a common humanity now drew me irresistibly to gloom. A fraternal melancholy! For both I and Bartleby were sons of Adam. I remembered the bright silks and sparkling faces I had seen that day in gala trim, swan-like sailing down the Mississippi of Broadway; and I contrasted them with the pallid copyist . . . (B 17–18)

What are we to make of this peculiarly confused outburst, full of contrasts and similitudes, flights and mutations? A pale copyist who suffers from the "black bile" of melancholy? A Broadway become the Mississippi, with all its racial connotations, and the "bright silks" that sail on it become *white* swans that somehow contrast with the "*pallid* copyist"? A narrator and master who, like any good abolitionist, declares his Adamic kinship with his slave? And all that expostulating only a little while before this brotherly compassion turns to "the old Adam of resentment" (B 25).

It becomes hard, indeed, not to read the narrator's displacement to the suburbs on what he happily calls "*fugitive* visits," or his escape along Broadway, as forms of "white flight" from the obdurate presence of the black man who will not have the good grace to disappear, whether into oblivion or back to Africa, as so many from Jefferson to Lincoln proposed. Bartleby remains, "a bit of wreck in the mid Atlantic," as if an obstinate remainder of the Middle Passage, until at last he can be buried back in the prison of the Tombs, the "Egyptian character" of whose masonry encloses him in its gloom (B 22 and 33). In this, too, he uncannily prefigures what will be the fate of all too many black bodies from Jim Crow down to the present. And yet he remains, in all the ambiguity of what it is that he represents, to trouble the stability of the figures of race. Or, as Colin Dayan has so appositely put it:

> Hovering obstinately at the interstices, at once a person and a thing, a body and a ghost, Bartleby destabilizes the definitions crucial not only to property in slaves but also to the regulatory beneficence of civil society. In a time of unrelenting taxonomies, when persons became things—either perishables in the market or fixtures on land—and where felons died in law but lived in fact, Bartleby stands between such categories as person and thing, life and death.[39]

To this list of crumbling taxonomies, we may add only that Bartleby is the flicker of black and white, shadow and light, dissolving into the blank margin of the text, there to remain.

Let us say, then, that Bartleby–Mangan is the negation that masks a black presence haunting both the text and the social, resistant by its very insistence on *remaining*, even if it remains only in the margins and as the trace of an erasure from the text. Buried, entombed, encrypted within the text that cannot name it, blackness is sublimated as and in the shadows of the "pallid margins" of this text. But Bartleby–Mangan is also the trace of a racial material that haunts *Howe's* text, just as the specter of what to do with free black labor haunted both abolition and slave society with its refusal to dissipate, evoking both compassionate solicitude and the violence of erasure, eviction, incarceration—and just as, on the far side of the Atlantic, and in the same moment, the redundant population of Ireland was scheduled for destruction by famine and emigration. The flicker of black to white, of white becoming black, black becoming white that is the fate of the text rhymes with the peculiar fate of the transatlantic Irish who haunt the text, finding no settled place there in the spectral, nomadic figure of Mangan, whose fate it is, at the edges of this text, to metamorphose into the ambiguous figure of Bartleby. Race is the nameless material that shadows the formal work of the text, its presence not so much named, represented, or experienced as that it shapes the dark margins that throw the work into relief. But in that case it ceases to be possible to think of race as either material or erasure: the very erasure of racial material suffuses the text with the haunting return of race as a medium in which the text emerges, the unspoken condition of its speaking, its "ghostly matters," in Avery Gordon's haunting phrase.[40]

And yet, from time to time, against the rhythm of this white song, the figure of blackness arises, manacled, "buckled to capital," untractable:

The salary coyly said yes
Drag handcuff along fence
or you in it all tractable
Awry pulled up by cinchstrap
yes buckled to the capital
green worth say yes English
a certain mock hobo bravado
mean scrip so solitary wroth
Darkening noon changed he s
untractable in darkness un
manacled beside the capital
he s waging political babble
a context goes awry in novel
He took out American money (MM 112)

Notes

1. Franco Moretti, "The Long Goodbye: *Ulysses* and the End of Liberal Capitalism." *Signs Taken for Wonders: Essays in the Sociology of Literary Forms.* Verso, 1983, p. 190.
2. Jacques Lacan, *The Four Fundamental Concepts of Psychoanalysis: Book XI of The Seminar of Jacques Lacan*, edited by Jacques-Alain Miller and translated by Alan Sheridan. W. W. Norton, 1981, p. 49.
3. Peter D. O'Neill and David Lloyd, editors, *The Black and Green Atlantic: Cross-Currents of the African and Irish Diasporas.* Palgrave Macmillan, 2009.
4. Ed Dorn, *The North Atlantic Turbine* (Fulcrum Press, 1967).
5. Frantz Fanon, *Black Skin, White Masks*, translated by Charles Lam Markham and introduction by Homi Bhabha. Pluto Press, 1986, p. 114.
6. Frantz Fanon, *Peau Noire, Masques Blancs*. Éditions du Seuil, 1952, p. 92.
7. Paraphrased from Frantz Fanon, "Racism and Culture." *Towards the African Revolution: Political Essays*, translated by Haakon Chevalier. Grove Press, 1988, p. 29.
8. Fanon captures precisely this mode of thinking in a critique of Sartre's introduction to the volume of negritude poets, *Black Orpheus*, citing the latter's contention regarding race versus class: "The first is concrete and particular, the second is universal and abstract ..." Fanon responds, "When I read that page, I felt that I had been robbed of my last chance." Fanon, *Black Skin, White Masks*, p. 133.
9. Immanuel Kant, *The Critique of Judgement*, translated by James Creed Meredith. Clarendon Press, 1952, pp. 104–5. For a fuller discussion of this passage and its implications for racial discourse, see David Lloyd, *Under Representation: The Racial Regime of Aesthetics.* Fordham University Press, 2019, pp. 29–33.
10. Fanon, *Black Skin, White Masks*, p. 129.
11. As Denise da Silva has put it, they remain subjects of affectability, as opposed to those subjects of transparency who legislate the hierarchy of

racial relations both sociologically and aesthetically. See Denise Ferreira da Silva, *Toward a Global Idea of Race*. University of Minnesota Press, 2007, pp. xxxv–xxxix and passim.

12. On this constitutive paradox of the aesthetic, see David Lloyd, "Kant's Examples." *Representations*, vol. 28, Fall 1989, pp. 34–54.

13. Dorothy Wang, *Thinking Its Presence: Form, Race and Subjectivity in Contemporary Asian American Poetry*. Stanford University Press, 2014, pp. xx–xxi.

14. Wang, *Thinking Its Presence*, p. 31.

15. Samuel Beckett, *The Letters of Samuel Beckett, Volume III: 1957–65*, edited by George Craig, Martha Dow Fehsenfeld, Dan Gunn, and Lois More Overbeck. Cambridge: Cambridge University Press, 2014, p. 377, in a letter to Israeli writer Matti Megged, November 1960. For further discussion of the paradoxes of reading Beckett in relation to Irishness, see David Lloyd, "Frames of *Referrance*: Samuel Beckett as an Irish Question." *Beckett and Ireland*, edited by Seán Kennedy. Cambridge University Press, 2010, pp. 31–55. But see further Emilie Morin, *Beckett's Political Imagination*. Cambridge University Press, 2017, and James McNaughton, *Samuel Beckett and the Politics of Aftermath*. Oxford University Press, 2018, works that have crucially remapped Beckett's work in relation to its political subtexts. McNaughton's work is far more successful in pursuing the political implications of Beckett's formal innovations.

16. Naoki Sakai, "Distinguishing Literature and the Work of Translation: Theresa Hak Kyung Cha's *Dictée* and Repetition without Return." *Translation and Subjectivity: On "Japan" and Cultural Nationalism*. University of Minnesota Press, 2008, p. 31.

17. Susan Howe, *My Emily Dickinson*. North Atlantic Books, 1985, p. 27.

18. John Wilkinson, "The American Tract." Review of *Souls of the Labadie Tract* by Susan Howe. *Notre Dame Review*, vol. 27, Winter/Spring 2009, p. 241.

19. Wilkinson, "American Tract," p. 242.

20. Howe, *My Emily Dickinson*, p. 29.

21. In the interests of full disclosure, I should note that among the materials that Howe draws on in "Melville's Marginalia" is my own *Nationalism and Minor Literature: James Clarence Mangan and the Emergence of Irish Cultural Nationalism*. University of California Press, 1987. See Susan Howe, "Melville's Marginalia." *The Nonconformist's Memorial: Poems*. New Directions, 1993, p. 105; hereafter cited in the text as MM.

22. See John Mitchel, editor. *Poems of James Clarence Mangan*. P. M. Haverty, 1859, p. 14..

23. See L. Perry Curtis, *Apes and Angels: The Irishman in Victorian Caricature*. Smithsonian Institution Press, 1971.

24. See Lloyd, *Nationalism and Minor Literature*, pp. 195–207, on Mangan's singular dandyism and Carlyle's connection of English dandies and Irish "Poor-slaves" or "White Negroes."

25. Mark Quigley, "White Skin, Green Face: House of Pain and the Modern Minstrel Show." O'Neill and Lloyd, p. 74.

26. Mieke Bal, *Quoting Caravaggio: Contemporary Art, Preposterous History*. Chicago University Press, 1999, p. 7.

27. Bal, *Quoting Caravaggio*, p. 1.
28. On Mangan's use of this line from Milton's *Paradise Lost*, "Within the lowest deep a lower deep," and the logic of citation in his work, see Lloyd, *Nationalism and Minor Literature*, pp. 182–7.
29. Although written "from the standpoint of her later writings," Gerald Bruns's thesis that "for Howe the texts that she reads and cites are pneumatic—inhabited by the ghosts of her authors" is germane here. See Gerald L. Bruns, "Voices of Construction: On Susan Howe's Poetry and Poetics (A Citational Ghost Story)." *What Are Poets For? An Anthropology of Contemporary Poetry and Poetics*. University of Iowa Press, 2012, p. 35.
30. Herman Melville, "Bartleby the Scrivener: A Tale of Wall St." Dan McCall, editor. *Melville's Short Novels*. W. W. Norton, 2001, p. 34; hereafter cited in the text as B.
31. Michael Paul Rogin, *Subversive Genealogy: The Politics and Art of Herman Melville*. Alfred A. Knopf, 1983, p. 194.
32. Rogin, *Subversive Genealogy*, p. 196.
33. This reading of the story has long been available. See, for example, Leo Marx's argument that "Bartleby" "is a parable about a particular kind of writer's relations to a particular kind of society": Leo Marx, "Melville's Parable of the Walls." *Sewanee Review*, vol. 61, no. 4, Autumn 1953, pp. 602–27. Reprinted in McCall, pp. 239–56.
34. Martin Heidegger, *What is a Thing?*, translated by W. B. Barton, Jr. and Vera Deutsch, with analysis by Eugene T. Gendlin. University Press of America, 1967, p. 191.
35. Walter Benjamin, "Critique of Violence." *Selected Writings: Volume 1: 1913–1926*, edited by Marcus Bullock and Michael W. Jennings. Belknap Press, 1996, p. 240. The German text is "Zur Kritik der Gewalt." Walter Benjamin, *Angelus Novus: Ausgewählte Schriften 2*. Suhrkamp, 1966, pp. 47–8. *Gewalt* is a more ambiguous term than the English "violence" conveys, running a gamut of meanings from authority or power to coercive force, to violence itself.
36. Giorgio Agamben, "Bartleby, or On Contingency." *Potentialities: Collected Essays in Philosophy*, translated by Daniel Heller-Roazen. Stanford University Press, 1999, p. 254.
37. On the labor and employment problems raised by emancipation in the West Indies and by the "redundant" population in Ireland, see Thomas C. Holt, *The Problem of Freedom: Race, Labour, and Politics in Jamaica and Britain, 1832–1938*. Johns Hopkins University Press, 1992. Thomas Carlyle's infamous essay "The Nigger Question," published only a few years before Melville's "Bartleby," is only the most virulent expression of the anxieties provoked by the specter of redundant racialized labor in both Ireland and the Americas. See Thomas Carlyle, "The Nigger Question" [1849]. *Critical and Miscellaneous Essays*, vol. 4. AMS Press, 1969, pp. 348–83. (Reprint of Chapman and Hall, 1899), pp. 352–3 and passim.
38. As Leo Marx comments, "the difference in colour is less important than the fact that what we see through each window is only a wall." See Marx, "Melville's Parable of the Walls." Reprinted in McCall, p. 241. The walls are blank. The dialectic in "Bartleby" of black and white, apparently unrelated to the racial concerns it at once masks and figures, could be compared

to the similar figures in black and white that Toni Morrison identifies in Poe in her pioneering *Playing in the Dark: Whiteness and the Literary Imagination.* Vintage Books, 1992, pp. 32–3. Needless to say, my reading of a blackness obscured in texts of whiteness is thoroughly informed by the reading strategies Morrison proposed. Melville is a writer exceptionally attuned to color values as markers of a social consciousness saturated with an often unacknowledged if pervasive racial text. See, for example, the opening of his "Benito Cereno," where the disturbance of black and white that the slave mutiny inaugurates is figured in the pervasive grayness of the scene. Herman Melville, "Benito Cereno." McCall, p. 35. I am indebted to Sarita See for drawing my attention to this dimension of Melville's work.

39. Colin Dayan, "Melville, Locke and Faith." *Raritan*, vol. 25, no. 3, Winter 2006, p. 34.

40. Avery F. Gordon, *Ghostly Matters: Haunting and the Sociological Imagination*, 2nd edition, foreword by Janice Radway. Minnesota University Press, 2008.

Part II:

New Things That Have Happened

Chapter 5

New Things That Have Happened: Forms of Irish Poetry

One feature of Irish poetry and of the preponderance of the criticism it has spawned makes it singular among contemporary anglophone poetries: its resolutely anti-theoretical, not to say anti-intellectual bias. Where rigorous and sometimes acrimonious debate and radical formal variation has invigorated the post-war poetry and poetics in the United Kingdom, the United States or the Caribbean, to name only three anglophone contexts, Irish poetry has for the most part remained peculiarly sheltered from such challenges. Criticism, which ought to furnish theoretical stimulus and self-reflection, has tended to be at its most acrimonious the more it has advocated for a poetic conservatism whose time, one would have thought, is by now all too well outworn. This shell into which Irish poetry repeatedly withdraws in intellectual renunciation coincides with the niche that it has been assigned in the global market of anglophone poetry. Irish poetry occupies a peculiar nook, long secured for it by the retailing of rural and decaying industrial backdrops and by their correlatives, the insistent formalism and programmatic adherence to the constancy of "voice" that has dogged poetic production since Yeats, while tamely eschewing the rigorous violence that sustained his magisterial verse. Like deal dressers and hand-blown glass, Irish poetry offers a reliably commodified form of traditional craft, supplying a market segment within the larger global circuits of poetic production.

The latter components—formalism and the simulation of individual voice—have proven of greater importance and perdurability than the decor: Irish poetry has for the most part clearly survived the advent of Celtic Tiger neoliberalism and its post-industrial mode of production with little challenge to the established parameters. Likewise, its response to the counter-insurgency modernization that made Northern Ireland a laboratory for the surveillance industries of our moment has been for the most part—with exceptions to be considered below—an insouciant connivance in the violence of civility. Irish poetry continues to provide the anglophone world serviceable exhibitions of poetic craft with sufficient formal prowess to maintain its market niche and furnish a digestible alternative to postmodern economic and cultural dislocation even where its thematic material embraces the Irish diasporic experience, no longer in Paris alone, but from Prague to San Francisco.[1] As with Irish theatre, Irish poetry offers a convenient bridge between the reassuring recourse to traditional forms and the frisson of novelty that access to international residence and performance excites. The "mismatch" between the assurance of continuity that those forms symbolically communicate and the violent displacement that neoliberalism and its militarization of the globe have occasioned is rarely engaged.[2] The "fissure" between "an innovative strain in Irish poetry open to international influences" and a "liberal-conservative development of a self-consciously Hiberno-English poetic diction or prosody" is scarcely very evident here and Irish poetry seems to supply a moderate and moderating alternative to poetry that seeks to work through in its matter as in its form both the spectacular and the "slow violence" of global capitalist developments.[3]

This discrepancy is not new in Irish culture. As I already noted in the Introduction, Samuel Beckett distinguished in his early book review, "Recent Irish Poetry," between a poetry of convention and a poetry of the actual, the latter having apprehended "the new thing that has happened," that is, "the breakdown of the object" or "breakdown of the subject" and the "rupture of the lines of communication."[4] His remarks suggest at least one line of continuity between his modernist moment and our present. "Conventional" poetry gives the impression that its materials have been processed to furnish a convenient metaphorical or anecdotal vehicle—a "theme"—for the expression of a subject secure in its self-possession: contemporary Irish poetry offers all too many examples of the happy procedure of the poem that commences with a "vividly realized" experience, draws from it some metaphoric thread, and winds up with a moral payload, validated by a nice turn of phrase, that brings metaphor and experience into graceful concord again, often enough "clinched by final rhyme and a final perspective."[5] As Trevor Joyce put it, "this familiar marketable thing, the Irish poem, was invariably in the expressive mode: it took its theme from off the shelf, and told you, in lyric fashion, what the poet felt on the subject."[6] The procedure of the "well-made poem" is handily available for recycling, and the world yields ample material for exploitation in this mode. That material is certainly more various now than the "antiquarianism" that bothered Beckett: inane recourse to tribalist allegories to explain the Northern Irish Troubles, or suburbanite reflections on the transition from a past generation's rural customs into the land of breeze-block dance halls or IT have largely exhausted themselves in favor of a more cosmopolitan range of reference, if largely at the cost of any serious engagement with the legacy of colonialism in Ireland or its subsequent place in the global emergence of neoliberal techniques of surveillance and counter-insurgency. Ironically, the new cosmopolitanism, with its celebration of geographical mobility and consumerism, all too often acts as the alibi for a retraction from the new things that have happened in our own time and which have, as it happens, all too much to do with the old things that we may be blithely assured we have left behind.

The subject and its relation to its object remain secure within the enclosure of the well-made poem. It is a peculiarity of Irish formalism that its commitment to craft or technical virtuosity within traditional modes, from sonnet to sestina, remains largely uninterrogated, even by explicit opposition to the various possibilities opened up by more innovative poetic work in English or other languages. The "fascination with form" seems peculiarly unmotivated by any necessity in relation to the pressures that impinge on the language that is its material.[7] Likewise, critical appreciation tends towards the celebration of the "vividly observed," the "finely observant of the details," "the balanced detailing, the accurate and yet indulgent eye," "detailed descriptions," as if poetry were "a literature of notations" whose material is the image rather than language.[8] Irredeemably social before it enters the particular artifice of the poem, language as the medium of the subject's subjection to heteronomy imposes constraints on the individual's expression that are far more determining, if more habitually disavowed, than the obvious constraints of traditional forms. All language use is "under constraint"; the question is how the poet engages with a medium that is always in dialectical relation to the poem that, as artifice, marks its distinction from "ordinary language" use. As Adorno put it:

> The paradox specific to the lyric work, a subjectivity that turns into objectivity, is tied to the priority of linguistic form in the lyric; it is that priority from which the primacy of language in lyric in general (even in prose forms) is derived. For language itself is something double. Through its configurations it assimilates itself completely into subjective impulses; one would almost think it had produced them. But at the same time language remains the medium of concepts, remains that which establishes an inescapable relationship to the universal and society. Hence the highest lyric works are those in which the subject, with no remaining trace of mere matter, sounds forth in language until language itself acquires a voice. The unself-consciousness of the subject submitting itself to language as to something objective, and the immediacy and spontaneity of that subject's expression are one and the same: thus language mediates lyric poetry and society in their innermost core.[9]

Adorno's formulations are beautifully hedged: apparently subjective impulses are virtually products of the language, not spontaneous expressions of the autonomous subject; submission to the language proceeds in unself-consciousness—as he puts it just before this passage, the lyric "is socially motivated behind the author's back." Matter is so thoroughly worked into form that its apparent disappearance is its haunting return. But if it is not merely to reproduce the social language unwittingly, to be an unacknowledged instance of "forced poetics," poetry demands the utmost self-conscious vigilance.[10]

For Adorno, the principal symptom of the heteronomy imposed by language as the medium of sociality and concepts was its instrumentality, its subjection to communicative ends. Sixty years later, and in a location marked so deeply by the legacies of colonialism and counter-insurgency and absorbed by the depredations of neoliberal capitalism as Ireland, language perforce seems saturated with violence without having lost any of its instrumentality. The poet's motto might best be Maurice Scully's "I made a song in a murderous / time. Listen to the sound of that."[11] Not that this is by any means an unprecedented linguistic condition, though the casual brutality of daily speech might now make unselfconsciousness a peculiarly deluded state: the very spaces of domestication that seem to proffer shelter from violence are themselves shaped by the violent protections of civility. Civilization is not "the opposite of war," but each is the other's intimate condition.[12] This is the peculiar dialectic of the civility of the well-made poem that seeks, through "vivid observation," to save the object that it appropriates even as it affirms the stability of the subject whose perception apprehends it. It is a mode whose discretely didactic ends, as the pedagogical model at once for good poems and good subjects, demand repetition: the scene of wrought epiphany can only fulfill its function if it can be transferred to the reader. Its apparently chance occurrence serves a form that must be capable of recurrence; it is thus an empty form that can be filled indifferently with any phenomenal content. Once the pattern is established, the object of perception ceases to matter: whether a hawk or a handsaw, its gleam in the subject's eye is what counts. What is repeated and affirmed is the subject–object relation and its reproducible auratic effect rather than its content. Thus, in the face of the new things that have happened, the subject–object relation is reassuringly restored. But the object is there annihilated for the sake of the subject.

Michael Longley is probably the master of this mode among current Irish poets, as well as having emerged as the widely acknowledged master of Ireland's "singing school." He is capable of consummating the manner in a poem consisting of a single, crafted quatrain:

While I was looking for Easter snow on the hills
You showed me, like a concentration of violets
Or a fragment from some future unimagined sky,
A single spring gentian shivering at our feet.[13]

The poem is a condensed instance of impeccable craft: the gradual, whispering accumulation of alliterations on s- or sh-sounds that culminate in the final line, the careful delay of the climactic appearance of the gentian by the parenthetical similes, the canny transposition of the word "unimagined" from qualifying the future to qualifying the sky that introduces a religiose, possibly apocalyptic note concordant with the Easter setting, and the ambiguity that transposition then prepares in the word "shivering"—with cold, or for fear of being trodden, or for something a touch more portentous? Thematically, the scanning of the (presumably masculine) eye of the heights and horizon for a blanket phenomenon is countered by the close (detailed?) observation of the (presumably feminine) eye for the particular, ephemeral phenomenon, the irreproducible, unique, and entirely chance appearance of the flower. Except that nothing here is left to chance: the epiphany is thoroughly prescripted and anticipated in so far as the form of the poem itself requires it (and numerous instances of the same phenomenon can be identified in this and other volumes by the same poet). The object, shivering as it is, offers no resistance to its appropriation, is incapable of doing so by virtue of its very indifference for the accomplishment of the poem: any other object could take its place and satisfy the demands of the form. In this respect, the poem, appearing as it does to stand out in the name of the particular against the leveling of phenomena by their commodification, inadvertently reproduces the commodity form for which the exact quality of the object—its use value or the satisfaction it may bring to the user—is a matter of indifference so long as it can be exchanged for any other object meeting those conditions. Repetition and exchangeability are the unwitting terms of the form, "behind the author's back," as it were. The upshot of this contradiction is that language apparently imbued with signification becomes effectively phatic, gestures that signal compulsively a content that matters only because the form requires its presence.

Ciaran Carson long ago sardonically abolished the routines of the well-made poem in the title poem of his first volume, *The New Estate* (1976), capturing precisely its relation to the fetishization of the object and of the commodity form:

Forget the corncrake's elegy. Rusty
Iambics that escaped your discipline

Of shorn lawns, it is sustained by nature.
It does not grieve for you, nor for itself.
You remember the rolled gold of cornfields,
Their rustling of tinsel in the wind,
A whole field quivering like blown silk?

A shiver now runs through the laurel hedge,
And washing flutters like the swaying lines
Of a new verse. The high fidelity
Music of the newly-wed obscures your
Dedication to a life of loving
Money. What could they be for, those marble
Toilet fixtures, the silence of water-beds,
That book of poems you bought yesterday?[14]

More importantly, however, it was Carson's signal achievement to break with what was by now the formal shell of the epiphanic lyric whose standard inner development is here inverted and parodied as an object of nostalgia, better forgotten. Between *The Irish for No* (1987) and *Opera Et Cetera* (1996), Carson developed the long, sinuous, mostly blank-verse line that proved capable of integrating the colloquial rhythms of bar-stool or barbershop conversation with a playful, associative, and often tongue-in-cheek intellectuality: under the pressure of political violence and counter-insurgency, he forged a formal means to enact the attitude of ironic suspicion, visceral threat, and restless movement that are at once the conditions of survival in and the terms of a poetic critical address to a situation of state as well as paramilitary terror. It proved capable of absorbing and rendering the vernacular traditions of urban folklore that have long found the means to negotiate the unstable interfaces of potentially violent encounters alongside a citational practice that preserves an astonishing equilibrium between high intellectual parody and analytic precision. The mobility of the mode never congeals into the kinds of aesthetic condescension that is habitual in poems more convinced of their own civil superiority to the purveyors of violence but permits a peculiarly calibrated ethical work, at once ironic and empathetic:

As usual, the clock in The Clock Bar was a good few minutes fast:
A fiction no one really bothered to maintain, unlike the story
The comrade on my left was telling, which no one knew for certain truth:
Back in 1922, a sergeant, I forget his name, was shot outside the National Bank . . ..
Ah yes, what year was that they knocked it down? Yes, its memory's as fresh
As the inky smell of new pound notes—which interferes with the beer-and-whiskey
Tang of now, like two dogs meeting in the revolutionary 69 of a long sniff,

Or cattle jostling shit-stained flanks in the Pound. For *pound*, as some wag
Interrupted, was an offshoot of the Falls, from the Irish, *fál*, a hedge;
Hence, *any kind of enclosed thing*, its twigs and branches commemorated
By the soldiers' drab and olive camouflage, as they try to melt
Into a brick wall; red coats might be better, after all.[15]

Even so brief an extract from "Hamlet," the long concluding poem of
Belfast Confetti (1989), indicates the possibilities of Carson's formal
innovations, as the "enclosed thing" that is the poem opens up onto
what seems a potentially endless movement of interruption and displacement that interweaves temporal frames, not only through citing the
Belfast legend of the sergeant's ghost, which recalls *Hamlet* to mind in
the midst of Belfast's "troubled state," but also by invoking the "redcoats" who in the nineteenth century oversaw the evictions by which
the process of enclosure was enforced in Ireland. That violent process
introduced a money economy, the circulation of the pound, at the
expense of Ireland's subsistence agriculture and the people it supported.
The Falls, indeed, was historically the product of the settlement of a
displaced Catholic population on the western outskirts of the city. That
Northern Ireland served as the laboratory for the modes of surveillance
and urban counter-insurgency that have become ubiquitous phenomena
of neoliberal regimes and their new forms of accumulation underscores
the "rhyme" between the redcoats and their camouflaged descendants.[16]
Sometimes history rhymes not with hope but with the violent replay of
the violence of dispossession. Simile and resemblance function here not
in the service of identity but as relays that open one "scene" onto apparently disjunctive tracks that continually loop back with a new burden
of historical matter. What appears, in other words, as loose association
is seeded with precise and telling historical reference that, threading an
oral narration with all its digressions and interruptions, effects a spatio-
temporal account of political violence and its embeddedness in colonial
histories.

>   . . . So we name the constellations, to put a shape
> On what was there; so, the storyteller picks his way between the isolated
>   stars.[17]

Allen Feldman has commented on the violence of the Troubles as func-
tioning like a language. One could likewise see Carson's formal innovations as pursuing a language adequate to the everydayness of violence
and to the vernacular modes of responding to and accommodating its
constant imminence.

Between *The New Estate* and *Belfast Confetti*, Carson opened out the
domesticated shelter *from* violence into the public spaces of the pubs and

streets where violence is both staged and parsed. Carson's contemporary, Medbh McGuckian, is often cast as a poet of the "rich inner world of feminine sensibility" and as an unusually obscure writer, drawing on private or hidden allusions and exploring the supposedly enclosed world of women's experience.[18] As several critics have recently confirmed, what appears private and hermetic is often woven from found language, now easily identified online on the internet.[19] Her construction of poems out of appropriated language has exacerbated the reservations felt by some critics as to whether the poems mean anything at all, a reservation that could once be redeemed by the notion that these were instances of an *écriture feminine* and therefore absolved of needing to mean or that their meaning was subordinated to their musicality. The foundness of their language upset these somewhat patronizing recuperations of her work and seems to have led to a sense of disappointment hard to distinguish from the accusation of deceit. Leontia Flynn's book-length leave-taking of her fellow poet is the type of such disappointment:

> The links and associative points to which her work connects seem potentially endless, part of the poem's refusal to 'represent' without suggesting an awareness of dozens of divergent, specific other representations of the same thing. Such connections could expand beneath or around the poems ... to the point where the poem is more or less forgotten, if it is still relevant at all. These meanings then can now surely only fully be understood or *remembered* by the author herself. Moreover, none of this has anything to do with poetry, which has to generalise or 'represent' at least to the extent that it creates meanings for more than one person.[20]

This rather tight-lipped critical legislation of what poetry can be and how it can mean, of the relation of the poet's intention and consciousness to the verbal artifact of the poem, and of the latter's relation to the reader is, it must be said, severely impoverished and of doubtful value in reading McGuckian's work, let alone a wide range of post-Romantic poetry. Even William Empson faced the problem that, once set in motion, the movement of interpretation was "potentially endless": the only limit that so attentive a critic could pose to reading was "tact," an arbitrary closure of the reader's engagement in face of the uncontrollable dynamic that an active attention unleashes.[21] The demand for evident reference, for the anchoring of the poem in some kind of representation that can be "generalised" for the sake of communication, goes hand in hand with the poem's closure in the well-regulated fulfillment of the subject's expressive intention, one that can be recalled and "fully understood." It is hard to see how this fading echo of British empiricism "has anything to do with poetry" and its unsettling ways of meaning and unmeaning. Certainly it is of little help in actually reading McGuckian.

Flynn's sarcastic proclamation peculiarly extends several decades of efforts to domesticate McGuckian's work precisely by assuming its disconnection from the public world of communication and the political. But long before this, a more significant characteristic of McGuckian's work was identified by Clair Wills's pioneering study, *Improprieties*, that is, its capacity to weave together public and private experience in a way that dismantles the boundary that has long been supposed to separate the feminine domain of the home from the masculine public world, emphasizing instead "the interpenetration of these spheres on the social level" as a consequence of Ireland's colonial history.[22] Wills's brilliant reading of McGuckian preceded the latter's *Captain Lavender* (1995), the volume in which McGuckian's formal practices and material concerns seemed to come into their fullest articulation. Whatever may be said as to the extent to which the violence of the Troubles may have permeated McGuckian's earlier work—and it is often forgotten how the counter-insurgency tactic of "normalization" had the peculiar effect of domesticating terror, in the double sense of that term—*Captain Lavender* does not merely introduce the context of violence and political imprisonment as thematic material, but enacts its dissemination across the social and psychic fields. Indeed, without the publisher's blurb that comments on McGuckian's work as a teacher in the prisons, one might be hard put to grasp precisely how "the war is in" these poems, as her epigraph from Picasso puts it. For it is not "in" the poems as representational material, but dispersed rhizomatically across them, both within each individual lyric and across the book as a whole in a network of musical echoes and transformations. Across that network, imprisonment, colonial histories, and the politics of language and culture form nodes of connection that are also relays with what are usually taken to be other dimensions or spheres of experience: loss and grief, fatherhood and daughterhood, home-making and gardening or farming, religion and music. The procedure undoes the compartmentalization of those domains of experience that was constitutive of colonial modernity, in Ireland as elsewhere. McGuckian's poetry is, as has often enough been noted, political not by its proclamations, provisional or otherwise, but by the movement of its language, that is, poetically.

This makes the knowledge that a poem like "Elegy for an Irish Speaker" is composed extensively from phrases "found" in writings by Osip Mandelstam of little final help in reading it.[23] Poems move off from their occasions, whether those occasions are the stimulus of another's words, read or overheard, or of sensory or social experiences. They do not remain at their apparent point of origin (which is likely to have been determined in any case by prior inputs) but disperse or disseminate from them. Even the given materials may be transformed in the process: it is not Mandelstam's Word that is "born very slowly" in the poem's opening, but the date that will have marked an anniversary, the same day in the calendar but always differing from itself in its repetition:

> Numbered day,
> night only just beginning,
> be born very slowly, stay
> with me, impossible to name.[24]

Day cedes to night, the moment of either's becoming from out of the other "impossible to name," as any phrase differs from itself as it moves though time or place. As we have seen in both Mangan and Yeats, the date that appears to mark a definable, numbered series of returns—in this case, the reader assumes, the death of her father—instead marks the slippage of memory from its anchorages. In their inner difference, name and date shadow the displacement of the subject, at once self-identical and self-alienated, "in words, made of words, others' words," as Beckett's Unnamable put it.[25] Slippage of every kind is the principle of the poem, and not only the slippery misappropriation of another's words. In a possible echo of Sylvia Plath's "Lady Lazarus," death itself is feminized as "Miss Death" while the father appears successively as inseminator, embryo, and poetess:

> Are you waiting to be fertilized,
> dynamic death, by his dark company?
> to be warmed in your wretched
> overnight lodgings
> by his kind words and small talk
> and powerful movements?
> He breaks away from your womb
> to talk to me,
> he speaks so with my consciousness
> and not with words, he's in danger
> of becoming a poetess.[26]

The precise moment of change between states, which undermines both gender and biological identities, remains indeterminable, defying the differentiating functions of language itself.

The non-verbal play of non-identity—the domain of death itself—cannot be rendered in words, but here, as throughout McGuckian's work, is approximated by polysemy:

> Roaming root of multiple meanings,
> He shouts himself out
> In your narrow amphora,
> Your tasteless, because immortal, wine.[27]

"Multiple meaning" arrives in diverse forms, ranging from the pun to the buried metaphor, from ambiguity to indeterminate reference. Hesitation constantly dogs the reader's progress through the poem: is "tasteless" a gastronomic or an aesthetic term? Does "he shouts himself out" imply the exhaustion of expression or the will to exit confinement? But reading is also directed onto various simultaneous tracks by resurrecting dead metaphors: "the knitting together of your two spines / is another woman / reminding of a wife" shifts across at least three trajectories of the poem's layered matter—that of the biological, that of the materiality of the book, and that of the erotic—through which the dialectic of death and living-on plays out. These are not separable domains, any more than are the public and the private, but intersecting complexes that slip constantly between registers, fixed at one moment and unfixed at another. The amphora that contains—and seems to condense at once the funereal urn, the jar of wine, and the enclosure of the poem—is also the vessel that transports. The dialectic between the nomadic movement of dissemination and the settled, cultivating work of insemination courses constantly through *Captain Lavender* and constitutes another principle of the poetic work and of the reading it summons:

> Most foreign and cherished reader,
> I cannot live without
> your trans-sense language,
> the living furrow of your spoken words
> that plough up time.[28]

The movement of reading plays between a sense and the senses—the image that speaks to the eye is generally also a node for other tracks of meaning, so that the domination of the eye is undone by the displacement of meaning—as it also "translates" the poem into the afterlife that is, according to Walter Benjamin, the fate of any work, its dislodgement from the time of its occasion into a future in which the author and the referent are equally absent.[29] Mandelstam's phrases both live their afterlife here and are "trans-sensed," uprooted from their own soil and reseeded in a different field of associations.

Within the book itself, any moment of the figurative play of the poem is the "second half / of a poetic simile lost elsewhere":[30] the reader constantly picks up the trail of some metaphoric complex elsewhere in the text as the process of reading any poem is replicated across the book as a whole. In "The Albert Chain," the death of the father echoes and folds into the other deaths it is "chained" to, that of the author and those that compose the historical legacy of colonial violence:

> Like a dead man
> attached to the soil that covers him,
> I have fallen where no judgement can touch me,
> its discoloured rubble has swallowed me up.
> For ever and ever, I go back into myself:
> I was born in pieces, like specks of dust,
> only an eye that looks in all directions can see me.
> I am learning my country all over again,
> how every inch has been paid for
> by the life of a man, the funerals of the poor.[31]

Return into the self, which might seem to promise the affirmation of identity, meets only a further dissemination, "in all directions," that is also embedded in the history of the country and its people—dispersal, exile, migration having been the consequence of enclosure and settlement. What might quite rightly be read in one direction as a feminist poetic that critiques the fixation on gendered identity and gendered divisions of space folds over onto another that equally queers the political symbolism of the Republican prisoners in their "stored statelessness"—"men utterly outside themselves, with the taint of women."[32] It is a poetic that responds to the conditions of a very modern epoch of political violence and counter-insurgency not by recourse to colonial stereotypes that oppose civility to atavistic tribalism, but with a practice whose "trans-sense language" rebuffs all "attempts to seal its meaning."[33] It is a language acutely capable of absorbing the violent displacements of modernity and of imagining alternative languages of non-identity in which, indeed, one might "hear two voices without either / disturbing the other—four harmonies / where there was only one."[34]

Manifestly different as their poetic modes appear, and quite distinct in the demands they make on reading, what links Carson and McGuckian is the dialectic in their work between a form and the materials that determine it. Form, for each of them, is not an arbitrary or given container, but the specific shape poetic thinking takes in moving through the materials, linguistic and historical at once, that it takes on. If those materials include the political violence of the Troubles that so spectacularly dissolved the boundaries between public and private experience, it is important to recall the degree to which the techniques and technologies of counter-insurgency that were developed in the laboratory of Northern Ireland have become part and parcel of the regime of neoliberal capital that has extended onto a global scale the violent policing and containment of the populations it has displaced and made disposable in the service of accumulation. What appears to the uncritical observer to have been an unhappy interruption of an otherwise continuous liberal and civic existence by an alien violence in fact represents an irreversible moment in the generalization of colonial modernization processes. Thus the general conditions for the Republic's neoliberal boom are one moment of capitalist development of which Northern Ireland's experience of counter-insurgency technologies was another.

One of the more baleful effects of the partition of the island has been the perception of "separate development," culturally as well as economically and politically, that disjoins Northern Ireland and the Republic into distinct and non-communicating compartments.[35] That such distinct trajectories have left their mark on poetic practice and on conversations about poetry, despite continuous cross-border exchanges, cannot be ignored. Critically, however, it remains important to identify what one might call the "growth-points" of Irish poetry in relation to the formal engagement of poets with the "new thing that has happened," in this case, the continuing subsumption of Ireland as a whole into that global capitalist sphere. This is not because it produces new thematic material for poetic anecdotes, but because the conditions of the present challenge the conception of the acting and perceiving subject that undergirds the well-made lyric just as powerfully as the "breakdown of the subject" undid for Beckett the "antiquarianism" of Irish poetry in the 1930s. The subject implicit in the well-made poem and its various formalist variants is a subject secure in its freedom and in the domain of private experience, communicable precisely because of the formal identity among individuals of which the poem is the model. The question that has to be confronted, as a question that is fundamentally and not casually addressed to poetry, is that of how to find forms adequate to the conditions of unfreedom that the neoliberal transformation of society in all its domains has produced.

It is this question that links the poetic procedures of Carson and McGuckian to poets working predominantly in the Republic, like Trevor Joyce, Maurice Scully, and Catherine Walsh. Generally contained by terms like "innovative" or "experimental," their work might better be approached in terms of its pursuit of formal solutions that would allow poetry to address a moment when the anecdotal lyric that has been the typical Irish mode appears at best exhausted, at worst irrelevant and inauthentic. Joyce, the most theoretically self-reflexive of Irish "innovative poets," has articulated his fatigue with "lyrics of description and expression dressed in the most transparent of formal attire" and linked it not only to the necessity to find new kinds of formal constraint, but also to find in those constraints a correlative to the social condition of language in which, as Adorno also suggested, one is "governed by forces and concerns in which one has had no hand, act, or part."[36] Scully and Walsh are less committed to procedural writing or "composition under constraint," but they share a disinterest in hand-me-down forms and a commitment to the construction of works that are in different ways resistant to easy consumption. Scully's work, discussed in Chapter 6, was for twenty-five years dedicated to the production of an eight-book work, *Things That Happen*, assembled from continuously interwoven poems in a variety of forms. His emphasis is on the construction or assemblage of the book, not on the portable individual poem as an entity in itself. Walsh likewise constructs books out of an assemblage of diverse forms and of modes of language use, ranging from digressive prose "essays" or memoirs to "lyrics" composed largely out of apparently overheard speech.

Walsh's 2009 book, *Optic Verve: A Commentary*, opens with what appear at first glance like little lyrics, mostly six to ten lines long, interspersed with brief phrases in Spanish on some of the left-hand pages. These turn out not to be what she later calls "terribly intact box-like parameters / . . . processed packaging of eagerness curiosity / quick commodification arrogance attempting dominance"[37]—a sequence that might suggest at once the lyric enclosure or the spatial enclosures inhabited by the contemporary subject—but little units of radically dismantled language:

> best why which can call given
> away so undo better for which remember
> thin with likely of which in all
> only where day call and forget change
> it as last could all that get
> many asked no one might be just can
> should be should what in all out of
> neither with a glad either welcome to
> known day all can who will or see
> without no wonder (*OV* 17)

This poem, if such it is, presents as a lyric and, indeed, gestures towards the standard materials of the genre: memory and change, day met with gladness and wonder, call and questioning. It even invokes the buried performative forms of the marriage ceremony that bring about a change of state of man and woman into husband and wife—"for better or worse," "through thick and thin," "given away"—but such faint echoes here signal little more than the formulaic sedimentations in even the most deconstructed language. Not only are reference, representation, and meaning evacuated from it, but predication of any kind is avoided. What remain are uncertain grammatical fragments and even those are subject to multiple possible recombinations that might gesture towards a sense that is almost immediately withdrawn again. One can continue to grasp for ways to reconstruct some kind of continuous sense across the lines and phrase-fragments, concluding, perhaps, with an affirmation of illumination, volition, and wonder reminiscent of the epiphanic lyric: "welcome to known day: all can who will or [will] see with [out no] wonder!" might be one effort to recompose a sense for the final lines. All such efforts are frustrated and the text remains a shuttling assemblage of part phrases deprived of predicates, for the most part even of nouns and verbs.

And yet this and the corresponding texts retain a haunting subliminal charge: a thin utterance seems to struggle to articulate, to piece together an ethical and ontological response to the world between the gaps and silences: "One might be just. Can / should be. Should what? In all . . . Out of / neither . . . With a glad . . ." In its refusal of any subject–object relations, any attempt at dominance, the little bursts of language seem to mime the unclosed speech-gestures of a being scanning the world and its possibilities, but constantly stopping short, suspending, in what one is tempted to call stutterance. Deconstructing the language of propositions about the world, the text could be taken as the discourse of what Walsh later calls "this rattled subjectivity" (*OV* 62) in a poem also about stuttering, repetition, and recomposition. And yet, for all its fragility, for all the feeling that it is "governed by forces and concerns in which one has had no hand, act, or part," the text is resistant: it is resistant to appropriation by the reader, to the desire to offer a portable, paraphrasable meaning, as it is resistant to the instrumentalization and commodification of language and experience: this lyric renders no luminous sentiment for the market in epiphanies. Like Bartleby, it prefers not to.

As such, it is a minimal instance of the resistance that *Optic Verve*, which is made up in part of satiric prose and counter-history, poses to the neoliberal Celtic Tiger boom of the moment in which it was written. The little text just cited may invoke only to refuse the "given name," the "proper name," but a text only a little further on addresses explicitly the issue of naming as if in a commentary on the Irish language tradition of *dinnseanchas*, or place name poetry, that Carson and McGuckian also ironically invoke and which is a staple of the Irish lyric standard. But gentrification, demolition, and speculative development have put paid to the affective relation between the name and what it designates. Writing of the projected demolition of Dublin's working-class Fatima Mansions in one of the many prose texts that intersperse the lineated pages, Walsh asks:

What will they call it? How can it not be Fatima, right there by Maryland? If there were no Luas [light-rail] line nearing completion (or bankruptcy) would anyone with access to power have given a damn?

Whose place was it? To say what is its name is not tantamount to saying I don't know what it is. Naming is not a speculative art and not necessary, as many seem to assume, to actual comprehension. Understanding. Naming makes communicative interaction a lot less tedious and time consuming. A coded shorthand of the specific, necessary component of the everyday dialectic of our lives.

Whose place was it? To say what its name is is saying I don't know whose it is. There's a girl somewhere, in London or Birmingham, Madrid or Barcelona, who says what its name is every time she tells her story. She says its name in her head, to hear the vowel sounds echo right; aloud they must be adapted for the pertaining local influence, to be understood, superficially. (*OV* 23–4)

Two versions of naming contradict one another here, in this passage that might itself be a reading of the lyric just quoted: the name that designates, abbreviates, facilitates communication, and the name that resonates as sensuous material, reverberates with affective associations, echoes in the body and the ear, its enunciation bearing local inflection and intonation, accent and accident, in different languages. If the former lends itself to instrumental purposes—mapping and planning, surveying and surveillance—and can be torn from place, the latter's resonances persist beyond its scheduled erasure, as a ghost that haunts the demolished site or, indeed, the dead body of the vagrant on the doorstep of the block whose lifelong home it had been.[38]

Walsh's work in its multiple modes reminds us that what reads as formal innovation is equally the means to imagine or recuperate "structures of feeling" and forms of living that resist the unfreedom of universal commodification, producing a medium that itself defies easy subsumption: as in other "semi-colonial" locations, there may be less contradiction between the most radical of modernist experiment and the non-modern practices in which the residual becomes emergent by virtue of its persistence than there is with the so-called traditional forms that actually accommodate the ongoing leveling of difference.[39] Innovative poetics spills over into the utopian projection of past possibilities as potentials that live on in the present, in the body as in the memory. *Optic Verve* culminates in diary entries that pose the surviving practices, language, and forms of sociality that persist in an unevenly and recently modernized culture like Ireland's:

Baking to go, making dough. One hundred years ago the same. The one I know without having to look it up. My hands, after years away from this particular activity, take off in a rhythmical series of sequential movements each designed to fulfill a certain function necessary to the act of breadmaking. My head wanders through layers of thought while processing sudden vivid visuals that pop up in time, it seems, with my hands. It's soothing, restful, satisfying. Tasty. I learned this process from two or three, assistant to my grandmother, in the new store, the room that opened off the back of the ancient dairy. (*OV* 119)

Bread-making and butter-churning are both "functional processes" (*OV* 120) with an aesthetic subordinated to those functions, and also practices in which memory is embedded. This is not merely a domestic memory: as Leopoldina Fortunati has taught us, the "feminine" scene of reproduction is no less integrated with capitalist modes of production than what the Marxist tradition has seen as productive, proletarian labor.[40] The domestic, precisely as a site of cultural reproduction, has also been a principal target of colonial modernization, along with indigenous languages, replaced by "that of commerce and international trade" (*OV* 123). This is, as Walsh remarks, "not new colonialism," but "very old, traditional, unchanged" (*OV* 123), and at once global and profoundly intimate in its reach. Walsh's writing, which often works through the historical transformation of such spaces by technology and shifting modes of reproduction, is peculiarly alert to their juncture with capitalist and colonial modernization. While much of her work is composed with an ear to the alienation and isolation of the suburban domestic space, it does not register it solely as a domain of unfreedom or of closure, but as a locus of survival in every sense. Sites of memory, they are also sites of possibility that challenge the relegation of older practices to obsolescence, "outmoded by commercialization" (*OV* 120):

> These matters are not just still within living memory or testament here in Ireland as in so many parts of the world, they are a crucial determining factor in how people choose to interact socially, what they aspire to attain, how they use language and how they view language. (*OV* 124)

The radically mixed-genre work of *Optic Verve* styles itself neither as poetry, nor memoir, nor "impositional narrative," but as "A Commentary" (*OV* 54), thus knitting together the old medieval practice of annotation and glossing with the contemporary practices of critical reading. Challenging "authorship   authority   absolutism" (*OV* 54), it also challenges the prejudice that the innovative or experimental is necessarily bad cosmopolitanism, deracinated, abstracted from history. As the work shows, and as Ireland's own history constantly testifies, it is possible to innovate, or renovate, to the fullest extent while still engaging with the potentials that are embedded in the cultural practices that live on in defiance of domination. This is what we would mean by alternative modernities or what Trevor Joyce nicely dubbed "alternative planes of cleavage."[41] Any Irish poetry adequate to our moment is obliged to take on if not to emulate the example of such historically attentive, formally alert alternatives to poetic business as usual.

Notes

1. J. C. C. Mays has been critically alert to Irish poetry's paradoxical relation to commodity culture for several decades now. See his "Flourishing and Foul: Six Poets and the Irish Building Industry." *Irish Review*, vol. 8, Spring 1990, pp. 6–11 and "The Third Walker." *Irish University Review*, vol. 46, no. 1, Spring/Summer 2016, pp. 48–62.

2. "Mismatch" is Mays's term for a comparable contradiction between form and occasion. See his "Third Walker," p. 60.

3. Matthew Campbell, cited in Fran Brearton, "The 'nothing-could-be-simpler-line': Form in Contemporary Irish Poetry." *The Oxford Handbook of Contemporary Irish Poetry*, edited by Fran Brearton and Alan Gillis. Oxford University Press, 2012, p. 630. The term "slow violence" is Rob Nixon's. See his *Slow Violence and the Environmentalism of the Poor*. Harvard University Press, 2013.

4. Samuel Beckett, "Recent Irish Poetry." *Disjecta: Miscellaneous Writings and a Dramatic Fragment*, edited with a foreword by Ruby Cohn. Grove Press, 1984, pp. 70–1.

5. Edna Longley, "'Altering the past': Northern Irish Poetry and Modern Canons." *Irish Writing Since 1950, The Yearbook of English Studies*, vol. 35, 2005, p. 5.

6. Trevor Joyce, "The Point of Innovation in Poetry," cited in "Irish Terrain: Alternative Planes of Cleavage." *Assembling Alternatives: Reading Postmodern Poetries Transnationally*, edited by Romana Huk. Wesleyan University Press, 2003, p. 157.

7. Brearton, "Form in Contemporary Irish Poetry," p. 631.

8. The cited phrases come at random from a handful of pages in Justin Quinn, *The Cambridge Introduction to Modern Irish Poetry, 1800–2000*. Cambridge University Press, 2008, pp. 204–9. But such terms of critical commendation could be replicated in almost any work on Irish poetry and are the stock-in-trade of the poetry workshop. "A literature of notations" is Beckett's phrase, from "Proust," in *Proust and Three Dialogues with Georges Duthuit*. John Calder, 1976, p. 76.

9. Theodor W. Adorno, "On Lyric Poetry and Society." *Notes to Literature*, vol. 1, edited by Rolf Tiedemann and translated by Sherry Weber Nicholsen. Columbia University Press, 1991, p. 43.

10. See the Introduction for a discussion of Édouard Glissant's concept of "forced poetics."

11. Maurice Scully, *Livelihood*. Wild Honey Press, 2004, p. 270.

12. Michael Longley, "All Of These People," from *The Weather in Japan*, 2000. *Collected Poems*. Jonathan Cape, 2006, p. 253. The citation, unat-

tributed in the poem, appears to come from Ursula LeGuin, *The Left Hand of Darkness*. Futura, 1981, p. 91, where its meaning is considerably more unstable, possibly ironic.

13. Michael Longley, "At Poll Salach. Easter Sunday, 1998," from *The Weather in Japan* (2000). *Collected Poems*. Jonathan Cape, 2006, p. 253.

14. Ciaran Carson, "The New Estate." *The New Estate*. Blackstaff Press, 1976, p. 41.

15. Ciaran Carson, "Hamlet." *Belfast Confetti*. Wake Forest University Press, 1989, p. 105

16. On both the economic and the counter-insurgency developments for which Ireland served as laboratory, see David Lloyd, *Irish Culture and Colonial Modernity, 1800–2000: The Transformation of Oral Space*. Cambridge University Press, 2011. Carson's story of the sergeant's ghost finds correspondences in Allen Feldman's ethnographic *Formations of Violence: The Narrative of the Body and Political Terror in Northern Ireland*. University of Chicago Press, 1989, pp. 65–8.

17. Carson, "Hamlet," p. 107. On the formal and thematic characteristics of Carson's Belfast poetry, see Eric Falci, "Carson's City." *Continuity and Change in Irish Poetry, 1966–2010*. Cambridge University Press, 2012, pp. 120–51, and Julia Obert, "Ciaran Carson: Sounding the City" and "Ciaran Carson: From Song to Stutter." *Postcolonial Overtures: The Politics of Sound in Northern Irish Poetry*. Syracuse University Press, 2015, pp. 22–76.

18. I deliberately draw the cited phrase from the fine if brief British Council web-page note on McGuckian by Eve Patten, which is one place where the baffled reader is first likely to turn for an introduction to the poet's work: https://literature.britishcouncil.org/writer/medbh-mcguckian (last accessed July 29, 2021).

19. Shane Alcobia-Murphy, *Sympathetic Ink: Intertextual Relations in Northern Irish Poetry*. Liverpool University Press, 2006, ch. 2, is the most exhaustive account of McGuckian's borrowings. The unsettlement that this practice and its extent in McGuckian's work has caused is somewhat odd in the Irish context, where practices of unoriginal writing, from fake translation to transcription and parody, have an honorable lineage from James Clarence Mangan through James Joyce and, more figuratively, Samuel Beckett.

20. Leontia Flynn, *Reading Medbh McGuckian*. Irish Academic Press, 2014, p. 173.

21. William Empson, *Seven Types of Ambiguity*. New Directions, 1966, pp. 244–7.

22. Clair Wills, "Women Poets: The Privatization of Myth." *Improprieties: Politics and Sexuality in Northern Irish Poetry*. Oxford University Press, 1993, p. 67. Wills's overall argument is a brilliant demonstration of the "colonial consequences" that have determined a different historical trajectory of social experience in Ireland and represents an exemplary case for the intellectual necessity of postcolonial arguments about Irish culture. For a recent study of McGuckian that compellingly extends Wills's early insights to read both her citational practice and her silences in the context of trauma theory, see Maureen E. Ruprecht Fadem, *Medbh McGuckian:*

Iterations of Silence and the Borders of Articulacy. Lexington Books, 2019. Fadem's study has the virtue of furnishing a broader comparative context for McGuckian, including Paul Celan, than most Irish-based studies can claim.

23. On McGuckian's use of Mandelstam in this poem, see Alcobia-Murphy, *Sympathetic Ink*, pp. 236–7.

24. Medbh McGuckian, "Elegy for an Irish Speaker." *Captain Lavender*. Wake Forest University Press, 1995, p. 42. For the borrowing from Mandelstam, see Flynn, *Reading Medbh McGuckian*, p. 155.

25. Samuel Beckett, *The Unnamable* in *Molloy, Malone Dies, The Unnamable*. Calder and Boyars, 1973, p. 390. On the differentiating return of the name and the date, and on the "departure" of poem from occasion, see Jacques Derrida, "Shibboleth: For Paul Celan." *Sovereignties in Question: The Poetics of Paul Celan*, edited by Thomas Dutoit and Outi Pasanen. Fordham University Press, 2005, pp. 1–64. These issues are also discussed in Chapters 1 and 2.

26. McGuckian, "Elegy for an Irish Speaker," p. 42.

27. McGuckian, "Elegy for an Irish Speaker," p. 42.

28. McGuckian, "Elegy for an Irish Speaker," p. 43.

29. Walter Benjamin, "The Task of the Translator," translated by Harry Zohn. *Selected Writings: Volume 1: 1913–1926*, edited by Marcus Bullock and Michael W. Jennings. Belknap Press, 1996, p. 254. See Chapter 1 for a fuller discussion of this passage.

30. McGuckian, "Elegy for an Irish Speaker," p. 43.

31. Medbh McGuckian, "The Albert Chain." *Captain Lavender*, p. 68.

32. Medbh McGuckian, "Flirting with Saviours." *Captain Lavender*, p. 53.

33. Medbh McGuckian, "Dante's Own Day." *Captain Lavender*, p. 34.

34. Medbh McGuckian, "Black Note Study." *Captain Lavender*, p. 39.

35. On the two states' separate development, cultural as well as economic and political, see Joe Cleary, *Literature, Partition and the Nation State: Culture and Conflict in Ireland, Israel and Palestine*. Cambridge University Press, 2002, p. 77.

36. Trevor Joyce, "The Phantom Quarry: Translating a Renaissance Painting into Modern Poetry." *Enclave Review*, vol. 8, Summer 2013, p. 6. Archived at http://enclavereview.org/the-phantom-quarry-translating-a-renaissance-painting-into-modern-poetry/ (last accessed July 29, 2021). Joyce gives in this essay a meticulous account of his poetic procedure, based on a transformation for spreadsheet composition of the traditional sestina. See also his "Poetry, Form and Meaning." *Cork Caucus: On Art, Possibility & Democracy*. National Sculpture Factory and Revolver—Archiv für aktuelle Kunst, 2006, pp. 371–8. The latter essay elaborates the procedures through which he constructed his "The Peacock's Tale." The difficulty of locating these low-circulation publications is an index of the inhospitability of such writing to easy commodification and a perhaps unwished-for sign of their success in that regard.

37. Catherine Walsh, *Optic Verve: A Commentary*. Shearsman Books, 2009, p. 39; hereafter cited in the text as *OV*.

38. See Clare Bracken's beautiful commentary on the final paragraph of this prose segment that narrates the death of a homeless young man in

"Nomadic Ethics: Gender and Class in Catherine Walsh's *City West.*" *Irish University Review*, vol. 46, no. 1, Spring/Summer 2016, pp. 75–6. Bracken's essay insightfully elaborates the connections between Walsh's work and the Celtic Tiger. With regard to Fatima Mansions, Walsh comments, "local efforts for Regeneration process have come through, building is complete and there is a strong community-based focus/ethos in running services and activities there": personal communication, October 3, 2018. The persistence of resistance and autonomous initiative as a community-based phenomenon is, as I argue further in the Conclusion, essential to Walsh's counter-word to neoliberal development in *Optic Verve.*

39. On the "residual" and the "emergent," see Raymond Williams, *Marxism and Literature.* Oxford University Press, 1977, pp. 121–7. I have commented on the need to see residual formations in colonial spaces as furnishing the means to shaping emergent and resistant ones in David Lloyd, *Ireland after History.* Cork University Press, 1999, p. 78. The term "semi-colonial" is borrowed from the Peruvian poet César Vallejo, who thus described his nation. On Vallejo's use of the term "semi-colonial," see Adam Sharman, "Vallejo, Modernity and Poetemporality." *Tradition and Modernity in Spanish American Literature: From Darío to Carpentier.* Palgrave Macmillan, 2006, p. 90.

40. Leopoldina Fortunati, *The Arcane of Reproduction: Housework, Prostitution, Labor and Capital,* edited by Jim Fleming and translated by Hilary Creek. Autonomedia,1995.

41. Joyce, "Irish Terrain." *Assembling Alternatives*, pp. 156–68.

Chapter 6

Intricate Walking: Scully's *Livelihood*

> The book
> is fat, contains code. The world,
> the water planet. The code contained in
> this thing in the world, the book, changes
> the things, the world.[1]

Livelihood challenges reading. Like any important work of poetry, it poses immediately the question of "how to read." That question ultimately resonates for poetics in general, that is, for our habits and customary formulations about reading and about what a poem is as it lays itself open to, or troubles, or even forecloses our reading practices. More than any other volume of Scully's to date, *Livelihood* announces itself forcefully as a book: in its heft, its substantiality in the hand, in its imposing material presence, this is a very different object than the slim sheaf of carefully arranged poems that the prevalence of lyric forms has led the reader to expect will be the format in which poetry arrives. The materiality of the book as object is not irrelevant: it embodies and announces the gravity of the project *Things That Happen*, a twenty-five-year-long process of writing aimed at what Scully has famously described as constructing or assembling books rather than composing poems.[2] *Livelihood*, as a book constructed of five books, stands as the centerpiece of that project, transforming the previously published chapbooks or booklets that it assembles into parts of an imposing whole, making a "fat book" that communicates a certain monumentality.

Yet its monumentality and its gravity as an object in the world are counterpointed at once by its title, *Livelihood*. A livelihood is a means to life, but it is not a career, in the sense of a curriculum vitae that suggests a life that is a developing whole, an achieved and coherent vocation shaped by a singular plan or intention: say, "a 'career in / "development"', the 'management of the poor'" (*L* 186). A livelihood does not lend itself to any idea of an opus, to a corpus of work bent on totality or monumentalizing a "life work." It connotes, rather, a casual relation to gaining a living, an occasional relation to work and to the material necessity of some source of income in order that the work of writing might proceed. *Livelihood* reflects often enough and intimately on this conundrum of living and dwelling poetically:

> my wife & I worry about our debts & spirited
> baby daughter. & the difficulty of getting out of
> this mess & learning the language & dodging the main
> streets at rush-hour so as not to run into anybody
> we might owe money to. (*L* 97)

The scenarios of various modes of casual but still mostly male-gendered labor—"working as a / teacher / porter / watchman / noteman / manman" (*L* 23)—and of the reproductive labor of raising children and making a home somewhere, somehow, counterpoint those of the poet at work, at, one is tempted to say, the real work:

> This is my desk. This is where I work.
> . . .
> I work hard in my corner, any chance I get,
> really I do.
>
> . . .
>
> And I've been busy. Busy eating, drinking, giving ear,
> Listening to repetitive nonsense, setting out, getting
> a living, watching my children, teaching my children,
> making Lesson plans, filling paper. . . . (*L* 134)

In this counterpoint of labor and the work, where "getting and spending lays waste our lives," chance governs the construction of the poem, the snatched moment of writing and the moments written of. However impressive the scale of the accumulated work, *Things That Happen* foregrounds happenstance, chance observation and encounter, the fleeting occasion, in defiance at once of necessity and of the Protestant ethic that responds to necessity with the injunction to steady labor. Scully's writing has, as Romana Huk has emphasized of another volume of Scully's, a lightness of touch that counterpoises gravity if it does not defy it altogether.[3]

Opening the volume more or less at random, the reader is faced with what appear to be some variety of lyric poems that often bear generic titles or subtitles that indicate one or other of the modes that form the repertoire of lyric poetry—sonnets, ballads, songs, rounds, and even, for the Hibernophile, the aisling. Despite their highly various arrangements on the page, their allergy to the regularities of quatrain or tercet, they mostly share the visual form of lyric poems, sparse texts on the page descending through white space. At times, they even deploy moments of "vivid immediacy" and the invocation of the second person that, as Jonathan Culler has recently argued, is the typical apostrophic stance of the lyric that floats ambiguously between self-reference (signifying "I") and address to the other:[4]

> **sonnet**/the way the peachtree branches are
>   loaded at the tip. I will please you
>   with pattern & no one will read you
>   no one will read you until you've been
>   chopped & laundered. no one. if this
>   worries you. someone will attempt
>   taking the money if someone thinks
>   they will read you. it's 4.02. dove-
>   coo & the toilet tank filling & the cock
>   crowing: nobody could say it's not
>   music, picking up the pattern by which
>   to please the process receptors. . . . (*L* 26)

This eighteen-line poem is scarcely a sonnet in any conventional sense, though closer to one in its appearance on the page than many so titled in the book. And yet, just as the rhyme scheme or the relation between octet and sestet in the sonnet establish patterns that, as formalists like Roman Jakobson have demonstrated to almost manic extent, operate across the whole sonic and semantic space of the sonnet, this poem establishes its own complex set of patterns, patterns that *please*. These patterns are indifferent to the tonal or social registers of the materials they orchestrate—"dove- / coo & the toilet tank filling & the cock / crowing" (with a buried pun on ball-cock and a deft allusion to the aubade)—and accommodate the most diverse materials without imposing hierarchies of taste or decorum. Indeed, characteristically the poems of *Livelihood* swerve and dip through multiple registers and levels, refusing both the high seriousness or tonal consistency by which the lyric generally distinguishes itself and the alternative and equally consistent effects of comic bathos by which another vein of contemporary versifying stakes its claims on a democratic undoing of poetry's earnest moral pedagogy.

But what differentiates this "sonnet" most of all from its archetype is its refusal of any closing *fabula* or *sententia*: the poem does not even conclude; at most, it may revert to its opening peachtree branches. It does not culminate in any rendering of epiphany or ironic reflection on the insights that its transformation of experience into figure has yielded. Rather, it splits its sides:

>   . . . then I
> said. then a choir, I could hear it
> through the doors, windows, fly-mesh &
> burglar bars, walls, tin roof,
> the page place—each filter in quiver—a
> choir, a magnificent hosanna, ooo ha-ha-ha
> a-appy day! blooming, spread. (*L* 26)

Much as a home may be penetrated by unearthly or disruptive musics from beyond that overwhelm its defensive "filters," the poem ceases to be a self-contained artifact and opens itself to connections and relations infiltrating any closed structure that might even provisionally be thrown up. The apparently immediate image of the arching branches of the peachtree is not fulfilled in this poem but is picked up again in the following "sonnet":

> peaches whose fur   sweet fruit smell
>   curved groove   three senses
>   then taste one (*L* 27)

Likewise, the tin roof is taken up again in a new conjunction across the page:

> tin roof + rain = tinroof rainmusic. (*L* 27)

In the subsequent "sonnet," the apparently imagistic tree opens once again, but now as matter for a school "nature walk" with all its pedagogical intonations:

> **sonnet/**(we went out to look at the tree.
>   we formed a circle around it.
>   this is the Bole, these the Branches, that the Canopy—
>   stand back. Underneath you know
>   is where the Roots go
>   to live & hold the ground together.
>   & look at the Top
>   how compliant it is to the weather. (*L* 28)

If I dwell on the recurrence and transformation of motifs among the poems—or verse units—from which the book is constructed on this local scale, it is to open the question which the book constantly poses, which is at what scale one is to think of pattern occurring, emerging, or being woven. Repetitions across one or a handful of pages are relatively easily attuned to. When repetitions, echoes, or variations chime across the distance of some hundred or even two hundred pages, how is one to think of poetic structuring?

Case in point: another sonnet placed early in the book captures a glimpse of a gull, that ubiquitous Dublin bird, perched on a roof:

> **sonnet/**There is a grey sky.
>   there is a white gull
>   on a black aerial
>   on a black roof
>   opening its yellow beak
>   wide & silently
>   calling calls. (*L* 21)

As if to arrest the reader's attention, a gull appears again at the opening of the following sonnet, where:

> neon flecks join & pass
> on the black water
>   gull
>   teal
>   but ons in special in thyn arraye
> I see well
> it passes
>   clamp
> two luminous blanks   rainbow splotch (*L* 22)

We are now all the more likely to recall this gull then, when some twenty pages later, it reappears in a further sonnet, but in language that slightly rearranges the initial version:

> there is a grey sky.
> there is a white gull
> on a black aerial
> on a black roof
> opening its yellow
> beak wide & silently
> calling
> calls. (*L* 45)

It takes a greater effort of attention for the reader to recall this when, on p. 205, the same scenario recurs, once again reconfigured and revised:

> low sky
> gull   aerial
> head that way
> this
> beak wide
> calls (*L* 205)

Likewise, the allusion to Thomas Wyatt's "They flee from me" in the second of these poems recurs within that poem as a kind of parodic commentary on contemporary club-goers' fashion:[5]

& close up
the Little Barrel's sexy sketches in thin array
     gullwing
      head flicking
        claw in glove
though all curve & flow
stiletto clack   HEY   tap
the seam of the knickers showing through
       then not
engage the array of the discarded on the streets to live (*L* 22)

But allusion to Wyatt also detaches itself from this context and recurs over two hundred pages later as an echo indexed only by the little phrase "in speciall" (*L* 252), a reverberation so faint as to make one wonder whether in the complex array of the book's construction one has missed other iterations—as on p. 96, "where their dance in special," or the simple word "array" in "a life an array of related mistakes" (*L* 48). Missed patterning or mistaken patterning: in either case, the "pattern-ache vanishing into life's pixels" (*L* 49) that the book both reflects on and induces in the reader is always in question. Pattern we inevitably, achingly seek, in the poem or book, in the world and in a life, ours or another's, haunted by the possibility that the patterns we decipher at any moment will the next dissolve into the pixelated textures of a world recalcitrant to processing by its very abundance and mobility.

 This is therefore the most unmemorable of poetry, in the best sense. It resists easy appropriation and mental processing, proving almost impossible to commit to memory, "FORGETTING EVERYTHING" (*L* 303). It refuses the moralization of poetry as a mnemonic vehicle for crystallized *sententiae*. That is not to say that *Livelihood* abandons structure or the iterative patterning on which memory relies. Repetition is the condition of (having) experience: without repetition in memory or as a condition of learning itself ("repetitive nonsense" being the teacher's bane) there could be no experience, only a continuous influx of sensations and percepts; repetition is in the service of establishing relation and pattern, of making sense of and arresting what Beckett's Neary, stealing from William James, called "the big blooming buzzing confusion."[6] Experience likewise requires relation among its parts: "A mess of reminiscence is nothing" (*L* 130). Repetition is by the same token, in its various forms, the very condition of poetry, at times formally evident in devices like rhyme and meter, at others to be apprehended in the overall echoic structure of the work, what Scully calls variously the weave, the mesh, the net, or the lattice, "the impossibly repeating lattice" (*L* 43). Multiple "fibrous" connections proliferate across the poems that construct the book as a whole, producing a web of repetitions and resemblances that—for this reader at least—constantly multiply on each reading, overlooked on prior occasions and gradually generating an ever more complex tissue—or weave—of connection.

Scully has commented on this aspect of the structure of his work:

> Now, broadly speaking, for me, an entry into form in poetry would be to think of it as two kinds, the architectural and the fibrous—two distinct ways of looking at it. Most of mine is fibrous—structure below ground. But *structured* for sure. The mycelium, the threaded web, connecting roots over long distances. Symbiotic not parasitic. My poetry has that sort of fibrous connectedness. It's all part of the way we experience the world, I think.[7]

Scully's preference for the fibrous structure reflects not only "part of the way we experience the world" but also an everywhere implicit aesthetic ethics of living. Anyone looking for a "politics" of Scully's writing might find it in that opposition of the symbiotic to the parasitic: the work refuses the relation of settling and colonization of the other, the exploitation of the host, in favor of a mutually supportive and constitutive relationality, in a "meshing" that can at moments become emphatic:

> when threads mesh as they cross
> over they sing to us.
>
> this is how to live. (*L* 219)

One is reminded that the sonnet (etymologically *sonitus*, little sound or song) was the form that inaugurated a Western poetics of interiority, adapted to ethical self-interrogation and the inner voice.[8] Its cellular space of enclosure is the image of that interior space in which the project of self-possession unfolds. Scully's deconstructed sonnets—or song-nets—are lyrics that open out to let the world enter, analogues of the porosity of the subject to the world that may even open the body to cosmic as well as mundane forces, its threads pulled even as it pulls on threads of interconnection:

> From
> the outside of your life, a pattern threaded
> through, to the inside of your life, what at
> the back of your mind coming to the front,
> tautens. Look, I move my fingers. Oh. Feeling
> the pull of that nearby star the river twists
> and spins. Then I begin to walk about with
> my body again. (*L* 199)

In one respect, the net or web furnishes a correlative to and attends an apprehension of living that is fundamentally generous, "giving back" in both a phenomenological and an ethical sense:

> Love plants peace. Not a catalogue of manipulative
> fairytales. The sky gives back. Gable-shape, tree-lines.
> The way the sunlight is, the way it comes down
> through leaves, and spider-silk gleams and
> doesn't suddenly, between lightly moving branches
> in the morning to be still. The order of the stones
> in the wall beside the yellow dust-track magnified,
> the insect ready, then away over and through a light
> dustfall in a sideways breeze gone but, very small,
> is noted . . . (*L* 163)

But the web or net, as Harry Gilonis has noted, is also a snare: both capture and entrap, as the multiple references in *Livelihood* to the spider's lethal webs and insect prey remind us.[9] But the patterns and systems of patterning that web and net stand for are no less perceptual or cognitive traps. Gilonis acutely poses this issue as "the question of how to understand the world without clinging to, peering through, being jailed behind, some conceptual lattice."[10] For Scully, the question seems to arrive more as a problem of how to register the appearance of patterns, grasp them "precisely" (a term that echoes throughout the book), and yet not get trapped into mistaking the momentary or provisional pattern for a fixed and conclusive identity: how, in other words, to keep "moving in the weave" (*L* 128). Indeed, the untitled opening poem of the section "Prior" seems to map the relation between the "mis-taking" of the world and the "weave" that tries to make some momentary sense of it:

> Hopeful human mistakes. I think I see what I think
> (sometimes), but mostly I imagine where I am
> in the dark, feeling around, moment to moment,
> ready to respond to elastic surface, do you see what
> I hope I mean? A tap on the pipe, an insect clicks;
> deep in its pulp, the seeds start out. It's a long
> fantastic journey and nobody *really* believes the
> details. (*L* 129)

Mistaking is a function, on the one hand, of the slippage between names and phenomena, sense and signification:

> The name of the noise of what they were saying doesn't
> contain this or that web of the meaning of what they
> were saying and this together, shimmering, terrific,
> in the grass somewhere. (*L* 128)

On the other hand, whatever web of meaning is constructed, precisely as it offers the indubitable aesthetic pleasures of fit and harmony, confirms the distance of observer from world and carries the potential for complacency, another mode of mistaking the world— snug is a precise anagram of sung:

> When the pieces fit moving in the weave they make a
> Noise together, snug in Disaster Depicted, not Disaster. (*L* 128)

The intrinsic distance of the poem from the world it orchestrates is at once its condition of possibility and its burden. The poet's stance at the window, catching glimpses of the world, or at the doorway, looking out at the rain-drenched or sunlit ground, is both a vantage and a threshold that hedges against "the strong tang / of the world impacting its *itself* on you, a / tide of smallest simplest things" (*L* 208). The cascade of the real overwhelms and demands the response of a patterning that is, by the same token, defense and rage for order, conducing to limitation and the deadening of receptivity. "Habit," as Beckett's Vladimir said, "is a great deadener,"[11] the product, in Beckett's own terms, of "a compromise between the individual and his environment."[12] For Scully, the deadening effect is that of interpellation, the recruitment of the subject to the social order by the impact of instruction and media, for "If the system locks you to the screen / it directs your life" (*L* 186):

> learning to follow
> the way you hear the talk
>
> you will learn to follow
> the ways you see the talk
> deployed
>
> & learn to initiate deployments
> in surprise
> measuring surprise
> crestfallen by the word *is*
>
> & this habit
> will facilitate & hinder
> yr ideas about the world
> skintight   to itself
>
> in the darkness
> (&) in the light. (*L* 189)

Scully's own relation to the interpellating effects of habit is not, however, to claim some ironically distantiated perspective that sees through the net of ideologies, but to recognize the constant possible oscillation between one's snug or smug satisfaction with the world as known and classified and the capacity of the world to derange or "dis-cord" that certainty, to slough the "skin" we stretch over its constantly shifting appearances:

> the problem
> was how the question was the
> more I thought I knew the more I
> "knew" I sank into the relative
> shadows that seem to cover the a-
> symmetrical skin that one begins
> to suspect anyway covers everything.
> full of. Everything differently
> precisely in each different net.
> full of the tiny bright word*ks* of
> discorded invention. our lives,
> glittering, reticulated. & from in
> here that edge where what you've
> been taught to imagine you know
> meets more . . . (*L* 29)

Scully's initially stumbling and ambiguous syntax betrays here the awkward incoherence that attends any effort in *Livelihood* to "cover everything": nets are necessarily gapped. And the nets that are potential snares are countered by the "glittering, reticulated" nets that are *differential* in their function, establishing provisional constellations of the most disparate and disjunctive materials, assemblages whose momentary patterned stabilities are "discorded" at every moment by the insistence of the "more" that has necessarily been excluded from them.

Like constellations, then, Scully's weaves are the effect of a specific stance or angle of vision, an angle that shifts and changes with greater frequency than can that of any earthly observer of the heavens, but which are no less arbitrary than the arrays of stars that seem so persuasively to organize the night sky into constant and perduring figures. The poem as constellation, or as an assembly of constellations, speaks necessarily from what Paul Celan—one of the tutelary presences of *Livelihood*— called that "angle of reflection which is [the poet's] own existence, [the poet's] own physical nature."[13] Scully does not seek to "fly by those nets,"[14] in Stephen Dedalus's expression, but rather captures himself as a constitutive presence in the nets that he weaves, no more nor less entrapped there than the reader or the friendly fly that each in their way find themselves "landing on the page" (*L* 7).

Dependent as they are on the particular "angle of reflection" of the poet, the patterns that form the local and extended constellations of *Livelihood* are nonetheless never understood to be the singular production of a peculiarly human capacity. On the contrary, the figures for the poems' and the book's structure are drawn from both organic and inorganic as well as artifactual phenomena: not only nets and weaving, but webs, crystals, honeycombs, and birds' nests furnish the analogues for Scully's sense of structure throughout *Livelihood*. Additionally, the poems constantly stage the arrest of the subject's attention before the momentary, fleeting patterns that recur throughout, the net-like interference patterns of light reflecting on water or of the concentric ripple, also interfering wave patterns, caused by a pebble dropped in water, or the sunlight's dapple among leaves, or even the sudden, peripheral passage of a bird across the sky. Whether understood as architectonic forms constant in nature—like crystals or webs—or as fleeting effects of no less constant physical laws, pattern and structure seem to exist independent of the human observer. To Pound's triumphant "O splendor it all coheres!" and subsequent, repentant "I cannot make it cohere,"[15] Scully responds with the architecture of the weaver bird in a passage of singular beauty:

> listeners there
>   are &
> steady hey but
>
> cohere? Go there
> look: hanker after
>   people or a
>
>   god or a blinding
>   pattern
>   one of the
>
>   smallest birds in
> the world its
>   nest the size
>
>   of half a
>   walnut shell
>   built to such
>
>   deft such delicate
> these feathers
>   leaves even telltale
>
>   flower-petals moss
>   hair feet
>   bill spider-thread
>
>   weaving or the
> bird's own saliva
>   together or both
>
>   dancing in despite of even

out over
    mimosa flicker past
    the village to
    the mountains

their eggs even
    their eggs themselves
stuck down fast

against gales one
flat yes precision

    stuck down
        fast   (*L* 272–3)

Pound's sublime ambitions here meet, perhaps in an echo of the *Pisan Cantos'* humble "lone ant," with the miniature architect in nature whose delicate, deft operations find their equivalent in the minimal architecture of the poetic lines.[16] Analogously, Gilonis cites Marx's famous remark that "a spider conducts operations which resemble those of a weaver, and a bee would put many a human architect to shame."[17]

Both the architectonic forms that appear in organic and inorganic nature and the beauty that the human eye may perceive in them raise more fundamental, and fundamentally aesthetic, issues than the humbling of human skills. In so far as they are regarded not with respect to any function they may have, but simply as patterned objects, things like webs, crystals, honeycombs, or nests correspond to what Immanuel Kant in the *Critique of Judgement* terms "free or self-subsisting beauties":

> Flowers are free beauties of nature. Hardly anyone but a botanist knows the true nature of a flower and even he, while recognizing in the flower the reproductive organ of the plant, pays no attention to this natural end when using his taste to judge of its beauty. Hence no perfection of any kind—no internal finality, as something to which this arrangement of the manifold is related—underlies this judgement. Many birds (the parrot, the humming-bird, the bird of paradise), and a number of crustacea, are self-subsisting beauties which are not appurtenant to any object defined with respect to its end, but please freely and of their own account.[18]

Kant's point—which he extends to music and non-representational forms of decorative art and design—is that such "beauties" please independent of any concept we might have of what the object in question is *for* (its function or use) or of its adequacy to any moral idea (in particular with regard to human form). Nonetheless, they may still appear *as if* their form were "chosen as it were with an eye to our taste" (*CJ* I 217). Later, he will add to these examples what he similarly calls "free formations of nature," all described with considerable knowledge of the physical laws involved, that include inorganic processes like mineral crystallization, the formation of ice in freezing water, or snow, "frequently of very artistic appearance and of extreme beauty" (*CJ* I 219). Again the production of such formations in nature *appears* to suggest that nature has its own "aesthetic finality," that is, produces beautiful forms of its own volition (*CJ* I 219).

Still, according to Kant, to believe so would compromise not only the freedom of aesthetic judgment, but also the foundations of human freedom in general in the capacity for the free exercise of that power of judgment:

> For nature to have fashioned its forms for our delight would inevitably imply an objective finality on the part of nature, instead of a subjective finality resting on the play of the imagination in its freedom, where it is we who receive nature with favour, and not nature that does us a favour. (*CJ* I 220)

Nature's apparent conformity to human aesthetic judgments that have universal if subjective validity "cannot belong to it as its end": "For otherwise the judgement that would be determined by reference to such an end would found upon heteronomy, instead of founding upon autonomy and being free, as befits a judgement of taste" (*CJ* I 220).

Art for Kant is essentially a domain of freedom and, as such, a domain that must be divided by a carefully policed boundary from the operations of nature, however much these may appear to reveal the capacity of non-human animals to produce beautiful forms independent of any function they may have. Natural forms may be analogous to artworks (*CJ* II 23), but only for the free reflective judgment of the human observer, not in themselves:

> By right it is only production through freedom, i.e. through an act of will that places reason at the basis of its action, that should be termed art. For, although we are pleased to call what bees produce (their regularly constructed cells) a work of art, we do so only on the strength of an analogy with art; that is to say, as soon as we call to mind that no rational deliberation forms the basis of their nature (or instinct), and it is only to their Creator that we ascribe it as art. (*CJ* I 163)

As I have argued at greater length elsewhere, Kant's insistence on the realm of the aesthetic as that which grounds the very possibility of both human freedom and of the accord that guarantees the universality of the form of the Western human subject continues to shape a prevalent conjunction between aesthetic work and the ideal of human freedom and individuality. It cannot do so, however, without establishing differentiating thresholds between the free or autonomous subject and both natural phenomena and subordinate categories of humans, its racialized others.[19] Kant's *Critique of Judgement* thus inaugurates a tradition of aesthetic thought (which embraces poetics) that understands art to be the principal domain in which questions of human freedom and determination, subjectivity and universality are articulated. The artwork, in deliberate opposition to the products of nature, however beautiful they may be, is the archetype of human freedom from what Kant calls here "heteronomy."

In some respects, *Livelihood* might seem to extend that tradition: it is, as I have remarked, often scathing about the effects of a socially induced conformity, about subordination to the market (of labor and of poetry), and about the numbing impact of habits developed to survive in what the Frankfurt School named the "administered world."[20]

> It impinges to such a degree that the minimum
> function required to remain the anonymous
> human agent in the world exerts a pressure
> disproportionate to the results required. *Chiaro?*
> Birdsong. I am that perfect citizen. Nothing is
> nothing. Yes-ing and no-ing and on-the-other-hand-
> ing my way through the mesh. I mean mess. Just
> pre-set the dial for Discipline: palm-frond in
> Harare, a bridge in Cambridge shiver a synapse. (*L* 201)

One of the volume's recurrent concerns is with the attainment of the means to a livelihood that might safeguard space and time for the writing to proceed in the face of the pressures of need and want. Writing continues to seem like a space that opposes heteronomy, that depends on the freedom from necessity that has always found its image in the free creativity of the artist, dismally as the concept of "creativity" has been appropriated in the lingo of Silicon Valley and sports good manufacturers and as the instances of transitory beauty—palm fronds and bridges— have been transformed into the routine metonyms of Discipline for the predisposed nervous system.

And yet *Livelihood* as a whole does not frame the issue with such finality. On the contrary, it establishes a constant oscillation between freedom and constraint, figured often as the relation between chance and choice. The sudden motion of perception or insight with which so many of the poems open or around which their movement turns alternates with the selection and patterning obliged by a world in which the poet "intent at desk" faces "the ten thousand / things that convene / shine escape / intermittent material" (*L* 279). In a world that is—to scale up and down—the product not of nature's subjective or objective finality, but of the accretion of dust particles through random collisions (*L* 168) or "colliding / high energy particles" (*L* 130), pattern and order are arbitrary or provisional, resembling the rules of a game that constitute the space and the instruments for a mesh (or mess) of chance outcomes:

> Giving back a black mesh, all the rules together, connected,
> or if all the rules together, dilated, make a path out then/
> Then the rules get up and shake hands. Game, set. No
>
> I mean yes . . . .
>   If, stepping inside around and then
> outside and then again inside the circle of the rules of
> the game is the game, what then? Got that? *Chak*. But that's
> a new game. Turn dance. . . . (*L* 192)

Not only the game—including the "language game" of poetry—but even the players themselves are constituted by the rules of the game for the duration of the game. But in *Livelihood*, the rules of the game keep changing, shifting, the diverse units of the book refusing to stabilize into a single set of procedures ("Game, set. No . . .").[21] Any reader of Scully's work may have been struck by the extent to which the "second person address" characteristic of the lyric warps into the imperative mood, as if each verse unit required the iteration of "the basic instructions" (*L* 127) in order for poet and reader to proceed: begin, listen, turn, leave, breathe, step, open the book, close the book.[22] The instances proliferate so extensively across the book that citation would be redundant. What matters is the function of the imperative mood and its relation to the order of poem that *Livelihood* enjoins the reader to engage with.

Critics have noted often enough Scully's antipathy towards the "well-made poem" that has dominated the Irish poetry industry and for which there seems an ever-avid market:[23] product of what he dismisses as "the Gem School" (*L* 18), it circulates "bottled poetry" (*L* 132) whose characteristics he satirizes more than once in *Livelihood*, at times in terms that recall Beckett's enumerative comic turns in *Watt*:

> A mess of reminiscence is nothing. I was living
> on a small half-empty island, cold and wet, and
> many poets making much of their mothers and fath-
> ers and grandfathers and grandmothers and fields
> and ploughs and pigs as deeply gouged lies—the
> surface of Jupiter's Ganymede as I remember it—
> in the same breath, phrase-packets, a very I must
> say very slowed poetry: this was not Africa.
> Procumbent. I left. A weave is something. (*L* 130)[24]

This is telling satire, directed at a familiar enough mode of Irish poetry, structured around the usually displaced, educated poet's reminiscences of rural childhood transformed into metaphors of belonging and cultural continuity. But there is more at issue than the anecdotal matter of poems that perpetually reiterate the conditions of deracination that have affected an agricultural economy undergoing rapid modernization, only to reassure the reader of the snug fit between the modern subject and the rural past. Ultimately, it is more about the inadequacy of a reproducible and widely reproduced poetic mode to the economic and social conditions of the present:

> I mean: everything run through this tensely amalgamated
> shadow-corps so that so many young practitioners
> don't even know how much's been filtered out or that
> anything has been *erase/erase* in the first place.
> Contact. Toy-like parallel movements. So complete, so
> concerted has been the walling round. To call repetitive
> clones "innovators" & get away with it. To inculcate
> a pathologically low tolerance threshold for complexity,
> & be thought intelligent. . . . (*L* 107)

Generic ossification induces a kind of sclerosis of the attention, a "toy-like" automatism in which the poetic conformism of the clonic "shadow-corps" produces a "walling round" that peculiarly emulates the forms of enclosure that destroyed Ireland's rural communities and imposed the conditions for the emergence of an Irish version of the possessive individual of modern capitalist society.[25]

Irish poetry may be the immediate object of Scully's critique, but the critique is framed in such a way that it extends far beyond the poetic automatisms specific to Ireland's poetic culture. It aims at the ethical and aesthetic assumptions that are embedded in the "well-made poem." Scully has expressed often enough his distaste for metaphors and similes "(I dislike / similes, Mary, you know me.)" (*L* 235).[26] Metaphorization is a fundamental operation or action of language and *Livelihood* is by no means devoid of either metaphor or simile. The antipathy is rather to the overall function of metaphor/simile within the "well-made poem" and the model of the autonomous subject whose formation such poetry continually reinscribes, long after the conditions for autonomy have been eroded both by the thorough saturation of the social with the "codes" of automated responses ("repetitive cloning") and by the pervasive heteronomy of late or neoliberal capitalism. The rote reproduction of lyric forms is symptomatic of a situation of unfreedom that Scully's fellow poet Trevor Joyce, no less dismayed by the automatisms of Irish lyric, has described acutely in terms already cited. The typical language of the lyric, that of "description, expression, aspiration," as Joyce puts it, "is constantly being sucked down the sink of calculated, monetized use. Moreover, even our means to refresh it have been appropriated."[27]

Both Joyce and Scully point to a larger predicament of lyric form than that evidenced in the routinized subject matter and "shape on the page" of the exhausted Irish mode. The so-called well-made poem reproduces the preset pattern of formation of the subject that integrates individual autonomy with the appropriation of the world. Its typical pattern is framed around metaphor: a vividly felt and particular moment of experience is rendered or recalled, usually in an ongoing present tense, only to be transformed—mostly by way of metaphor—into a figure for a generalized moral sentiment. The genealogy of the contemporary lyric may be traceable back to its Romantic forebears, but as an exhausted form it finally fails to partake of the imaginative imperatives that it now clones: both the illumination and the free relation to the social whole that it promises have declined into predictable "phrase-packets." What the form retains, however, is a specific economy of appropriation that informs the idea of the individual as autonomous or independent entity and an implied relation of author to reader in which the reader repeats the insight of the former in the interest of cultivating in turn his or her own self-formation. The poem stands as an act of appropriation that is in its turn appropriated or internalized by the reader as a model and vehicle of subjectivity. It thus lends itself consummately to the institutionalized practice and ends of the pedagogy of New or Practical Criticism, in which the student reader is formed as the self-possessed and morally discriminating subject. Metaphor is the vehicle by which experience is possessed and accumulated—"owned," as the current expression has it. Experience appears as a kind of raw material from which the individual is constituted in repeated acts of possession and processing *as* the "possessive individual." The type, however, is standardized and the poem that time and again relays the process by which experience is laid hold of is likewise standardized, offering the little "shiver" of recognition that fires the synaptic chains of pleasure. What appear as individual and spontaneous acts of perception in fact represent programmed responses played out according to a fixed and pre-set pattern.

The correlative of that pattern and its capacity to circulate a standardized model of self-hood is money, the universal equivalent that succeeds in transforming every particular thing into a commodity form: money is, so to speak, the ideal form of metaphor, transforming difference into identity for the sake of realizing the potential exchange value that can be extracted from any thing, as the lyric transforms the specific moment of perception into a general equivalent. Scully makes the association explicit:

> Years ago one winter evening travelling
> through Ireland on a bus I watched a
> moon like money in the sky. (I dislike
> similes, Mary, you know me.) The moon
> was like money. Like money. Pulsing in
> my breast-pocket, bright sterile dust—
> rock, just like money. Circular shine
> against black, a brilliant silver, crystals,
> poison. (*L* 235)

Against the toxicity of money, transforming everything into sterile identities, the poem here seems to pose particular things—"that tree, this lake" (*L* 235)—if at the risk of transforming them in turn into "likenesses," metaphors rather than instances of particularity. More consistently, and more profoundly, *Livelihood*—and Scully's poetics as a continuing project—counterposes to the "money form" of the contemporary lyric an ethics and aesthetics of dispossession, one of whose crucial tenets is the refusal of a metaphoric poetics that converts its percepts into likenesses or equivalents, the mis-taking or misappropriation of one thing for another. The latter process repeats poetically the labor of global capital's sweatshops where everything, including human effort, is commodified in the entrapping net or web of circulation in exchange.[28] Gaining a livelihood obliges the writer to engage in this dark parody of the poetic weave:

> I look at the thread. I watch, I hope, doing the sweatshop
> rag (pick up the whisper-movements of the grass, the
> insane harmonies of money) and in my hand
> mistake everything for everything else: floodlit factories,
> fences, dogs, men, uniforms. (*L* 127)

In this dark weave, the hopefully watchful attention of the poetic gaze at the world is perilously matched by the surveillance that guards the productive forces and fences the world into its enclosures. The "watchman" occupies the thin strip that divides these counter-domains of production and watching the world: his shed is the convertible site of watching and writing that generates the antithetical space of a counterpoetics that radically opposes the value system of accumulation and exchange.[29] One of the recurrent locations of the writing throughout *Livelihood* furnishes also one of its pervasive puns: the shed where the writer produces his work, the shed where his writing accumulates along with other "clutter" (*L* 195), simultaneously and antithetically offers the term for this aesthetic of continual dispossession, its ongoing "shedding" of the particulars that risk being appropriated into congealed patterns and enclosures:

Two or three small things, smaller, smaller, enmeshed.
Shed! Shed it all! sings the strange bird I know of
in the banyan tree. Quietly, quietly . . . (*L* 151)

Shedding counters the potentially endless round of "making and saving"
where the appearance of choice manipulates the consumer-worker's
desire:

Does matter stop at its edges? In a forest of false
options your picture of the world inside your head is
manipulated from outside to sell you a kind of hell:
step onto the Desire-Wheel and start making and saving,
making and saving, losing and making and losing again
over the checkerboard. (*L* 151)

Shedding is the refusal of a fixed pattern in which it might seem that
"matter stops at its edges," congealed in images of desirable commodities.
It makes space for the renewal of attention to an unpossessed and
unpossessable world of moving phenomena, of listening, of watching
without desire to fix or appropriate:

nervure of a fly's wings
to blur the lens, difficult,
working through, watching,

taking note, watching, puzzled,
delighted, in a presence
(never anything by rote)

beyond sense, sentient.
Black green
blue (*L* 249–50)

The composition of the weave of *Livelihood* out of such moments of
precise, close-in attention, "puzzled" by fleeting and ephemeral glimpses
of the world, its counter-sublime refusal of grand narratives or dwelling
on historically significant events or figures, might seem to belie the
immediate appearance of this "fat" book's epic scale. That is not to say
that *Livelihood* is anything other than "a poem including history,"[30] in
Pound's sense, but its inclusion of the historical is not a matter of the
citation of events but of being "in history" (*L* 61): as a poem, as a whole,
it registers at every node of its net the pressures and possibilities of its
actual historical moment, from personal and social economic constraints
to the universe of theoretical physics, but with an ear attentive to what
passes and, at times, "lodges   obdurately (in the net)" as history (*L* 61).
Likewise, in its adherence to "writing at the edge" (*L* 130), always at

the cusp of what is emerging into attention, it honors its debt to Charles Olson's notion of "projective verse," but without the shadow of imperial desire that always haunts Olson's formulations, the desire for the work to match up to nature in its scale, to achieve "projective size" that belies the "humilitas" Olson espouses.[31]

Not that Scully's work is devoted to any kind of false modesty or minimalist reserve. It is, rather, a different conception of the projective that is at work here, one that connects Olson's injunction, "one perception must must must MOVE, INSTANTER, ON ANOTHER!" to Scully's own suspicion of metaphor as an index of reduction to equivalence.[32] For him, indeed, "one thing leads to another," but by a more tentative, less declarative movement, hedged around by the possibility of mistaking simultaneity or sequence for identity:

what is the name of the sound of the rain?

     (none   a bell)
      or anything echoing
          between
    one thing & another

       one thing
       of course

       one thing

     cedes to another
      & stored
        in

   as a matter of

      certain

   coarsely sometimes
      strangely
        of

     (tap)

     course

  one thing leads to another

<blockquote>
fine
through certainty
in a sort of constricting ring.
</blockquote>

<blockquote>
I thought the other hammering
was the echo of another (tell/told)
until the first(which?)stopped (*L* 94–5)
</blockquote>

Here, indeed, one perception moves, more or less instanter, but hesitantly, towards another, or, more precisely, "one thing *cedes* to another," giving way as perception moves; and not only forward, but though interruption and the sideways flitting of the attention, *across* the field of composition, "mind skittering, touching/jumping / across a water surface" (*L* 321). Ceding is the antithesis of "holding," accumulatively, to what is, to the imposition of a progression or direction. Like yielding, its giving way is productive, even if, as Scully jests, what it produces, one thing after another, might be "a terminal spinney / of ampersands" (*L* 49). Its law is not that of subordination but of seriality, "One one one one one" (*L* 259) in irreducible contiguity, not by likeness or resemblance. One is not mistaken for an other one.

In this respect, Scully's compositional practice seems radically musical, though not necessarily in the manner of the round or ballad forms his titles occasionally invoke, forms that depend on closed patterns of repetition. On the contrary, just as he deconstructs the sonnet form to open out its interior enclosures, so his musicality approaches rather the procedure that Adorno attributes to Alban Berg, and with similar demands on the "attentive listener":

> Even pointing to the presence of repeats does not count for much where the repeated elements are themselves so dissolved and transformed that they are scarcely perceived as an identity, and where no appeal is made to a feeling of architectonic symmetry. The complexity of the motivic elaboration, as well as the overlapping of formal ideas, transform the work into a piece of free prose despite, and because of, the bound nature of every note. The only listener to take it in properly will be the one who follows its flow from one bar to the next, following wherever it chooses to lead him. The attentive listener must expand and contract with the music, instead of listening attentively for correspondences.[33]

Livelihood is, of course, threaded through with repetition, but Adorno's description of repeated elements "so dissolved and transformed that they are scarcely perceived as an identity" could not better characterize the way in which Scully repeats motivic elements in *Livelihood*, suggesting itself as a very precise description of the musical function of a section like the *Postlude*, composed almost entirely of elements repeated from earlier in the book. Indeed, Adorno's provocative expression "free prose" might well characterize large parts of *Livelihood* where the patterning of the verse moves not through interwoven sound- or imagescapes, but in a series of self-interrupting visions and revisions.

Adorno's description of Berg's method is no less apt in its application to Scully's refusal of subordination of the elements that compose the field of the poem:

> Berg does not begin by defining figures graphically in terms of rhythm, and then using them as models to be subsequently modified. Instead, one aspect of a complex, no matter what, is singled out because it is felt to contain seminal force. It is then spun out and transformed into the next one, without reference to any fixed point. The whole thing develops in a quite unschematic way. This may serve as the technical formula for that rampant proliferating growth in Berg's work, for that sense of an impenetrable undergrowth which may have been the core of his nature.[34]

Certainly, the reader of *Livelihood* is constantly aware that its structure refuses any central organizing motifs, no matter how often recurrences of materials may be noted. What is repeated does not organize the meaning or even the form of the whole metaphorically. Brief comparison with a more or less contemporaneous long poem, Derek Walcott's *Omeros*, may help to make the point, not least because so many of the figures that Walcott deploys find correspondences in *Livelihood*. For Walcott such elements as the African swallow that flies between Africa and the Caribbean, or the fishing nets of the islanders, or the criss-cross patterns of the waves are metaphors that undergird the larger moral significance of an epic that aims at reconciliation with the violent colonial past of the West Indies. Scully's repeating elements scrupulously refuse recruitment into such an epic resolution. One is not continually directed to contemplate the weave of the poem as an expression of the final harmony of both its structure and its evolution towards a well-prescribed and redemptive conclusion. Indeed, however much one is drawn to admire the sheer "craftsmanship" and technical achievement of the poem, sustained over so large a scale, *Omeros* inevitably feels archaic, not because of its allusions to Homer or Dante, but because it is so resolutely, even obstinately, committed to resurrecting an exhausted form.

Adorno's remarks on modern compositional form remain relevant here also, additionally offering another way than Olson's to think of "composition by field":[35]

> Composers now work in terms of "areas" [*Felder*], instead of themes and thematic complexes. A path leads from each area to the next, but none is the

logical inference or result of its predecessor. They all have equal status and stand on the same plane. They serve as prototypes of what must become of the symphonic form once the sonata system, and even more importantly, the spirit of the sonata, has been exhausted. The units within the movements are segments. They are connected by motifs which are divided up and shared between them.[36]

It would not be wrong to consider the sonata form as the musical counterpart of the "well-made poem," each with their dominant thematic material, development towards resolution, and metaphors or motifs that organize the progression throughout. If both are "exhausted" forms, it is not only because the techniques have come to seem so familiar as to appear rote, but also because their "spirit," the historically informing logic that dictates the laws of individual development that each obeys, no longer seem adequate to the condition of heteronomy that prevails in late capitalism. Adorno's subsequent analysis of the formal difficulty presented by the exhaustion of developmental forms, the danger of their reduction to stasis, incidentally offers remarkably relevant terms for describing the overall construction of *Livelihood*:

> Where music does not unfold entirely according to the laws of development, but is composed, as with certain derivatives of dance, of segments whose meaning is not altered all that much if their sequence in time is changed, then a static architecture is not only possible, but it also assists in the articulation of events.[37]

Ultimately, in Berg as in Scully, "the organized chaos of overlapping lines and sounds" allows for the "energy stored up in the simultaneous" to become "that of succession."[38]

Adorno's remarks throw into relief the tension throughout *Livelihood* between its peculiar stasis and its constant, restless forward movement, the way in which the poet's attention seems always "on the edge," alert at every moment to shifting movements internally and externally and propelled forwards or sideways by each instant of perception or apperception: reading through the poem, for all its lively movement, does not subject even the most attentive reader to the ironic effects of cumulative revisions of mistaken conclusions. This is not a poem "with designs on the reader,"[39] moral or pedagogical, but a labyrinthine lattice, a "web of meaning" (*L* 128) across which connections may be made in any direction. Touring its lattice, to borrow Scully's expression (*L* 17), one reads and thinks across and around the poem, not through it to its destination: any node in the net is the switch to another point and a sum is never the product of its parts. The reader steps in and out of the poem in the tracing of the dance that is one of Scully's privileged figures for the patterns discovered in the natural world and in the movement of perception:

```
the dance of rain
snow     discovery
taking in     letting
go     molecular pavanes
in rings & chains
     pistons  combustion
reading  doubt
     day/night  chequerwork
cloud-dance     tidal-
dance     dance of the whale
     ants & bees     dance
of the binary
systems     dance of the
regenerating
lithosphere     things
in relation     rippling
wing-edges
dance of energy
dance of the
blood
          the dance
of the
          blood
slow sets
     shimmering nets
mountains
     moving.
     So. (L 268)
```

The dance, however, does not propose to be a Platonic idea of the harmonious universe, whatever harmonies may on occasion be descried among its "free beauties," constellations, webs, crystals, or ripples. The dance is not an Order, even if lining things up produces momentary orders. On the contrary, the mis-step and the missing figure are as much part of Scully's complex weave as are things in their places, while order appears only in the commitment to the writing and its often uncanny moments of recognition:

```
adding (down) leaning to that law that
each thing in its number its place
between the/because of the shadows
interlocked and separate figures
things missing or things wedged side-
ways that remind us that all orders
have their justification in the end in
an order of orders only our faith as
we work, addresses – oh! – (L 260)
```

The poem is not the imitation of the Idea of Order; rather, the poem orders and in ordering changes what it orders. Not according to the model of exchange, where one thing may become any thing according to the law of equivalence for which money is the ultimate idea, but according to the model of intervention, where every thing, including the poem, acts as a thing in the world, changing and changed by what it changes:

> when the dance changes the world
>   changes the dance
>
> changes the dance changes: broken
> bits make a mosaic, mosaic a
> picture, picture a blur falling
> into darkness, darkness folded on
> darkness, old places shot through
> multiple veins of new surfaces
> in old places: (*L* 292)

As the foot moves through the dance, it leaves its trace, a vestige, like the prints in the snow or sand that pace through the poem, like the breath that mists the pane and in which other traces are inscribed, momentarily. Or like the handprint on rock: as the mosaic that forms a picture blurs and falls away, it falls down into the cavernous darkness whose rock-faces bear the imprint of the oldest human traces—artworks, perhaps—like those whose figures furnished the frontispiece and backpiece of the first volume of *Things That Happen, Five Freedoms of Movement*.

As Jean-Luc Nancy has argued, such traces or vestiges are not mimetic, not efforts to present an idea of the world in sensible form or incarnation, but "present nothing other than presentation itself, its open gesture, its displaying, its aperity, its patefaction—and its stupefaction."[40] As he continues, these prints of hands are the signs of passage, not of grasping the world:

> the hand posed, pressed against the wall, grasps nothing. It is no longer a prehensile hand, but is offered like the form of an impossible or abandoned grasp. A grasp that could well let go. The grasp of a letting-go: the letting go of form.[41]

In its "intricate walking" (*L* 257), *Livelihood*, we could say, is the vestige of the poet's passage through the world, a letting-go of what passes into the poem, not as an array of things appropriated, nor as a presentation of ethical or political designs, but as a movement that sheds as a hand scatters what it holds in passing. It is a work that withdraws from all those forms in which writing has participated in the domination of the world and of the reader, offering itself instead as "the most estranged simplicity of presence":[42] of presence in the world of which it is part and to which it is always "next," "deep in the world, / open, touching" (*L* 284). It offers us an unprecedented poetics of displacement and of dispossession, a weave for readers to lose their way in. We might say that therein lies the Irishness of Scully's counterpoetic work, but that no such identity category survives its shedding.

Notes

1. Maurice Scully, *Livelihood.* Wild Honey Press, 2004, p. 228; hereafter cited in the text as *L. Livelihood* is now available, together with all the other previously published books that make up the whole multi-volume work, in *Things That Happen*. Shearsman Books, 2020.
2. Like many other critics of Scully's work, Harry Gilonis comments on this defining aspect of Scully's procedure in "The Spider, the Fly and Philosophy: Following a Clew through Maurice Scully's *Livelihood*." Nate Dorward, editor, *The Fly on the Page*, special issue of *The Gig*, no. 3, November 2004, p. 29. Scully recently described his work as "not making collections, but constructing books" at a reading in Cork, June 21, 2018. Author's recording.
3. Romana Huk, "'Out Past/Self-Dramatization': Maurice Scully's *Several Dances*." *Irish University Review*, vol. 46, no. 1, Spring/Summer 2016, p. 105.
4. Jonathan Culler, "Lyric, History and Genre." *New Literary History*, vol. 40, no. 4, Autumn 2009, pp. 887–91. Kit Fryatt makes a similar comment about Scully, writing of the later volume *Humming* (2009): "Scully frequently employs, in place of the lyric 'I', a semi-imperative generalized 'you' . . ." Kit Fryatt, "The Poetics of Elegy in Maurice Scully's *Humming*." *Irish University Review*, vol. 46, no. 1, Spring/Summer 2016, p. 101.
5. Thomas Wyatt, "They flee from me, that sometime did me seek." *Silver Poets of the Sixteenth Century*, edited by Gerald Bullett. J. M. Dent, 1947, p. 15.
6. Samuel Beckett, *Murphy*. Picador, 1973, p. 6.
7. Marthine Satris, "An Interview with Maurice Scully." *Contemporary Literature*, vol. 53, no. 1, 2012, pp. 13–14.
8. Paul Oppenheimer, *The Birth of the Modern Mind: Self, Consciousness and the Birth of the Sonnet*. Oxford University Press, 1989, pp. 183–5.
9. Gilonis, "Spider," p. 30.
10. Gilonis, "Spider," p. 39.
11. Samuel Beckett, *Waiting for Godot*. Faber and Faber, 1981, p. 91.
12. Samuel Beckett, *Proust and Three Dialogues with Georges Duthuit*. John Calder, 1976, p. 18.
13. Paul Celan, "The Meridian." *Collected Prose*, translated by Rosemary Waldrop. Carcanet Press, 1986, p. 49.
14. James Joyce, *A Portrait of the Artist as a Young Man*, edited by Seamus Deane. Penguin, 1992, p. 220.
15. "What splendour, it all coheres!" are the words of the dying Herakles in

Ezra Pound's translation of Sophocles' *Women of Trachis*. Ezra Pound, translator, *Sophocles: Women of Trachis*. Faber and Faber, 1956, p. 50. The lines "I am not a demigod, / I cannot make it cohere" are from canto CXVI of the *Drafts and Fragments of Cantos CX–CXVII*, that is, from the virtual conclusion of the work. Ezra Pound, *The Cantos*. New Directions, 1972, p. 796.

16. Pound, *Cantos*, p. 458.

17. Gilonis, "Spider," p. 30.

18. Kant, Immanuel. *The Critique of Judgement*, translated by James Creed Meredith. Clarendon Press, 1982, Vol. I, p. 72; hereafter cited in the text as *CJ*.

19. David Lloyd, *Under Representation: The Racial Regime of Aesthetics*. Fordham University Press, 2019. See further on Kant, race and aesthetic judgment in Chapter 4.

20. For the notion of the "administered world," see in particular Max Horkheimer and Theodor W. Adorno, *Dialectic of Enlightenment*, translated by John Cumming. Continuum, 1972, p. x and passim.

21. See also Gilonis, "Spider," pp. 35–6, for a luminous discussion of this and related passages and their relation to Wittgensteinian "language games."

22. Fryatt, "Poetics of Elegy," p. 101.

23. Satris, "Interview with Maurice Scully," p. 1. For a critique of this by-now received idea of Scully's practice, see Huk, "'Out Past/Self-Dramatization,'" p. 105.

24. Compare this passage with Samuel Beckett's rather more extended routine of the Lynch family in *Watt*. Grove Press, 1953, pp. 101–11.

25. On this transformation of Irish culture in the nineteenth century, driven by political economists' commitment to the formation of Irish possessive individuals, see David Lloyd, *Irish Culture and Colonial Modernity, 1800–2000: The Transformation of Oral Space*. Cambridge University Press, 2011, ch. 1.

26. In the reading cited above, Scully also reiterated his hatred of metaphors, introducing a poem in which he claimed, he wanted to see what he "could squeeze out of the damn thing."

27. Trevor Joyce, "The Phantom Quarry: Translating a Renaissance Painting into Modern Poetry." *Enclave Review*, vol. 8, Summer 2013, p. 6. Archived at http://enclavereview.org/the-phantom-quarry-translating-a-renaissance -painting-into-modern-poetry/ (last accessed July 29, 2021).

28. Gilonis, "Spider," p. 37, refers to the networks "of electronic communication carrying signals, moving money and information." Given the important place in *Livelihood* of the net or web as an analogue of natural and human patterning, including poetry, it may seem surprising that Scully does not play more with the idea of the internet or world-wide web, whose forms were coming into being even as the book was being constructed, between 1992 and 2004.

29. Mairéad Byrne also riffs on the locus of the shed in Scully's work, remarking that: "The shed is a redolent fact. There's more than a grim satisfaction in this being the marginalised space for a marginalised art in a marginalised tradition, not just poetry or Irish poetry in English—but experimental Irish poetry in English. . . . There is no rent to pay. No-one wants to work here.

It is absolutely ideal for the purposes of invention . . ." Mairéad Byrne, "The Shed of Poetry." *A Line of Tiny Zeros in the Fabric: Essays on the Poetry of Maurice Scully*, edited by Kenneth Keating. Shearsman Books, 2020, p. 165.

30. Ezra Pound, *ABC of Reading*. Faber and Faber, 1973, p. 46.
31. Charles Olson, "Projective Verse." *Modern Poets on Modern Poetry*, edited by James Scully. Fontana, 1973, pp. 247–8.
32. Olson, "Projective Verse," p. 240.
33. Theodor W. Adorno, "Berg's Discoveries in Compositional Technique." *Quasi una Fantasia: Essays on Modern Music*, translated by Rodney Livingstone. Verso, 1992, p. 188.
34. Adorno, "Berg's Discoveries," pp. 189–90.
35. Olson, "Projective Verse," p. 239.
36. Adorno, "Berg's Discoveries," p. 190.
37. Adorno, "Berg's Discoveries," p. 191.
38. Adorno, "Berg's Discoveries," p. 193.
39. This comment is cited by Alex Davis in "Coda. 'No Narrative Easy in the Mind: The Irish Neo-Avant-Garde." *A Broken Line: Denis Devlin and Irish Poetic Modernism*. University College Dublin Press, 2000, p. 167, from an essay by Scully, "As I Like It," that appeared in his journal *The Beau*, no. 3, 1983/4, p. 10.
40. Jean-Luc Nancy, "Painting in the Grotto." *The Muses*, translated by Peggy Kamuf. Stanford University Press, 1996, p. 72.
41. Nancy, "Painting in the Grotto," p. 72.
42. Nancy, "Painting in the Grotto," p. 72.

Chapter 7

Rome's Wreck: Joyce's Baroque

In a review of Trevor Joyce's first collected poems, *with the first dream of fire they hunt the cold*, I suggested that the poems collected in his early volume *Pentahedron* (1972) could be seen as

> mannerism in the best sense that designates an art tired of the habits of a style that has become commonplace in its very common-sensicality and that forces the limits of style at the risk of excess and artificiality. Mannerism as one recognizes it in Baudelaire, Kafka, Mangan, the early Beckett, all of whom used conventions to burst conventions.[1]

The limits of a newspaper review did not give me space to elaborate that comment, one that might all too easily be misread as implying a negative judgment of the achievement of the poems, given the still prevalent critical assumptions that associate "mannerism" with stylistic artificiality and poetry itself with sincere subjective expression. In the present chapter, I want to explore further this association of Joyce's early work with mannerism and to devote some sustained attention to the singular and important achievement of that early work in its moment, an achievement that has frequently been too easily undervalued in light of the subsequent direction of his work as a whole. I also hope to add to that still inadequately developed judgment some further reflections on what I continue to consider the "baroque" elements of Joyce's work that are as striking now as they were in his early poems. Once again, the colloquial association of that term with over-elaboration or excessive ornamentalism demands a richer specification of the term as I intend it here.

In the first instance, both Mannerism and the Baroque most commonly refer to the stylistic unities of art historical periods and characterize the common traits of various arts in those periods. Mannerism designates the period of the sixteenth century that emerged between the classicism of the Renaissance and the seventeenth-century Baroque. Strongly associated with Michelangelo's late work, as with his imitators, it is characterized by stylistic self-consciousness and by the extreme awareness of the conventions within which its formal elaborations take place. In a certain sense, one might say that Mannerism involves the deliberate exaggeration of the traits of a received style, in this case, those of Renaissance classicism, even to the point of being a criticism of them. It is on account of this stylistic self-consciousness that, on the one hand, Mannerism is often regarded as demanding a very high degree of intellectuality and, on the other, is associated so strongly with being "mannered," that is, as betraying insincerity or inauthenticity. A more sophisticated but still pejorative usage of Mannerism would be the acute remark of Samuel Beckett's friend, the painter Avigdor Arikha, that by the late 1950s, abstract painting had become a form of mannerism, in the sense that it was "painting from painting."[2]

A quite different understanding of mannerism, however, is that of Arnold Hauser who, drawing on pioneering work by Ernst Curtius, argued that mannerism should be seen not so much as a single stylistic epoch, but as a recurrent, critical moment in the dialectical oscillations of Western art forms. Whereas for Curtius, mannerism became a generalizable set of stylistic traits, for Hauser, it names formal attributes that emerge quite specifically at certain moments of social transition in which accepted conventions lose their legitimacy. He reads Mannerism in its strict art historical sense as symptomatic of the cultural impact of the rise of capitalism in the sixteenth and seventeenth centuries and then understands its recurrence as bound to similar moments of crisis in later centuries. If, as Hauser argues, mannerism, with its exacerbated tension between subjection to convention and its exaggeration into excess, is correlated to a destabilization of the relation between the individual and traditional institutions, then any consistent projection of mannerism as a term applicable to other historical moments would have to be grounded in an apprehension both of the moment of transition itself and of the stylistic or aesthetic institutions that are, for any given moment, in dominance. That is precisely the kind of context I will want to give for what I understand as the mannerism of Joyce's *Pentahedron*.[3]

Art historically, the Baroque follows Mannerism and is usually understood as a stylistic period marked by the intellectual moment of the Counter-Reformation and bounded by the eighteenth-century resurgence of neo-classicism. Accordingly, it is marked by the tension between the new, propagandistic requirement of the Catholic Church to produce work legible to the illiterate, which demanded dramatic and often sensational depictions, and the tendency to a visual grandiosity, especially in architecture, that emphasized the power and opulence of Church and State. One could say that its extreme tendencies would be represented by Caravaggio, on the one hand, with his emphasis on the worldliness of his religious subjects, and Bernini, on the other, whose grandiose architectural projects and exuberant sculptural forms synthesized the Baroque emphasis on the passions with its orchestration of masses and perspectival effects. There are, however, other and less official modalities of the Baroque, a Baroque of the margins, one might say, such as the colonial Baroque forms that characterize the religious architecture and sculpture of Latin America or the Philippines, with an intense emphasis on human suffering and on ornate, almost labyrinthine forms. Here the Baroque lends itself to the articulation of what may be quite different, more subversive affects, often associated with melancholy and resistance, and with a far less bounded periodization.[4] Like mannerism, the Baroque suggests (as its colloquial usage implies) not so much a bounded period as the recurrence of formal and affective motifs whose elaboration—in the sense, as we already saw in Chapter 1, of their rigorous working-out rather than their excessive ornamentation—undercuts the institutional functions in which they may have originated.

So much is already implicit in even the most conventional characterizations of the Baroque:

> Classical compositions are simple and clear, each constituent part retaining its independence; they have a static quality and are enclosed within boundaries. The Baroque artist, in contrast, longs to enter into the multiplicity of phenomena, into the flux of things in their perpetual becoming—his compositions are dynamic and open and tend to expand outside their boundaries: the forms that go to make them are associated in single organic action and cannot be isolated from each other. The Baroque artist's instinct for escape drives him to prefer "forms that take flight" to those that are static and dense; his liking for pathos leads him to depict sufferings and feelings, life and death at their extremes of violence, while the Classical artist aspires to show the human figure in the full possession of his powers.[5]

In a somewhat more sober account of the Baroque, which derives its aesthetic principles less from Counter-Reformation religious requirements and more from philosophical and mathematical foundations that cut against a later, post-Kantian aesthetic, Gilles Deleuze characterizes the Baroque in terms of a certain "operative function" rather than a historical period:

> The Baroque refers not to an essence but rather to an operative function, to a trait. It endlessly produces folds. It does not invent things: there are all kinds of folds coming from the East, Greek, Roman, Romanesque, Gothic, Classical folds. . . . Yet the Baroque trait twists and turns its folds, pushing them to infinity, fold over fold, one upon the other. The Baroque fold unfurls all the way to infinity.[6]

Formally, Deleuze associates the enfolded traits of the Baroque both with the labyrinthine, composed of multiple folds, and with a peculiar characteristic of its disposition of material, where "matter tends to spill over in space, to be reconciled with fluidity at the same time fluids themselves are divided into masses" (*F* 4). Stone floods, one might say.[7] These formal traits of the Baroque, independent of its periodization, permit Deleuze to think of the Baroque as a concept that "can be stretched beyond its precise historical limits" (*F* 33), and which, indeed, by its very definition as "enfolding," must always exceed the limits prescribed to it by a concept. Hence, for Deleuze, it includes not only Tintoretto or El Greco, but also Mallarmé, or the Boulez who composed the song-cycle "Pli Selon Pli" ("Fold upon Fold") after the former's poems, or the contemporary Hungarian-French artist Simon Hantaï, with his techniques of folding, or even the Bauhaus modernist Paul Klee (*F* 30–8).

This emphasis on the definition of the Baroque through a specific trait or "operative function" could run the double risk, as Deleuze well knows, of seeming at once overly reductive and too all-enfolding. While Deleuze does continue to specify at some length the particular differentiating elements of the Baroque through which it recurs at various moments (*F* 34–8), here I want to follow him rather in his emphasis on what he calls the baroque "division into two levels," the high and the low, its "two stages or floors: the pleats of matter, and the folds in the soul" (*F* 35; 3). This principle of severance, "between the lower floor, pierced with windows, and the upper floor, blind and closed, but on the other hand resonating as if it were a musical salon translating the visible movements below into sounds above" (*F* 4), furnishes an architectural "allegory" (as well as an actual architectural paradigm) that grounds the opposition between the Baroque and the Classical. In place of a stable harmony and proportion between the world and its sense, the elaborated fold of the Baroque "moves between the two levels" (*F* 35) in a potentially infinite process. If, for Deleuze, this division produces, not a direct conciliation, but a *process* of harmonization, "a perfect accord of severing" (*F* 35), it is not hard to see how so rigorous a principle of division could equally produce, in another key, so to speak, an apprehension of a world utterly sundered between sense and matter, the redeemed and the fallen, the historical and the absolute.

It is on this point that Deleuze's reflections converge, if only tangentially, with those of that other great theorist of the Baroque, Walter Benjamin. As is well known, Benjamin's work focuses not on architecture or the visual arts, but on that "minor" dramatic form, the *Trauerspiel*, or "mourning-play" that flourished not amidst the material and religious triumphs of Counter-Reformation Rome, but in the wake of the crises of sovereignty provoked by the Thirty Years War in Northern Europe. Accordingly, the Baroque in Benjamin's work takes on a quite different and darker tonality, even as he equally envisages it as a stylistic or formal tendency that exceeds its historical moment and furnishes an analogy for the expressionist work of his moment.[8] Though Benjamin does not stress this, and cites critical work from an earlier decade, the conjunction he perceives between the *Trauerspiel* and Expressionism may well be driven by the analogy between the effects of the Thirty Years War and those of the First World War, which likewise threw into question the sovereignty of empires and nations in the wake of catastrophic violence.[9] This emphasis on the recurrence of formal traits in analogical moments, on the concept of the Baroque as one that exceeds its temporal boundaries, clearly connects Benjamin to both Hauser and Deleuze.

At all events, it is on the baroque sense of the catastrophic rather than the harmonic that Benjamin focuses:

> The religious man of the baroque era clings so tightly to the world because of the feeling that he is being drawn along to a cataract with it. The baroque knows no eschatology; and for that very reason it possesses no mechanism by which all earthly things are gathered in together and exalted before being consigned to their end. The hereafter is emptied of everything which contains the slightest breath of this world, and from it the baroque extracts a profusion of things which customarily escaped the grasp of artistic formulation and, at its high point, brings them violently into the light of day, in order to clear an ultimate heaven, enabling it, as a vacuum, one day to destroy the world with catastrophic violence. (*OGTD* 66)

We may recognize here the negative version of Deleuze's "perfect accord of severing" with its Leibnizian optimism: Benjamin's baroque severance is between an unredeemed thingly or creaturely finite world and an abstract and perhaps absconded absolute. This irrevocably fallen world is "haunted by the idea of catastrophe" (*OGTD* 66); it is the temporal world of "natural history," that is, of a creaturely history subject to nature rather than to a redemptive eschatology; its predominant affect is the perpetual mourning of melancholy, "the state of mind in which feeling revives the empty world in the form of a mask" (*OGTD* 139) and which "emerges from the depths of the creaturely realm" (*OGTD* 146). Its privileged material figures are stone and ash, or the ruin that is the sign and remnant left by the process of "irresistible decay" that is natural history (*OGTD* 177–8).

"Allegories are in the realm of thoughts what ruins are in the world of things" (*OGTD* 178): for Benjamin's baroque theatre and its ruined, fallen world, allegory is the dominant tropological mode. In part, this preference for the allegorical explains the modern disquiet in the face of the Baroque and its typically pejorative usage as a term. As Benjamin may have been the first to articulate critically, it is with Romanticism that allegory was subordinated and marginalized by the discourse of the symbol. The symbol "as it were categorically, insists on the indivisible unity of form and content," thus distorting "the unity of the material and the transcendental object" in the theological symbol (the transubstantiation of bread and wine in the Eucharist) into a secularized "relationship between appearance and essence" (*OGTD* 160). Benjamin cites Goethe's antagonism to allegory:

> "There is a great difference between a poet's seeking the particular from the general and his seeing the general in the particular. The former gives rise to allegory, where the particular serves only as an instance or example of the general; the latter, however, is the true nature of poetry: the expression of the particular without any thought of, or reference to, the general. Whoever grasps the particular in all its vitality also grasps the general, without being aware of it, or only becoming aware of it at a late stage." (*OGTD* 161)

As anyone who has ever been subjected to the study of poetry in college will recognize, Goethe's pronouncement stands even now as an unassailable orthodoxy. It is not only an aesthetic, but also a categorically moral orthodoxy that organizes both the relation of the particular to the general in post-Romantic theories of representation and the idea of the individual's development from partial fragment to participation in the whole with which it is one: "What is typically romantic is the placing of this perfect individual within a progression of events which is, it is true, infinite but is nevertheless redemptive, even sacred" (*OGTD* 160). The symbol, the part which represents the whole in a "momentary totality" (*OGTD* 165) that anticipates an infinitely deferred reconciliation or redemption, lies at the core of a whole pedagogical theory, aesthetic, moral, and ultimately political, of the modern human under whose sway we continue to live.

Allegory, on the other hand, describes a dialectical "movement between extremes" (*OGTD* 160), a movement that partakes of the violence of an unredeemed world:

> Whereas in the symbol destruction is idealized and the transfigured face of nature is fleetingly redeemed in the light of redemption, in allegory the observer is confronted with the *facies hippocratica* of history as a petrified, primordial landscape. Everything about history that, from the very beginning, has been untimely, sorrowful, unsuccessful is expressed in a face—or rather in a death's head. And although such a thing lacks all "symbolic" freedom of expression, all classical proportion, all humanity—nevertheless, this is the form in which man's subjection to nature is most obvious and it significantly

gives rise not only to the enigmatic question of human existence as such, but also of the biographical historicity of the individual. (*OGTD* 166)

Allegory resides in the severance of extremes, both in its formal antinomy "between the cold, facile technique and the eruptive expression of allegorical interpretation" (*OGTD* 175) and in the gulf it registers between the worldly and the transcendent. Both that formal technique, which may arbitrarily lay hold of any thing and force it violently into the sign of another (allegory is the domain par excellence of substitution), and in the division of spheres it signifies, allegory consigns things to a realm of indifference utterly divorced from the domain in which they attain significance or redemption:

> Any person, any object, any relationship can mean absolutely anything else. With this possibility a destructive, but just verdict is passed on the profane world: it is characterized as a world in which the detail is of no great importance. But it will be unmistakably apparent, especially to anyone who is familiar with allegorical textual exegesis, that all of the things which are used to signify derive, from the very fact of their pointing to something else, a power which makes them appear no longer commensurable with profane things, which raises them onto a higher plane, and which can, indeed, sanctify them. Considered in allegorical terms, the profane world is both elevated and devalued. (*OGTD* 175)

Of this allegorical domain where the indifference or devaluation of the object is the condition of its signifying, the skull or death's head is the apt figure, as a fragment of the dismembered body consigned to a contemplation for which the individuality or particularity of the human no longer matters.

This relation between allegory and the fragment is constitutive and profoundly opposed to the symbol, the part fully integrated or translucent with the whole: "It is not possible to conceive of a starker opposite to the artistic symbol, the plastic symbol, the image of organic totality, than this amorphous fragment which is seen in the form of allegorical script" (*OGTD* 176). Fragmentation, the reduction of the body to its severed parts, is the very condition of allegory, for

> the human body could be no exception to the commandment that ordered the destruction of the organic so that the true meaning, as it was written and ordained, might be picked up from its fragments. Where, indeed, could this law be more triumphantly displayed than in the man who abandons his conventional, conscious physis in order to scatter it to the manifold regions of meaning? (*OGTD* 216–17)

If Isis is the allegory of the allegorical interpreter, it is Osiris who figures allegory itself. Only when broken and scattered into its constituent parts, like language itself after Babel, can the material enter into the domain of meaning and value: "the image is a fragment, a rune," and "the false appearance of totality is extinguished" (*OGTD* 176). It is this state of dissolution, of a radical separation of the elements, rather than through particularity and individuality, that things can come to point to or substitute for one another.

Any reader of Marx might recognize in this description of allegory's tropological system an allegory of capitalism as a system of exchange. Transposed from the theological terms which, not yet secularized, formed the interpretive matrix for the crises of sovereignty and political power, into those of the critique of political economy, the movement of the fragment from fallen, natural history to the elevated domain of signification where substitution is the rule replicates that of the commodity from a thing in use to the domain of exchange value. In the realm of exchange, any thing's operative function is to substitute or be substituted for another, as its being as a particular thing succumbs to indifference in the face of its circulation as a sign of value. In that domain it becomes, as Marx put it, "changed into something transcendent," into "a social hieroglyphic," an allegory for the social process.[10] Allegory as an aesthetic mode recurs as the correlative of reification, where the very arbitrary violence of its appropriation of the thing as figure is the mark of a totality that is instituted through coercion rather than through the organic integration that the symbolic falsely promised. The melancholy of the Baroque, as it appears in Benjamin's critical construction, is the melancholy of a persisting attachment to things that have become devalued as the means to their abstraction as signs of value, in a world where "the frenzy of destruction, in which all earthly things collapse into a heap of ruins" (*OGTD* 232) furnishes both the limit and the necessity of allegory.

It is within this double construction of the Baroque, as a formal elaboration or folding–unfolding of the severance of matter and meaning, and as the recurrence of an allegorical mode that registers the effects of a contemporary intensification of reification, that I wish to situate Joyce's poetry and its critical practice. It was not, however, in the first instance in its formal or rhetorical procedures that I initially observed the baroque or mannerist dimensions of the earlier work, especially *Pentahedron*. It was, rather, in the insistence of certain elemental figures that underlie the bleak urban lyrics of that volume, figures that recur throughout Joyce's work no matter what procedures he employs in its production. Throughout *Pentahedron*, stone, water or river, ash, moonlight furnish the underlying ground of lyrics that foreground the histrionic images of a derelict humanity—drunks, beggars, mad men and women, and children whose uncanny, shrieking laughter furnishes a kind of inarticulate chorus seaming the poems. The volume's central preoccupation is the severance of an indifferent, cosmic or geological time from the "natural history" of human or biological decay:

> Cold and opaque
> as a chunk of river quartz,
> the town that inroads these eyes.
>
> The effort to impress
> rock results
> in the quick fixed,
>
> or a fossil mote
> sprouting in our late
> damp climate.
>
> The hazel leaves,
> the hazel wands
> scream in storm winds.
>
> Words are blown
> in the storm like old saurian
> down.[11]

The city itself in its architectural decay becomes a kind of parody of such geomorphic forces, a petrification of human design and labor that has become an alien rather than a lived landscape:

> Each individual limestone cuboid
> Chisel-squared and weathered
> Rough and grimy, holding on its face
> All its past history and the threat
> Of its future. Streams
> Of rust-brown rain had stained
> The entire wall; each
> Block realized its presence
> In this pattern and the wider
> Patterns of sunlight, shadows, tone
> And the complete distributed
> Weight of rock
> Combined for the present.[12]

Against the backdrop of this stone geometry, where cobblestones resemble skulls and seem to undergo a slow, vegetal decay, the volume's personae appear as little more than types, allegorical *faciei hyppocraticae* that render the sheer disposability of mortal flesh:

All forms are savaged as they come:
   maimed men who limp on club-leg,
   garrotted men with meths-blue faces,
   women whose secretive survival
     shuns the predatory light,
   and all the ashen faces of the dead.[13]

The title of this poem, "Dynamic," is surely ironic: such savaged forms of the human are not parts in a dynamic whole, but fragments any one of which could substitute for another—madman for maimed man, beggar for drunken woman—in the hostile city whose emblem may be the "countless wheels" that "revolve / on distant rails" (*WFDF* 71).

The icon of the volume as a whole is the skull, through whose "ruined jaw" the lips fall (*WFDF* 77) and whose "cage of bone" forms the cell or crypt of the monadic subject's anxious circulations. The skull, a *memento mori* that represents the human reduced to its inorganic substrate, is not a symbol, offering no prospect of reassembly into a living whole of which each part is the representative. By the same token, *Pentahedron* as a book is rather "a ruined web / bent with death's freight" than the progressive cycle of poems its recurrent, desiccated figures might suggest. The finest single poem in the volume, the unrhymed sonnet "Christchurch. Helix. 9th Month," seems to thematize the impasse of the volume:

Passages of labyrinth repeat;
the crypt gives vellum thighs to the dead,
mark our return in this way;
again we hollow dust-caves, ankle deep.

Paths are furrowed by rats' feet,
scribbled as cryptic schemes, motifs
of death and propagation;
here the fruit of death dilates.

Arid courses interplay, rivers of dust,
graphs wrought in frost, dust-falls interpret sunlight.
a cat plays knucklebones with something grey
and we move into daylight. (*WFDF* 68)

The poem plays knowingly with the relation between the crypt as site of burial and the cryptic scripts or graphs it may secrete. But what it elicits, in this space where both human flesh and the rivers of life revert to dust, is a subjectless reading of allegories that encrypt only their evacuation. And the return from this cave to the light in turn yields no Platonic truth, only the dazzle of light on surfaces: "for mornings the roads are chrome / and the sun is a citron stain on a limed wall" (*WFDF* 68.)

There is a relation between this labyrinthine repetition of familiar passages and the evacuation or desiccation of the form. "Christchurch" mimes perfectly the characteristics of the fully achieved lyric poem, with its steady conversion of the elements of the real place into laden metaphors, prepared for by felicitous adjectives like "vellum," its movement from dark to light that apparently parallels a movement from sensuous immersion to sense. Its formal qualities are no less striking: the turn to the sonnet form (the "narrow room" or "cell" of Wordsworth's metaphor), the internal rhymes and half-rhymes that echo the repetitions and turns of its thematic statement [dead-deep, feet-motifs], the double anapaests of the twelfth line that might imitate the upward movement that the line describes. As does any high parody, the poem repeats the lyric mode in a way that emphatically betrays its exhaustion as a form. And what it repeats, with precise knowledge of the conventions, was certainly the dominant manner of Irish lyric of the moment—one has only to evoke a poem like Seamus Heaney's "The Forge," another sonnet, from his 1969 collection *Door into the Dark*, to instantiate perfectly the ideal type of that mode.[14]

As we have already seen, Joyce has since expressed often enough his dissatisfaction with that mode of poetic writing, the "well-made," subjective, and expressive lyric, what he has recently called "the standard Irish bag of tricks: lyrics of description and expression dressed in the most transparent of formal attire; the emphasis being almost entirely on the language as carrier of information, with little heed to other possibilities."[15] That "bag of tricks" we might consider an etiolated offshoot of the Romantic symbolist tradition as Benjamin describes it: the descriptive element corresponds to the moment of the particular through which the subjective experience is elevated to a generalizable, transferable meaning whose continuity with the experience is guaranteed by the function of metaphor (etymologically the trope that performs transfer). In its late usage, however, what had in Romanticism represented the revolutionary value of the emancipated individual whose unique particularity was an embodiment of universality betrays its secret tendency: rather than conveying the universality of the particular, the expressive lyric obeys the laws of general equivalence that were always the occult condition of the individual's emancipation. The exhaustion of that mode of which Joyce had grown tired was also its declension into untruth, the falsity of putatively spontaneous or free lyric expression or the fallacy of the analogy of poet with craftsman (as in "The Forge") in an era of intensified commodification. The "originality" of the subject that finds expression in the symbolist lyric succumbs to the automatism of repetition as the particularity of the experience described becomes merely the alibi for the momentary reproduction of a totality that is over and again the same.

Joyce's achievement in *Pentahedron*, which certainly exceeds the mere reproduction of this "standard bag of tricks," is that of a very specific mode of mannerism. And, in keeping with Hauser's understanding of mannerism's recurrences, it emerged at a moment of transition, when the Irish state's commitment to economic modernization seemed to have produced more devastation than progress and had consigned to redundancy, along with much of the nationalist tradition, the conventional forms of lyric subjectivity and the ideological assumptions they embedded. Thus, in place of the conventions of Renaissance classicism that art historical Mannerism extended and challenged through exaggeration, Joyce exaggerates the tendencies of the Irish lyric in such a manner that symbol and metaphor pass over into allegory, bearing with them the specters of ruination and petrification for which the skull is the just emblem. The disjunctions of the poems, between their fleeting and derelict human figures and the chill simulacra of geological permanence against which they appear, between the decay of natural history and the cycles of cosmic time, mark a severance of spheres that no symbol could bridge. Nor do they affect a "natural" or ordinary language use. Benjamin remarks on what links the language of baroque *Trauerspiel* and that of German expressionism—with whose rhetorical traits Joyce's early style has much in common—that "Exaggeration is characteristic of both" (*OGTD* 54).[16] That quality of exaggeration in Joyce is manifest both in the somewhat hyperbolic emphasis on figures of death, deformity, and decay that endow the poems with a certain grotesque quality and in the pushing of metaphor into deliberately tasteless terrain:

Acts are expectorated,
and when the spittle hardens
into facts, our lives
are emerald threads of mucus.[17]

The tastelessness of such a hyperbolic metaphor nonetheless remains true to the logic of metaphorization: it merely projects comparison beyond the bounds that convention usually sets. In that process of projection, the poems of *Pentahedron* perform a kind of anatomy of the contemporary Irish lyric, one that exposes its structure like a skeleton it then reduces to fragments.

Projection, in the mathematical sense, is itself a metaphor entirely in keeping with similar figures that punctuate the poems: construction, geometric planes, gnomon, surd, spiral, diagram, circle, graphs, parallax, and, of course, in the title poem itself, pentahedron. Such terms, in most cases separated from the body of the poems to function as titles, work to suggest an abstract, formal dimension of the poems that is the correlative of their thematic emphases on abstraction and reification. But they remain metaphors, signaling a tendency that the poems are unable to realize formally, working as they do still in a lyric mode of expression that has yet to be fully subordinated to the kind of algorithmic constraint that would exhaustively determine the disposition of the poems' linguistic materials. The pursuit of such forms of constraint, it is well known, would preoccupy Joyce through the next decades, including those of his virtual silence as a writer between the publication of *The Poems of Sweeny Peregrine* in 1976 and that of *stone floods* in 1995. What is less often observed is that Joyce's turn to successive modes of procedural production, restlessly experimented with in various versions and combinations, is intimately linked to his perception of the socio-political bankruptcy of the expressive lyric and the subjective spontaneity it assumes. As he would put it, reflecting on his three-decade-long elaboration of the "hyper-sestina":

> My approach was to try to set up certain constants of texture or structure, and then to set loose within those constraints an apparently free subjective voice, the intent being to simulate in various ways the common experience of seeming to act freely and spontaneously, while even a minimal self-awareness reveals that this freedom is to a great extent generated and governed by forces and concerns in which one has no hand, act, or part. Without some reframing of this sort, I fear that the language of description, expression, aspiration, is constantly being sucked down the sink of calculated, monetized use. Moreover, even our means to refresh it have been appropriated.[18]

Assumed in the relation between "description" and "expression" is the movement from outer to inner that is at once the movement from material to value, matter to sense, establishing the subject as a kind of processing plant for its raw experience. Constraint and procedure do not abandon the idea of a material that is subjected to labor; on the contrary, the working of a variety of materials, from found language like legal phrasing or astronomical terminology to others' poems, is crucial to their concept, for which the autonomy of the poem derives from its formal operations rather than from original subjective utterance. What they do contest is the naturalization of that work either as craft or as spontaneous expression: constraint is the foregrounding of the mediation of the material in a fully intentional formal structure. It requires what Benjamin described, in relation to the kinship of the Baroque and Expressionism, as an "unremitting artistic will" (*OGTD* 55). What Benjamin ascribes to specific periods of artistic production may in fact be the formal condition of modern art in general. As Adorno put it of the new music:

> Competence is no longer what it was once supposed to be, but in reality never was, namely a treasure trove of acquired methods that could be exploited by talent. Instead, every element of the structure, from the smallest up to the totality, has to spring from the sustaining intuition of the specific musical insight, without regard to traditional skills. And conversely, every musical intuition, every involuntary, subjective impulse, must be transmuted into the rule-bound procedure that retroactively takes over what had started out as an irrational origin.[19]

One might correspondingly understand Joyce's poetic career after *Pentahedron* as involving an unremitting pursuit of procedures that would allow the material to be mediated through the form with ever-increasing thoroughness, from the mostly binary "axes" around which, as he explained to Michael Smith, *stone floods* was structured, to the assemblages of found language from which *Trem Neul* is constructed, with the aim of producing "an extended autobiographical essay … from which everything personal has been excluded."[20]

At least one phase of this pursuit culminates in *Syzygy*, with its thoroughly musical elaboration of its elements in the medieval form, the *cancrizans* or "crab canon." Any reader of *Pentahedron* would recognize in the later poem the continuities of tone or theme, the recurrence of certain elemental figures and of the severance between cosmic time and natural history:

> exposure to the extreme
> stillness of fire
> the flickering rock
> disturbs
> all night across an empty sky
> the high frosts creak
> and strike the clumsy sun
> leaves on the grass
> the shadow of the vaulting white
> beyond the bounds
> no silence no noise[21]

The "voiceprint" of these almost obsessive figural motifs remains, as if deeply inscribed in the DNA of the work: it is their formal disposition that has changed and transformed them. In *Syzygy* and other procedural poems, the figural elements cease to be the mannered remnants of referential signs, and are certainly no longer representations of "particulars" elevated to generality. Its very deliberate detachment from any directly representative function, its increasingly thorough mediation, produces the characteristic austerity of Joyce's mature language, as if it echoed with the sound of high cosmic winds and "grows to take in snatches / from high stars from elsewhere," as the opening stanza of *Syzygy* puts it (*WFDF* 136).

As the fugal form of the *cancrizans* suggests, the procedural forms that Joyce invents are—like the baroque compositions of which Bazin writes—"forms that take flight," from *Syzygy* to the thirty-six worders that spin off from the extended hypersestina project of the last decades. The non-referential language generated by these algorithmic forms is no less a language in flight, determined not by its anchorage in the real and the particular, but by a series of departures that take place as words take off in a "cascade of splayed ambiguities" from their signifying function into an autonomous realm through which their relation to the world is thoroughly mediated.[22] This is not at all to say that the works bear no relation to the world and are merely "language games." The apt figure for this detached and mediated relation of the formal work of the poem to its world is another cube than that of the four-dimensional hypersestina, that of the closed room into which light filters indirectly. Joyce uses this figure at least twice. One is in connection with the poem "Approach of Bodies Falling in Time of Plague," of which he explains that the poem takes off from Isaac Newton who, during the London plague of 1665, "locked himself up and excluded the world" in a room that became a kind of camera obscura, illuminated by a small slit that admitted a ray of light which he then split with a prism.[23] Newton's experimental practice resembles the use of the camera obscura by Baroque painters to which Joyce alludes in the beautiful, transitional poem, "Mirror: of Glazier Velazquez":

> Where shutter, wall, and lock
> exclude the casual sun
> a new light illuminates
> long darkened and abandoned rooms.
>
> Light that is natural has failed;
> an angular course delivers this
> through systems of reflections,
> enfilading in its route
> chambers where pose manifold
> still dwarf and her princess
> introvolute and incessantly,
> or where, upon a bed, a graceful girl
> approves herself in slender contemplation. (*WFDF* 88)[24]

This "closed arcanian space" forms a kind of passage between the failed natural light that still fitfully illuminated the poems of *Pentahedron* and the cryptic later work whose autonomy from the real is established by the absolutely systematic determination of its materials.[25] For Deleuze, the baroque camera obscura is the closed space of the monad, "a cell" or rooms "with neither doors nor windows, where all activity takes place on the inside" and yet where "a crushing light comes from openings invisible to their very inhabitants" (*F* 28). Composed of grids and "linear and numerical tables" (*F* 27), this Leibnizian monad resumes a variety of interior spaces of display or performance—"a cell, a sacristy, a crypt, a church, a theater, a study, or a print room"—to destroy the traditional model of representation as a window opening on the outside: "The painting-window is replaced by tabulation, the grid on which lines, numbers and changing characters are inscribed" (*F* 27–8). Emancipated from capture by the external "model," in which the Platonic Ideal is always secretly at work, these monadic forms are enabled to take flight, "introvolute and incessantly."

Resumption of these closed spaces as it may be, the monad, however, is also their ruination. We might say that the sealed interior of the hermetic room bears the same relation to the ruined building as Giovanni Battista Piranesi's series of etchings, *I Carceri* (The Prisons), do to his other series, *Vedute di Roma* (Views of Rome) that depicts the ruins of ancient Rome. If the one dwells almost claustrophobically on the unfolding of obliquely illuminated spaces, in flight on flight of perspectival elaboration, the other exposes through the ruin the inner structure of repetitions, passages, apertures, that underlies the facade of the intact edifice. "In the ruins of great buildings," as Benjamin puts it, "the idea of the plan speaks more impressively than in lesser buildings" (*OGTD* 235). Both are anatomies, analytical procedures that reveal a structure through fragmenting and reassembling it, "articulated with a precision characteristic of the analysis of a skeleton."[26] The features of the ruin are predicted by the structure itself, and the principle of ruination, the condition of always being a fragment, as opposed to a part representative of a whole, is contained in the very idea of the procedural in poetry, even as it operates through the closed monadic chamber of the work. The constraint, like the *stretto* of the fugue, intensifies the flight of signification beyond its function of containment. Accordingly, the structural capacity of the procedure to generate forms and variants exceeds the actual realization of work that can never exhaust its productive potential, such that the work is always a fragment, the ruin of a never completed plan. Always, the work that results "remembers the calculation and ruin which generated it."[27]

One of the modes of constraint that Joyce has favored from his earliest work is translation. Like "writing through" or the lattice works constructed in relation to poems by other poets that appear at the end of *with the first dream*, translation in the first place obeys the non-expressive constraint of inhabiting another's language, perhaps the most rigorous and fundamental prescription possible. Furthermore, as Joyce has put it, "any translation now must take its place within a recursive series of previous versionings, each with its own significant subtractions and additions."[28] Here the crypt or chamber becomes a box within other boxes, or a series of enfoldings. We have seen already in Chapter 2 Benjamin's striking simile for translation: "While content and language form a certain unity in the original, like a fruit and its skin, the language of the translation envelops its content like a royal robe with ample folds."[29] In a Deleuzian sense, then, translation is baroque, a matter of folds. It is also a process of ruination: every translation is a shadow of the original, at its best laying bare the latter's inner structure or isolating its context. Moreover, translation works in the shadow of the ruined Babel. Its recursive force is not only to be a fragment in itself, but to reveal the original as such also:

> a translation, instead of resembling the meaning of the original, must lovingly and in detail, incorporate the original's mode of signification, thus making both the original and the translation recognizable as fragments of a greater language, just as fragments are part of a vessel.[30]

Translation is thus not as bound to the original as its initial condition of constraint might suggest: its departure from the original is an intrinsic quality of translation, rather than the index of inept execution of the task. That in translation language takes flight from its original was signaled in the resonant pun that Joyce embedded in the title of his version of the *Buile Suibhne*, *Sweeny, Peregrine*: Sweeny who wanders, peregrinates, and Sweeny who, in his becoming-bird, takes flight. And flight itself, the poem reminds us, is double: a horizontal movement of displacement and a vertical movement of elevation or metamorphosis.

Sweeny, Peregrine, Joyce's first published work of translation, was already a version of a ruin or fragment subject to "significant subtractions and additions": its original is a distressed text, "somewhat the worse for *lacunae* and the pious interpolations of monks" (*WFDF* 236). His more recent work of translation, on the other hand, operates by distressing an existent and complete text, which is itself already a translation. In *Rome's Wreck*, Joyce "translates" Edmund Spenser's English translation of Joachim du Bellay's *Les Antiquités de Rome* (1558), *The Ruines of Rome* (1591).[31] Rather than an interlingual translation, then, Joyce's is a translation from one English into another, subject to a singular constraint: that it be completely done over into monosyllables. My reference earlier to Piranesi's *Vedute di Roma*, usually referred to as *The Ruins* (rather than *Views*) *of Rome*, was not arbitrary: like Piranesi's etchings, *Rome's Wreck* is a kind of anatomy of an anatomy, of both Du Bellay's and Spenser's descriptions of Roman ruins and of their moral meditations on fame and mortal decay.[32] In a fashion familiar from Renaissance *aere perennius* poetic convention, Spenser follows Du Bellay in invoking the possibility that his own written language might outlive in fame that of Rome itself:

> If vnder heauen anie endurance were,
> These moniments, which not in paper writ,
> But in Porphyre and Marble doo appeare,
> Might well haue hop'd to haue obtained it.
> Nath' les my Lute, whom *Phoebus* deignd to giue,
> Cease not to sound these olde antiquities:
> For if that time doo let thy glorie liue,
> Well maist thou boast, how euer base thou bee,
>   That thou art first, which of thy Nation song
>   Th' olde honor of the people gowned long.[33]

Joyce's austere rendering—to use that term in its industrial or culinary as well as poetic sense—of the poems into octosyllabic verse almost automatically ironizes that desire for elevation, reducing Spenser's tentative triumph and steady pentametric beat to faltering rhythms and emphasizing both the secondariness of his language and the rift between spoken and written words:

> The skies grow dark. No fame stands fast
> or these stones spread round, clean cut, cold
> and hard, dressed by sharp steel, so far
> less frail than script, should have it made.
>   I use the tools I've got: hard words
> passed down, passed on, may speak on some
> days when the live voice breaks.
> Not all words bear the weight. I mean;
>   but they may not. And these? Pen's mark
>   lives on, but not the mouth that sang.[34]

Joyce's ear for ambiguity in colloquial phrasing is here fully at work, as in "should have it made" or in the reader's momentary hesitation as to the possible and expected predicate of "I mean," which surely brings to mind Browning's "Fra Lippo Lippi": "The world's no blot for us, / Nor blank; it means intensely, and means good: / To find its meaning is my meat and drink."[35] Just as surely, "I use the tools I've got" resonates both with Clov's "I use the words you taught me" in Beckett's *Endgame*, that ultimate drama of ruination, and with Caliban's "You taught me language," to which Beckett alludes.[36] In turn, the complicated plays in "Hard words / passed on, passed down, speak on . . ." run the gamut of meanings from transmission through tradition, with its connotations of descent and then decline, to death ("passed on") as opposed to the continuity of voice ("speak on")—a meaning suspended and completed in turn by one of the more aggressively interruptive enjambments in the poem: "speak on some / days when the live voice breaks," an odd six-syllable line that does indeed break off.

Joyce's rendering of Spenser thus performs a double operation: on the one hand it radically simplifies the diction of the poem by confining its linguistic options so radically; on the other, with half an eye on Borges's Pierre Menard, it subjects the poem to a recursive cascade of accreted possible meanings along a line of flight that splays and frays, unraveling the texture of the original. That Joyce's rigorously monosyllabic rendition is so analytical in its effect may seem paradoxical. It is, after all, a deeply held prejudice that the monosyllabic element represents the most fundamental layer of English, its roots in Anglo-Saxon, as opposed to the later Latinate vocabulary that enters with Norman French and with the learned speech of the educated or professional classes. The putative "earthiness" of Anglo-Saxon is, by way of a metaphor that becomes an implicit assumption, associated with its status as the most primitive and therefore most authentic, if less developed, part of the language. The metaphor obscures the fact that if Anglo-Saxon appears to be "basic" English, that is only because of the reduced social and cultural status of its speakers in the wake of the Norman conquest. Spenser himself may have had no small part in the shaping of such assumptions, given his own studious incorporation of older English words, like "wight" or "shreik," into the verse pattern of this and other poems. This practice gives rise to some of the odder energies of *The Ruines of Rome*:

> If so be shrilling voyce of wight aliue
> May reach from hence to depth of darkest hell,
> Then let those deep Abysses open riue,
> That ye may understand my shreiking yell.[37]

Behold what wreake, what ruine, and what wast. . . .[38]

It was also a practice which, much like Du Bellay's ambitions for French poetry, was at once nationalist and imperialist, aimed at producing a distinctively English vernacular literary language that might accord with the rising nation-state's visions of empire. The language, unifying the various historical strands that composed the national culture and furnishing a fully adequate medium for poetry, might rival Latin even as the nation's expanding territory and geopolitical power seemed set to rival Rome's imperial expansion.

Joyce's monosyllabic text works peculiarly in an opposite direction, its effect being not only analytical, but abstract, rarefied even. Compare Spenser's lines with Joyce's:

> Triumphant Arcks, spyres neighbours to the skie,
> That you to see doth th' heauen it selfe appall,
> Alas, by little ye to nothing flie,
> The people's fable, and the spoyle of all. . . .[39]

> arch that's pure win, spires shot up so
> they scare the sky, tick tick, too bad
> that bit by bit you end in ash,
> scarce worth a laugh, you spoil our source.[40]

The spare economy of Joyce's diction succeeds simultaneously in appearing to impoverish the language and in exhausting all its resources. Spenser's "spoyle" becomes at once an allusion to Joyce's travesty of his source, *The Ruines of Rome*, and the analogous process of despoiling that led to Rome's ruin, the cannibalizing of the ruined buildings as materials for new structures. Thus it is that the passage of time—condensed here ironically to a Baudelairean "tick tick"—that "bit by bit" Rome "ends in ash," and thus it is that Joyce's appropriation of Spenser's text not only "spoils its source" but furnishes the materials for a renewed text. That text in turn seems to obey Goethe's dictum that the ideal translation does not domesticate its original, but draws the translator's language into the orbit of the original's, thus estranging the former from itself. This, Goethe claims, is achieved by going back "to the primal elements of language itself."[41] Joyce's reduction of the resources of English to its supposedly monosyllabic "roots" performs a parodic version of such estrangement on Spenser's translation and on the English language. In a certain respect, *Rome's Wreck* performs on Spenser a work analogous to that which Joyce performed on his own *Pentahedron*: where Spenser creates a kind of triumphal progress while invoking ruin, naming ruination as a figure, but still standing off from it, Joyce reworks Spenser's poem by drawing ruination into the very process and language of the poem. The elements that resonated as figures throughout *Pentahedron*, constituting its affective palette—ash, stone, dust, flood, ruin, the whole natural history of decay—recur in *Rome's Wreck*. In the latter, however, they are integrated into the very process of the poem, as the rationale of its desiccated language.

Joyce's procedures in *Rome's Wreck* remain thoroughly baroque, both in the persistence of certain fundamental affective registers and in the procedures that renovate the allegorical and reaffirm the validity of a poetics of fragmentation and of "forms that take flight." But that it should be a reworking, and quite a violent reworking, of a poem by Spenser may remind us that this is a baroque of the margins, rather than one of the expanding, imperial Europe of the seventeenth century. Spenser was, after all, a colonial servant, dispatched to County Cork in order, as Joyce himself puts it, "to wreck the lineage [Aogán] O'Rahilly praises."[42] Counterpart to those other forms of colonial baroque of Latin America and elsewhere, and sharing in their sense of ruination and in their melancholic refusal to abandon the fragments that history has stranded, Joyce's Irish baroque constitutes a counterpoetic with its own broken and dispersed lines of transmission. This is a baroque in which Benjamin's crisis of sovereignty, of the subject no less than of the state, remains in play because it has never ended. If this poetic "remembers the calculation and ruin which generated it," we should perhaps recall that the ruination that afflicts it is not only an effect of its procedural destruction of all naturalized models of reference and representation, but also an echo of unrelenting historical catastrophe. The wager of this counterpoetic is that it may be the black box of the crypt, the monad only obliquely penetrated by the real it refracts, that furnishes the most adequate echo chamber for the reverberations of a disaster that remains unfinished.

Notes

1. David Lloyd, "An Impressive Collection." Review of *with the first dream of fire they hunt the cold* by Trevor Joyce. *Irish Times*, September 8, 2001, p. 10. In part, my observations drew on my earlier study of James Clarence Mangan, in which I argued that his work should be regarded as mannerist in the strict sense I elaborated there and further in this chapter. See David Lloyd, *Nationalism and Minor Literature: James Clarence Mangan and the Emergence of Irish Cultural Nationalism.* University of California Press, 1987.
2. Maurice Tuchman, "A Talk with Avigdor Arikha." *Arikha*, edited by Richard Channin. Hermann, 1985, p. 44.
3. Arnold Hauser, *Mannerism: The Crisis of the Renaissance and the Origin of Modern Art*, 2 vols. Routledge and Kegan Paul, 1965. For an extended discussion of Arnold Hauser's approach to mannerism, see Lloyd, *Nationalism and Minor Literature*, pp. 197–200.
4. Germain Bazin, *Baroque and Rococo Art*, translated by Jonathan Griffin. Praeger, 1964, p. 7, points out that in Latin America, the Baroque persists well into the nineteenth century, and one might argue that in popular forms, baroque elements persist, at the risk of kitsch, down

to the present in many regions where the effects of colonialism persist. John D. Blanco's discussion of mid-twentieth-century Filipino writer Nick Joaquin as an instance of colonial Baroque proposes that Joaquin's "countermodern" work "corresponds to the experience of modernity as the immanence of disaster and disenchantment." See John D. Blanco, "Baroque Modernity and the Colonial World: Aesthetics and Catastrophe in Nick Joaquin's *A Portrait of the Artist as Filipino.*" *Kritika Kultura*, vol. 4, 2004, p. 7. The title of Joaquin's collection of short stories strongly suggests the self-consciousness of his association of the Philippines with Ireland.

5. Bazin, *Baroque and Rococo Art*, pp. 6–7.

6. Gilles Deleuze, *The Fold: Leibniz and the Baroque*, translated by Tom Conley. University of Minnesota Press, 1993, p. 3; hereafter cited in the text as *F*.

7. *stone floods* was the title of Trevor Joyce's second book-length collection (New Writers' Press, 1995), a collection that inaugurated his return to publication after an almost twenty-year silence.

8. Walter Benjamin, *The Origin of German Tragic Drama*, translated by John Osborne, introduction by George Steiner. Verso, 1985, p. 54; hereafter cited in the text as *OGTD*.

9. For a discussion of Benjamin's concern with the question of sovereignty in this and other contemporaneous works, and in particular his debate with the political theorist, Carl Schmitt, see Giorgio Agamben, *State of Exception*, translated by Kevin Attell. Chicago University Press, 2005, pp. 52–64.

10. Karl Marx, *Capital: A Critique of Political Economy*, vol. I, translated by Samuel Moore and Edward Aveling. Lawrence and Wishart, 1954, pp. 76 and 79.

11. Trevor Joyce, "Surd Blab" III. *with the first dream of fire they hunt the cold.* New Writers' Press and Shearsman, 2001, p. 57; hereafter cited as *WFDF*.

12. Trevor Joyce, "Construction." *WFDF*, pp. 52–3.

13. Trevor Joyce, "Dynamic." *WFDF*, p. 71.

14. Seamus Heaney, "The Forge." *Door into the Dark*. Faber and Faber, 1972, p. 19.

15. Trevor Joyce, "The Phantom Quarry: Translating a Renaissance Painting into Modern Poetry." *Enclave Review*, vol. 8, Summer 2013, p. 6. Archived at http://enclavereview.org/the-phantom-quarry-translating-a-renaissance-painting-into-modern-poetry/ (last accessed July 29, 2021).

16. In an interview with Marthine Satris, Joyce remarked on his intense interest in the German expressionist poet Georg Trakl at this time, when "it was sort of a little bit rarefied as a taste." Marthine Satris, "Interview with Trevor Joyce." *Journal of British and Irish Innovative Poetry*, vol. 5, no. 1, 2013, p. 19.

17. Trevor Joyce, "The Importance of the Bells." *WFDF*, p. 48.

18. Joyce, "Phantom Quarry," p. 6. It would require another essay to elaborate the ways in which Joyce's developing poetic is embedded within the history of the Republic of Ireland's efforts and failures at capitalist modernization during the 1960s, '70s, and '80s, projects with which his own career as a computer systems analyst was intimately bound up. There is certainly a

close relation between the branding of Ireland as simultaneously a space of surviving traditionalism and one ready for development and the lyric forms that continued to dominate in the face of the monetization and capitalization of the Irish economy. Robert Kiely's *Incomparable Poetry: An Essay on the Financial Crisis of 2007–2008 and Irish Literature*. punctum books, 1996, is a valuable contribution in this direction. On the relation of tradition to modernization, see Luke Gibbons, "Coming Out of Hibernation? The Myth of Modernization in Irish Culture." *Transformations in Irish Culture*. Cork University Press, 1996, pp. 82–93. For an account of Ireland's economic modernization and its cyclical failures, see Peadar Kirby, *Celtic Tiger in Collapse: Explaining the Weaknesses of the Irish Model*, 2nd edition. Palgrave Macmillan, 2010, pp. 13–68.

19. Theodor W. Adorno, "Criteria of New Music." *Sound Figures*, translated by Rodney Livingstone. Stanford University Press, 1999, p. 150.

20. See Trevor Joyce, "On *stone floods*: A Commentary from a Letter to Michael Smith." Nate Dorward, editor. *The Fly on the Page*, special issue of *The Gig*, no. 3, November 2004, p. 3, and anonymous jacket note to *with the first dream of fire they hunt the cold*.

21. Trevor Joyce, *Syzygy*, "The Drift." *WFDF*, p. 141.

22. Joyce, "Phantom Quarry," p. 7.

23. Trevor Joyce, "'Approach of Bodies Falling in Time of Plague' and 'Proceeds of a Black Swap': Some Explanatory Notes." Dorward, pp. 17–18.

24. This poem was initially not included in *Pentahedron* and was first published separately in *The Lace Curtain*, vol. 6, Autumn 1978, p. 8. It may be the last poem Joyce wrote prior to his return to the poetic work that became *stone floods*, hence its transitional status.

25. For the phrase "closed arcanian space," see Louis Marin, *To Destroy Painting*, translated by Mette Hjort. University of Chicago Press, 1995, p. 160: "The closed arcanian space is that of a black box. If we introduce a single light into that space, a ray of light emanating from a single source, this light has a maximum of potency and intensity. It creates a blinding effect—an effect of stupefaction."

26. Barbara Maria Stafford, *Body Criticism: Imaging the Unseen in Enlightenment Art and Medicine*. MIT Press, 1991, p. 69. On the relation of Piranesi's *Vedute* to actual anatomical drawing in the eighteenth century, see the brilliant pages of *Body Criticism*, pp. 58–72. I am grateful to Trevor Joyce for introducing me to this work.

27. Joyce, "Phantom Quarry," p. 8.

28. Joyce, "Phantom Quarry," p. 5.

29. "The Task of the Translator," translated by Harry Zohn. *Selected Writings: Volume 1: 1913–1926*, edited by Marcus Bullock and Michael W. Jennings. Belknap Press, 1996, pp. 257–8.

30. Benjamin, "Task of the Translator," p. 260.

31. Trevor Joyce, *Rome's Wreck*. Cusp Books, 2014.

32. As we worked on the visual design of *Rome's Wreck* for Cusp Books, Joyce and I discussed at length the appropriateness of working over fragments of some of Piranesi's *Vedute* in combination with anatomical drawings reproduced in Stafford's *Body Criticism*. Our thanks to Susan Guntner, the graphic designer, for the execution of this working over.

33. Edmund Spenser, "The Ruines of Rome," #32. *The Poetical Works of Edmund Spenser*, edited by J. C. Smith and E. De Selincourt. Oxford University Press, 1912, p. 514.

34. Joyce, *Rome's Wreck*, #32. That effect of halting or uncertain rhythm may derive straightforwardly from the monosyllabic texture of the verse. As Joyce comments to Marthine Satris, "How do you fix the rhythm of something that's monosyllabic?" Satris, "Interview with Trevor Joyce," p. 21.

35. Robert Browning, "Fra Lippo Lippi." *Men and Women*, 1855. Reprinted in *Poetical Works 1833–1864*, edited by Ian Jack. Oxford University Press, 1975 p. 576.

36. Samuel Beckett, *Endgame* in *Endgame and Act without Words*. Grove Press, 1957, p. 51, and William Shakespeare, *The Tempest*, I.ii.366.

37. Spenser, "The Ruines of Rome," I, 509.

38. Spenser, "The Ruines of Rome," III, 509.

39. Spenser, "The Ruines of Rome," VII, 510.

40. Joyce, *Rome's Wreck*, #7.

41. J. W. von Goethe, cited in Benjamin, "Task of the Translator," p. 262.

42. Joyce, "On *stone floods*," p. 8.

Conclusion. Conduits for the Humane: Walsh's *Optic Verve*

Throughout this book, I have argued that we need to understand the poetry of the SoundEye poets—writers whose work has retained a sense of the ethical as well as aesthetic obligations that drove modernism and occasioned the apparent difficulty of its characteristic works—as a counterpoetics of modernity. Their commitment to finding poetic modes adequate to "the new things that have happened," a commitment that, more than formal similarities or influences, forges their links to Samuel Beckett, is not in itself unprecedented in Irish writing. As I hope to have shown in the first part of the book, Irish poetry has always borne the marks of what Édouard Glissant calls a "forced poetics" that in turn shapes the conditions for any counterpoetics. Both Mangan and Yeats wrote in the shadow not only of language loss but also of the violence of a century of colonial modernization that sought quite expressly to destroy the Irish culture that had proven so recalcitrant to capitalist development. Like so many other colonized societies, Ireland long served as a kind of laboratory for the bureaucratic and institutional innovations that a colonial administration could impose and that forged the outlines of what the Frankfurt School would come to call administered society. As I have argued in the Introduction, Ireland's modernism was driven by the need to shape alternatives, both cultural institutions and forms of expression, to counter the imposition of British capitalist modernity. It is its virtue and not its shortcoming to be politicized through and through and to effect the integration of art and life in ways that sought to shape a different aesthetic sociality. If we have lost sight of this counterpoetic project of the Revival, after decades of a deliberately depoliticizing criticism, that is perhaps our loss rather than a failing of the work or of the Revival itself. This is not to say that the contemporary poets I have discussed see themselves as sharing that project or as working in continuity with the Revival in any direct way. On the contrary, the discontinuities that mark Irish poetic history, as I suggest in Chapter 1, are bridged neither by tradition nor by influence, but by a recurrent return to the impact of processes of modernization over which we have little control and which each time anew demand the reinvention of form in order to respond to the conditions of unfreedom they create.

Trevor Joyce has mused on the possible utopian capacities of contemporary poetic language, suggesting that: "Poetry seems to be one of the few areas where language, natural language, is used where it hasn't in any irrevocable way been contaminated and distorted beyond capacity to serve as a conduit for the humane."[1] This is not, as he makes clear, any kind of advocacy for the idea of the poem as a protected preserve within which humane values can be realized in isolation from the pressures that an over-administered society imposes on the language and on artistic practice in general. It is, rather, to insist that the poetry of our moment must take the measure of this "contamination and distortion" of the language and work with the knowledge of how easily affect can be commodified or the routinization of bureaucratic and media speech cast a euphemistic veil over the inhuman violence of the state and of capitalist modernity. What drives Joyce's poetry is not the effort to retain some residual conception of a free moral subject but

> the question of how, in the face of such constraints, one can best live and arrive at one's humanity (for lack of a better word). I use my characteristic toolkit to model the encroaching pressures on compassion, from business, politics, the managers of our society.[2]

Joyce's constant innovation as a poet over many decades is ill-served by the term experimental, which all too easily suggests an arbitrary play with formal possibilities for their own sake, abstracted from any motivating engagement with the social conditions that shape its essential material, language, in both its sensuous and its signifying aspects. It is precisely a counterpoetics, one that seeks to counter both the routinization of daily language practice, as bureaucratic locutions seep into common speech, and that of poetic forms themselves, as they simulate some apparently personal "poetic dialect" in what is nothing but "a reworking of old language and old collocations."[3]

By way of concluding what must in fact be the unending task of reading and rereading work whose ambitions and complexity demand our attentive engagement, I want to return to a work I have already discussed in Chapter 5, Catherine Walsh's *Optic Verve: A Commentary*. In *Optic Verve*, a work that is increasingly, if slowly, coming to be acknowledged as a major Irish feminist text of the post-Celtic Tiger moment of affective as well as financial deflation, Walsh engages in an extended interrogation of the conditions of writing from multiple and constantly shifting angles of approach and in no less polymorphous an array of styles.[4] By "conditions of writing" I mean both the conditions that inform choices of form and diction and those material ones that permit or hinder the actual physical act of sitting down to write. That concern may be communicated in the complex pun that forms the work's title, substituting "verve," with its connotation of a capricious inspiration that animates artwork and its derivation from the Latin *verba*, words, for the standard "optic nerve," with its peculiar mixed associations with receptive passivity and nervous energy. Verve is precisely what her situation would seem to disallow. The frankly adverse conditions for her writing furnish Walsh with a lens, to pun further on the title, through which to view the wider conditions of Ireland in the immediate wake of another faltering burst of modernization. That lens is distinctly feminine and feminist in its orientation, framed as it is within a context of domestic work. Indeed, Walsh's restless interrogations might even seem to recapitulate those of feminist philosopher Jane Flax in her classic *Thinking Fragments*:

> How is it possible to write? What meanings can writing have when every proposition and theory seems questionable, one's own identity is uncertain, and the status of the intellectual is conceived alternately as hopelessly enmeshed in oppressive knowledge/power relations or utterly irrelevant to the workings of the technical-rational bureaucratic state?[5]

But where Flax approaches the questions of writing and of feminine subjectivity through philosophy and psychoanalysis, Walsh's starting point is considerably more material, commencing again and again in this diaristic assemblage of fragments from the necessities and distractions of a domestic space that is at once the site of her work and that of the household chores that make it an utterly inhospitable space for writing. Yeats famously differentiated "the bundle of accident and incoherence that sits down to breakfast" from the subject of the poetic work "reborn as an idea, something intended, something complete."[6] The remade subject complements the well-made poem. Walsh's writing happens *at* that breakfast table:

> Whose small drafts were they among the litter debris of responsibility looming crumbs butterdish miscellaneous novels biographies sheets of oddly sized strangely assorted papers biro Tipp-Ex and marmalade dish the intrusive radio transmitter of the pulpit I am the epitome of authority in my chosen field/anything I care to fling my hat at voice the unbelievable lack of ability to cohere to pronounce to be stylistically or hey lets not ask for too much even grammatically cohesive . . .[7]

One's hesitation as to whether the sarcastic phrase "epitome of authority" fingers the pundit pontificating on the radio or the poet herself works to undercut what might be a tone of condescension pervading the work's fulminations against the decay of language in public media and daily usage alike: the inability to cohere or be stylistically or even grammatically cohesive reflects back on a work whose shifting forms and tones offer no appearance of a complete and intended subject, but rather play out the dispersed or scattered modes of attention that this journal performs in its extended "commentary" upon itself as well as its world. This domestic angel of hearth and history casts her appalled gaze not only at the catastrophic "pile of debris" that is progress and modernity, evident enough in her depictions of contemporary Ireland, but also at the mess that is her own workplace: "Day's debris littering floors, shelves, chairs, benches, stereo, footstools. Shoes, caps, hats, recorders, guitars, CDs, panpipes, harmonicas, bags, books, piano. Piano" (*OV* 88). Out of, and not apart from, such a space of chaos and "moidered" consciousness the writing emerges:

> That's what happens, you write books, chores lurch. Walking in, out of rooms, ostensibly busy, without any of what you came in for/still with that which you had wished to put away. Talking to yourself again. Drifting inaudibly though language/s, unfolding segments, scenes, rhythmical structures. Sifting. Realizing retrospectively three. To write (   ) which way the contraflow?
> An elegant silence? C'mon! I mean, what's that? . . . (*OV* 89)

The meditative silence that is the reserve of the poet fails to materialize in this space that is entirely porous—in a manner that had already been a constant of Walsh's writing in volumes like *City West* (2005)—to "noises off," the intrusions of household and external sounds: "Some days there is no greater silence. Typewriter stops. White machines can whoosh, click, cars pull up, doors bang, dogs bark" (*OV* 88).

This porosity of the writing subject is a core condition of the writing and the mixed-genre form that it assumes. Mixed genre is perhaps mis-leading, in so far as it might suggest an orderly alternation between, say, poetry and prose passages, or between journal entries and lyrics. This commentary that constantly glosses itself shifts far more unpredictably and without strongly marked borders between its restless prose ("If rest-less, move something/one/where": *OV* 85). Passages that are lineated as lyric and occasionally hover momentarily around an epiphanic stillness rapidly dissolve back into the meandering flow of the prose from which the lineated sections are often tonally indistinguishable. The text's dis-solution of generic boundaries corresponds with its dissolution of the division of spheres into which modernity has distributed both its modes of practice and the affective and discursive regimes appropriate to each, fragmenting the subject's experience and narrowing its potentialities:[8]

Imagine it
lower calibre critique makers pigeon holers
enough to be that
(there are always alternatives
boxin'
terminology cramping
(after the alternatives lads
attempting delimiting
proscription seeking
curtailment
bid for?
bounds of?
set by? (*OV* 107)

The specialization that increases the more the division of labor advances under capitalism has long been seen to "curtail" or "cramp" the potentials of the human subject. Historically, the aesthetic sphere was charged with redeeming that fragmentation of the modern individual by another partition, and another specialization, that installed the separation between artwork and life that the avant-garde eventually sought to undo. Whatever redemption takes place though the enclosure of aesthetic experience could —at a certain moment that Adorno historicizes in the essay "Lyric Poetry and Society" cited in Chapter 5—represent its social purpose and function as shaping a reserve for the still resistant subject. But at this stage of late modernity, the possibility of such a residually autonomous and innerly reconciled subject is radically reduced. Every domain of subjective experience has, in the gradual inroads of modernization, been colonized by forces beyond the subject, shaping the most private domestic spaces as it shapes the world of public discourse, the conditions of dwelling and consuming as of work, of language use as of emotional tone and response. Where *City West* enacted the almost passive responsiveness of the suburban subject to its undefended porosity to other(s') voices—the patter of domestic life, the constant chatter of the media, passing pedestrians and partying youths—*Optic Verve* raises the pitch to a nervously frenetic level in posing its "counterflow" in the form of what Dina Al-Kassim has termed the "literary rant." The literary rant is the medium of the writer's revolt against things as they are and, as such, is necessarily transgressive and insubordinate. At the same time, however, as Jean-Paul Sartre once remarked of Charles Baudelaire, the rebel requires the law against which she rebels. Even as "resistant speech" the rant testifies to the abjection of its subject before the law:

Neither a genre nor a reliable indicator of a psychological state, a rant is an event of address that irrupts in the modernist text of contestation. Dependent upon a fantasy, that one could speak in one's own voice and denounce the

law, the rant unwittingly constructs the law it seeks to rebuke. This paradoxical address, engaging as it does a fantasy of sovereign speech, establishes the
very symbolic order it resists for the rant must testify to its own abjection if it
is to accuse the law that orders it.[9]

In *Optic Verve*, the almost painfully forced efforts at rational response
to absurdity, hypocrisy, and stupefaction issue in the clipped speech
of a quasi-generic objective commentary. But that effort at control is
drowned out by the ready-made language of the commodity sphere,
mediaspeak and bureaucratic euphemism that has a peculiar helter-
skelter poetics of its own:

> take these words   access   review   media
> decline in service   costs   in other developments   initiative
> leadership   that failure   the expert   continuing   results   establish
>   risk   engage   attempts to restore   the issue   was still being
> considered arrangements will be necessary   the independent framework
>   warning acknowledged   it did not believe   they supported so the moment
> comes   however to be guardedly positive there is no going back   so
> interested applicants   choose from a huge   range   compromise agreed
> it is the place to be   talk to our professional doctors   confidence
> creativity   enjoy a well deserved   book now for best   awardwinning
> fun   formula   limited availability   new   exciting times   new
> experience awaits   anticipated yields   in the region   timing
> critical call today   all inclusive how do you spell due to power
> failure   are now poised   as a mark of respect   delivery within 1 week to
> capitalize on reservation recommended commercial enquiries   welcome
>   unprecedented growth only 45 minutes from   nationwide great location
> great food   lots to do after renovations   all should be back to normal
> by now   see website   subject to   to availability   choose from   selection
>   available now   fill the gap   sudden departure stock arriving daily
>   awardwinning complimentary car parking is this what we are reduced to
> (*OV* 114)

Indeed, the watchwords of modernist rebellion are reduced to this com-
modityscape of creativity, new experience, new exciting times, even as
the achievements of progress and modernity boil down to the indistinguishable patter of news announcer, politician, and marketer. Innovation
appears not as the quality of an inventive poetic writing, but as the
mind-numbing drumbeat of commodity production's need ceaselessly to
"make it new." The monumental and exhausting language slab of this
collage of pulverized overhearings that saturate the audiosphere of daily
life strangely resembles the phatic fragments that constitute the opening
"lyrics" of the volume discussed in Chapter 5: neither offer place to an
autonomous subject whose expressive resistance could challenge the
overbearing insistence of an utterly rationalized and atomized world.

Rant's rebellious counterpoint is the subjection of that world's linguistic tics to a parroting whose repetitions reduce it to the nonsense that it in any case already was.

In what seems to me a critical feminist work for the twenty-first century, critique—whose dismantling power assumed a disinterested or, at a minimum, residually autonomous subject capable of mediating the real—is displaced by a rant that constantly but haphazardly scans the catastrophe piling up at the writer's feet in an endless chaos of debris whose constituents range from the quotidian scatterings of personal objects to the larger spectacle of social violence in which persons are shattered into appendages of the machine, migrants displaced and exploited, children shot just "for being alive." In the face of such ubiquitous brutality, the elegiac contemplation of one individual's mortality verges on complicity:

> She'll say it had to come once she'd lived long enough. She is pleased, yet unmoved. That objectivity necessary to level the blows, leaven the day light leaves behind. Still, as she sits there, children are taken off the streets of Honduras, shot, for being alive. The Brazilian woman trafficked to Ireland, sold into prostitution, is rescued, no doubt for deportation. (*OV* 92)

Far from the private refuge from the trials of public workaday life of a previous domestic ideology, this room of her own that the woman writer labors to secure (and tidy) is itself penetrated relentlessly by a world that no longer respects any such divisions: its avatar is the constant background hum, the "Ceaseless noise of white machines," that seems to regulate the writer's work, which is no less subject than any other drudgery to mechanical demands in the era of digital reproduction: "Plugging. On. Plugging. In. Plugging. Out. Plugging. Along. A book on . . ." (*OV* 119; 85)

That book is a scarcely partitioned jumble of genres and languages, through which Walsh's "stutterance" labors to release poetic fragments, luminous moments that—like the glosses or lyric commentaries of Celtic scribes—are pushed to the margins by the mass of text. *Optic Verve* is the record of the *work* of writing whose exhaustive inventory is also its investigation of the contemporary *conditions* of writing. No longer either a vocation that, as an end in itself, transcends the constraints of modern labor relations, nor the specialized social function that that apparently free avocation always already was, the work of the writer is an act of survival and salvage, seeking to clear amid the rubble of modernity's passage the space for the subject's expression of its rage and protest. But its form can no longer be the momentary instant of lyric transcendence of the well-made poem: so relentlessly is the world of the writer—and of any late modern subject—driven and impinged upon by the heteronomous demands of the world that a space unbounded by the clutter of that world is no longer conceivable except by an act of self-consoling fraud. Walsh's various efforts to offer us her vision of communal well-being in opposition to the predatory and shabby provisions of neoliberal austerity tend to peter out in face of their ineffectuality: "sadly could go on and on and on so much room for improvement in the general every day welfare of children at school" (*OV* 66). The very language of well-meaning and even pragmatic social projects is already colonized by the vocabularies of past administrative state interventions: improvement, welfare, even "the general," a term for the collective debased into a homogenizing bureaucratic placeholder.

We could say then that an Irish counterpoetics of modernity reverses the tendency of the avant-garde as Peter Bürger theorized it.[10] Where the avant-gardiste seeks to collapse the boundary between the sphere of art and that of everyday life in the interest of an anticipatory revolutionary practice, this counterpoetics, with a greater sobriety of means and affective responses, apprehends all too well the fact that late or neoliberal capitalism has already effectively dissolved not only the boundaries of art and life, but even the partitions by which liberal modernity divided the social, reserving protected spaces for the performance, if not the actuality, of free subjectivity. Those discrete enclosures or enclaves into which, in the constructs of a liberal ideology, privacy and freedom could withdraw, from the domestic to the pedagogical, the recreationary to the aesthetic, are now thoroughly and, it would seem, irrevocably penetrated by the twin levers of financialization and commodification. The critique that Marxist feminism leveled at the delusory separation of the space of reproduction (that extends to the cultural as well as the domestic) from that of production has been overtaken by capitalism itself. The free space in which the autonomous subject of expression could realize itself as its own end—if indeed it ever did exist in practice—has by now been thoroughly colonized. Poetic speech frets in the shadow of others' words.

But this heteronomy of the means to expression is a not unfamiliar condition for a colonial culture: Samuel Beckett presciently intuited the inescapable fate of a language that has become the badge of unfreedom in generalizing a condition that Stephen Dedalus had resentfully attributed to the secondariness of a colonized Irish English. Joyce perfectly expressed the colonial consequence that makes of Irish writing an always "forced poetics." Stephen—dejected and disheartened—must acknowledge that the Englishman's language "so familiar and so foreign, will always be for me an acquired speech. I have not made or accepted its words." Beckett—for whom the "obligation to express" made all writing a forced writing—lets his Unnamable encapsulate this predicament more summarily: "Having nothing to say, no words but the words of others, I have to speak."[11] The condition of having to work within a "contaminated and distorted" language is no new thing in the Irish context, even if the forms in which it confronts the writer change: that is, as I have argued throughout this book, the fundamental situation of Ireland's cultural modernity.

The trajectory of the spell cast on free expression runs from language loss to the coercive automatisms of bureaucratic speech. In this respect, as Walsh's frantic catalog of ready-made language captures with the desperation of one always fleeing on the spot, the current phase of Irish modernity is little different from anywhere else. The paradoxically homogenizing atomization of the social that is the logic of capitalist reason was instrumental in the colonial destruction of unsubsumable cultural formations, but now extends its reach equally over the globe: "Hundreds of people a week remixed and labeling lots of pretty bleak forgettable sad / all over new york newry boston ballyhaunis barcelona ballymun paris piedmont / kilkenny knightsbridge" (*OV* 57). Drawn willingly into the circuits of transnational capital, Ireland is caught, as everywhere is, by the suffocating embrace of the Same: "a vast similitude interlocks all" (*OV* 129). What is it to "live and arrive at one's humanity" or to extend compassion under such conditions? Despite its frequent frustrations—"tediously, back to square one minus any resolution" (*OV* 101)—Walsh's text is seeded with the traces of alternative and mostly female practices of care that are at times somatic memories, at others the record of participation in communities and practices of mutual aid among the rural and urban working class. Such practices were not understood as separate economic functions, whether the "non-value" of reproductive domestic work or the specialized labor of underpaid "carers," but an integral element of a community still grounded in the moral economies of commoning that turn out to be inseparable from a vital, subversive language practice:

> Punning, a social art form. Once accustomed to expert purveyors of the pun diurnally, spoilt for life at any distance from them. That town Dublin hoarded caches of punners, they stood around bus stops on stormy days, queued for the dole in Thomas St., Werburgh St., Victoria St., pinched their fruit on Camden St., bought potatoes off prams, scrubbed doorsteps on their knees and put Grannies out on them minding babies, shelling peas, peeling potatoes, darning socks, knitting jerseys, at ease. Needed. Looked after, necessary. (*OV* 87)

The invocation of these grannies, "with quick wits, sharp minds, indeed, occasionally, loud mouths" (*OV* 87), like that of the physical gestures etched into the body by the repeated acts of baking or churning butter practiced by generations of rural women and learnt by Walsh from her own grandmother, might appear sentimental or nostalgic, idealizing the burdens and privations of premodern social life as a refusal of subsumption into capitalist labor processes. In the context of a lyric mode that might have made of them redemptive examples for a compensatory aesthetic preserve, that is exactly what they would be. In *Optic Verve*, however, such moments emerge within the jagged flow of a commentary on a damaged world in which "Wrong life cannot be lived rightly."[12] Such recollections and observations are thrown up, like flotsam, by the necessity to articulate a protest against the unfreedom which that protest itself confirms, much as the ghosts of Ireland's prehistoric past are unleashed from an archeological site revealed by the construction of a new road. It is a chance occurrence that haunts the text thereafter, recurring as a kind of burden that also offers a clue to the overall movement of the text:

a fortification   a round house
cremated bones in urns older than
the settlement as they were found
under the bank a broken skull
of a woman of around 40 years old in the
trench around the house   pre christian
late celtic   a ripe old age
charcoal   pottery   an iron knife   blade intact
a whetstone   a thumb scraper for curing
hide   and the ubiquitous and much more
recent   bowl of a clay pipe   mark intact (*OV* 71)

These traces of a never-written material history, disparate historical moments layered over one another, lead to a series of questions and speculations regarding its former inhabitants' daily lives and culture whose very possibility lies in the disappearance or erasure of the past:

whole episodes
  epochs
are   not retained
            in any conventional
memory
but   one   day
          years later a
line road   resonates   triggers
  incidents   places   people
reverberate   memory (*OV* 74)

"How much," the poet wonders, "is speculation?" (*OV* 74). The root of the word speculation in *speculum*, a mirror, is subtly picked up a moment later as a cluster of words arise, as if from nowhere, first in English and then in their Irish equivalents:

grange   day   light   snow
wind   sky   bird   night
   river
      abhann   oíche
eán   speír   gaoth
   sneachta   solas   lá   an ghrainseach

where did these words come
from?
proto what?
is this a series of articulated
sound the youngster hoeing the
small enclosed tillage would   have
recognized
would not have run from (*OV* 75)

"where did these words come / from?" is perfectly poised: is its reference etymological, querying their derivation in time past? Or is it a question of the present, asking from what space in the writer's head the memory of Irish might suddenly have returned? It may take a moment to realize that the Irish words are given in reverse order to the English terms, pivoting on river / abhann, to produce an effect of mirroring. Across the time-space of language loss and transformation that separates the poet and the long-dead youth, language reaches out the faint hope of an intimacy in recognition, less, perhaps, a ferry or a bridge carrying across than the reflection of two river-banks across the flow. Pointedly, the same passage recurs immediately after the collage of commodity-language quoted above (*OV* 114) as if to counterpoint its vacuous blather with another vision of language's potentials.

Clearly, though, this is no nostalgic idyll: the violence of the past, signaled in the "broken skull" of the buried woman, cannot be bracketed, and the language of the past survives only in the form of isolated words, glowing briefly within the constellation of a concrete poem, then swept away in the relentless onward movement of the text. Rather than affirming some lyric transcendence of loss, it underscores the impossibility of holding to enclosures of private or communal affect uncontaminated by the toxic language of modernity. *Optic Verve*, written under the sign of Walsh's dead grandmother, is a work saturated with loss, in which the private grief for foremothers and fellow poets—Ric, Cid, Bob, Gael, Brian (*OV* 109–10)—is braided with sorrow on another scale for the seemingly unending trail of indifferent destruction that modernity bears in its wake.[13] In this braiding, the images of the living and the dead overlie one another inexactly, as if in some faulty stereoscopy:

> The faces of the remaining mingle with those who are gone in more articulate ways than I would have expected. Almost credible, slight contextual warping, shifting. Clarity of such faces etched eyes, fleeting expression, meta-language I grew up in, learned to speak in, or not. Such voices practically elusive now. (*OV* 104)

This imprecise overlying could be read as the failure of transmission, refraction rather than mirroring, in which time and history spell irrevocable decay and displacement. But its proper image may in fact be the device that Walsh invokes, the thaumatrope (*OV* 70). The thaumatrope was a simple Victorian toy that consisted of a disc on either side of which two complementary images were imprinted, say, a bird and a rooftop. When the disc was spun rapidly by the cords to which it was attached, the two images appeared to combine into one. In *Optic Verve*'s temporal thaumatrope, the "wonderworld beyond the tangible" emerges in the juxtaposition of the present with the image of the past, "A reaching forwards/backwards into that non-thing called time" (*OV* 72; 121). In "the art of catoptrics," or speculative reflections, that threads through the text, mirroring across time shows "merging moments scenes / abandoning their moment for each / other proceeding into the next view" (*OV* 70). One might say that the thaumatrope operates visually on the same principles as the pun does verbally, holding together two distinct images in one perception. Where the pun asks us to grasp simultaneously two disparate senses of the same word, the thaumatrope, exploiting the persistence of an impression in the eye after the percept has passed, overlays two visual moments in one image.

The critical model for this thaumatropic merging of moments is suggested by the dialectical image that Walter Benjamin imagined in his *Arcades Project* or *Passagenwerk*:

> It's not that what is past casts its light on what is present, or what is present its light on what is past; rather, image is that wherein what has been comes together in a flash with the now to form a constellation. In other words, image is dialectics at a standstill. For while the relation of the present to the past is a purely temporal, continuous one, the relation of what-has-been to the now is dialectical: is not progression, but image, suddenly emergent.— Only dialectical images are genuine images (that is, not archaic); and the place where one counters them is language.[14]

As Benjamin goes on in a following note, "The image that is read— which is to say, the image in the now of its recognizability—bears to the highest degree the imprint of the perilous critical moment on which all reading is founded."[15] Walsh is utterly attuned to the perilous moment in which *Optic Verve* is being written, where language, life-in-common, compassionate togetherness, the very possibility of alternative imaginaries beyond capitalist modernity, are reduced to a relentless process of homogenization in the name of progress, while the past and its unexhausted repertoire of possibilities are threatened with erasure and forgetting, much as an archeological dig might "be covered with a new road" (*OV* 71) shortly after its discovery.

Walsh's insistence on holding steadily in mind the corrosive time of the now together with images of the past that in the resultant constellation paradoxically "attain to legibility" conjoins her work with that of Joyce and Scully in a common counterpoetics of modernity.[16] Across great divergences of form and language practice, and against any hankering after a continuous tradition, they share a corresponding commitment to reinventing the means and materials of poetry that make it adequate to the now. The newness of form that they persistently shape in this counterpoetic practice makes space for those sudden dialectical emergences of past and present potentials that lie athwart the ongoing flow of destruction that is the burden of modernity.

Notes

1. Marthine Satris, "Interview with Trevor Joyce." *Journal of British and Irish Innovative Poetry*, vol. 5, no. 1, 2013, p. 28.
2. Satris, "Interview with Trevor Joyce," p. 29.
3. Satris, "Interview with Trevor Joyce," p. 29.
4. For an important essay that considers how "Walsh's social critique in *City West* [2005] is also directed towards gender concerns," see Clare Bracken, "Nomadic Ethics: Gender and Class in Catherine Walsh's *City West*." *Irish University Review*, vol. 46, no. 1, Spring/Summer 2016, pp. 75–88.
5. Jane Flax, *Thinking Fragments: Psychoanalysis, Feminism, and Postmodernism in the Contemporary West*. University of California Press, 1991, p. 5.
6. W. B. Yeats, "A General Introduction for My Work." *Essays and Introductions*. Gill and Macmillan, 1961, p. 509.
7. Catherine Walsh, *Optic Verve: A Commentary*. Shearsman Books, 2009, p. 65; hereafter cited in the text as *OV*.
8. See David Lloyd, *Irish Culture and Colonial Modernity, 1800–2000: The Transformation of Oral Space*. Cambridge University Press, 2011, for an extended account of British "improvements" by which Irish space was rationalized and Irish subjects disciplined.
9. Dina Al-Kassim, *On Pain of Speech: Fantasies of the First Order and the Literary Rant*. University of California Press, 2010, p. 34.

10. See Chapter 1 for a fuller discussion of Bürger's theory of the avant-garde.
11. See James Joyce, *A Portrait of the Artist as a Young Man*, edited by Seamus Deane. Penguin, 1992, p. 205, and Samuel Beckett, *Molloy, Malone Dies, The Unnamable*. Calder and Boyars, 1973, p. 316.
12. Theodor W. Adorno, *Minima Moralia: Reflections from Damaged Life*, translated by E. F. N. Jephcott. Verso, 1978, p. 39.
13. A tentative identification of the poets mentioned in these pages might be Ric Caddel (1949–2003); Cid Corman (1924–2004); Bob Cobbing (1920–2002); Gael Turnbull (1928–2004); Brian (and Bridget) Coffey (1905–1995), all poets closely associated with Walsh and with SoundEye and the Irish and British innovative poetry. Tom Raworth and Roy Fisher, both still living at the time of *Optic Verve*'s publication, may be other poets memories of whom are invoked here.
14. Walter Benjamin, "Convolute N: On the Theory of Knowledge, Theory of Progress." *The Arcades Project*, edited by Rolf Tiedemann and translated by Howard Eiland and Kevin McLaughlin. Harvard University Press, 1999, p. 462.
15. Benjamin, "Convolute N," p. 463.
16. Benjamin, "Convolute N," p. 462.

Appendix to Chapter 2: Crossing Over

Auf der Überfahrt

9. Oktober 1823

Über diesen Strom, vor Jahren,
Bin ich einmal schon gefahren.
Hier die Burg im Abendschimmer,
Drüben rauscht das Wehr, wie immer.

Und von diesem Kahn umschlossen
Waren mit mir zween Genossen;
Ach! ein Freund, ein vatergleicher,
Und ein junger, hoffnungsreicher.

Jener wirkte still hinieden,
Und so ist er auch geschieden,
Dieser, brausend vor uns allen,
Ist in Kampf und Sturm gefallen.

So, wenn ich vergangner Tage,
Glücklicher, zu denken wage,
Muß ich stets Genossen missen,
Teure, die der Tod entrissen,

Doch, was alle Freundschaft bindet,
Ist, wenn Geist zu Geist sich findet;
Geistig waren jene Stunden,
Geistern bin ich noch verbunden.

Nimm nur, Fährmann, nimm die Mie
Die ich gerne dreifach biete!
Zween, die mit mir überfuhren,
Waren geistige Naturen.

Ludwig Uhland, *Dichtungen, Briefe, Reden: Eine Auswahl*, edited by Walter P. H. Scheffler (Stuttgart: J. F. Steinkopf, 1963), pp. 216–17. Reproduced by kind permission of Antiquariat Steinkopf e.K., Stuttgart, Germany.

Spirits Everywhere

A many a summer is dead and buried
Since over this flood I last was ferried;
And then, as now, the Noon lay bright
On strand, and water, and castled height.

Beside me then in this bark sat nearest
Two companions the best and dearest;
One was a gentle and thoughtful sire,
The other a youth with a soul of fire.

One, outworn by Care and Illness,
Sought the grave of the Just in stillness;
The other's shroud was the bloody rain
And thunder-smoke of the battle-plain.

Yet still, when Memory's necromancy
Robes the Past in the hues of Fancy,
Medreameth I hear and see the Twain
With talk and smiles by my side again!

Even the grave is a bond of union;
Spirit and spirit best hold communion!
Seen through Faith, by the Inward Eye,
It is *after* Life they are truly nigh!

Then, ferryman, take this coin, I pray thee,
Thrice thy fare I cheerfully pay thee;
For, though thou seest them not, there stand
Anear me two from the Phantomland!

James Clarence Mangan, translated from the German of Ludwig Uhland, in "Anthologia Germanica, No. XVI: Ballads and Miscellaneous Poems." *Dublin University Magazine*, vol. 18, no. 103, July 1841, p. 24, reprinted in John Mitchel, editor, *Poems of James Clarence Mangan*. P. M. Haverty, 1859, pp. 94–5.

Bibliography

Adorno, Theodor W. *Aesthetic Theory*. University of Minnesota Press, 1970.

—. "Berg's Discoveries in Compositional Technique." *Quasi una Fantasia: Essays on Modern Music*, translated by Rodney Livingstone. Verso, 1992, pp. 179–200.

—. "Criteria of New Music." *Sound Figures*, translated by Rodney Livingstone. Stanford University Press, 1999, pp. 145–96.

—. *Minima Moralia: Reflections from Damaged Life*, translated by E. F. N. Jephcott. Verso, 1978.

—. *Negative Dialectics*, translated by E. B. Ashton. Continuum, 1973.

—. "On Lyric Poetry and Society." *Notes to Literature*, vol. 1, edited by Rolf Tiedemann and translated by Sherry Weber Nicholsen. Columbia University Press, 1991, pp. 37–54.

Agamben, Giorgio. "Bartleby, or On Contingency." *Potentialities: Collected Essays in Philosophy*, translated by Daniel Heller-Roazen. Stanford University Press, 1999, pp. 243–74.

—. *State of Exception*, translated by Kevin Attell. Chicago University Press, 2005.

Alcobia-Murphy, Shane. *Sympathetic Ink: Intertextual Relations in Northern Irish Poetry*. Liverpool University Press, 2006.

Al-Kassim, Dina. *On Pain of Speech: Fantasies of the First Order and the Literary Rant*. University of California Press, 2010.

Allt, Peter and Russel K. Alspach, editors. *The Variorum Edition of the Poems of W. B. Yeats*. Macmillan, 1973.

Archer, Mark. "The Year of Globalization." *Wall Street Journal*, June 15, 2013, p. C5. http://online.wsj.com/article/SB10001424127887324299104578527420006048876.html (last accessed July 29, 2021).

Armstrong, Tim. "Muting the Klaxon: Poetry, History and Irish Modernism." Coughlan and Davis, pp. 43–74.

Arsić, Branka. *Passive Constitutions or 7½ Times Bartleby*. Stanford University Press, 2007.

Bal, Mieke. *Quoting Caravaggio: Contemporary Art, Preposterous History*. Chicago University Press, 1999.

Ballagh, Robert. *A Reluctant Memoir*. Head of Zeus, 2018.

Bazin, Germain. *Baroque and Rococo Art*, translated by Jonathan Griffin. Praeger, 1964.

Beckett, Samuel. *Disjecta: Miscellaneous Writings and a Dramatic Fragment*, edited with a foreword by Ruby Cohn. Grove Press, 1984.

—. *Endgame* in *Endgame and Act without Words*. Grove Press, 1957.

—. *Molloy, Malone Dies, The Unnamable*. Calder and Boyars, 1973.

—. *Murphy*. Picador, 1973.

—. *Proust and Three Dialogues with Georges Duthuit*. John Calder, 1976.

—. *Waiting for Godot*. Faber and Faber, 1981.

—. *Watt*. Grove Press, 1953.

Bell, Desmond. "Ireland without Frontiers? The Challenge of the Communications Revolution." *Across the Frontiers: Ireland in the 1990s*, edited by Richard Kearney. Wolfhound Press, 1988, pp. 219–30.

Benjamin, Walter. *Angelus Novus: Ausgewählte Schriften 2*. Suhrkamp, 1966.

—. "Convolute N: On the Theory of Knowledge, Theory of Progress." *The Arcades Project*, edited by Rolf Tiedemann and translated by Howard Eiland and Kevin McLaughlin. Harvard University Press, 1999, pp. 456–88.

—. "Critique of Violence." *Selected Writings: Volume 1: 1913–1926*, edited by Marcus Bullock and Michael W. Jennings. Belknap Press, 1996, pp. 236–52.

—. "Fate and Character." *Selected Writings: Volume 1: 1913–1926*, edited by Marcus Bullock and Michael W. Jennings. Belknap Press, 1996, pp. 201–6.

—. "On the Concept of History." *Selected Writings: Volume 4: 1938–1940*, edited by Howard Eiland and Michael W. Jennings and translated by Edmund Jephcott and others. Belknap Press, 2003, pp. 389–400.

—. *The Origin of German Tragic Drama*, translated by John Osborne, introduction by George Steiner. Verso, 1985.

—. "The Task of the Translator," translated by Harry Zohn. *Selected Writings: Volume 1: 1913–1926*, edited by Marcus Bullock and Michael W. Jennings. Belknap Press, 1996, pp. 253–63.

Bhabha, Homi. "DissemiNation." *The Location of Culture*. Routledge, 1994, pp. 139–70.

Blanco, John D. "Baroque Modernity and the Colonial World: Aesthetics and Catastrophe in Nick Joaquin's *A Portrait of the Artist as Filipino*." *Kritika Kultura*, vol. 4, 2004, pp. 5–35.

Bloom, Harold. *The Anxiety of Influence*. Oxford University Press, 1973.

Bracken, Clare. "Nomadic Ethics: Gender and Class in Catherine Walsh's *City West*." *Irish University Review*, vol. 46, no. 1, Spring/Summer 2016, pp. 75–88.

Brathwaite, Kamau. "History of Voice." *Roots*. University of Michigan Press, 1993, pp. 266–73.

Brearton, Fran. "The 'nothing-could-be-simpler-line': Form in Contemporary Irish Poetry." *The Oxford Handbook of Contemporary Irish Poetry*, edited by Fran Brearton and Alan Gillis. Oxford University Press, 2012, pp. 629–47.

Brown, Terence. "Ireland, Modernism and the 1930s." Coughlan and Davis, pp. 24–42.

Browning, Robert. "Fra Lippo Lippi." *Men and Women*, 1855. Reprinted in *Poetical Works 1833–1864*, edited by Ian Jack. Oxford University Press, 1975, p. 576.

Bruns, Gerald L. "Voices of Construction: On Susan Howe's Poetry and Poetics (A Citational Ghost Story)." *What Are Poets For? An Anthropology of Contemporary Poetry and Poetics*. University of Iowa Press, 2012, pp. 35–55.

Bürger, Peter. *Theory of the Avant-Garde*, translated by Michael Shaw, foreword by Jochen Schulte-Sasse. University of Minnesota Press, 1984.

Byrne, Mairéad. "The Shed of Poetry." *A Line of Tiny Zeros in the Fabric: Essays on the Poetry of Maurice Scully*, edited by Kenneth Keating. Shearsman Books, 2020, pp. 151–75.

Carlyle, Thomas. "The Nigger Question" [1849]. *Critical and Miscellaneous Essays*, vol. 4. AMS Press, 1969, pp. 348–83. (Reprint of Chapman and Hall, 1899).

Carson, Ciaran. *Belfast Confetti*. Wake Forest University Press, 1989.

—. *The New Estate*. Blackstaff Press, 1976.

Castle, Gregory. *Modernism and the Celtic Revival*. Cambridge University Press, 2001.

Celan, Paul. *Collected Prose*, translated by Rosemary Waldrop. Carcanet Press, 1986.

—. "Du liegst." *Gedichte*, vol. I. Suhrkamp, 1975, p. 334.

—. "In Gestalt eines Ebers"/"In the Shape of a Boar." *Memory Rose into Threshold Speech: The Collected Earlier Poetry*, translated by Pierre Joris, bilingual edition. Farrar, Straus and Giroux, 2020, pp. 402–3.

Césaire, Aimé. "Cahier d'un retour au pays natal." *The Collected Poetry*, translated by Clayton Eshleman and Annette Smith. University of California Press, 1983, pp. 32–85.

—. "Lay of Errantry." *Corps Perdu/Lost Body: The Collected Poetry*, translated by Clayton Eshleman and Annette Smith. University of California Press, 1983, pp. 254–9.

Cleary, Joe. "Capital and Culture in Twentieth-Century Ireland: Changing Configurations." *Outrageous Fortune: Capital and Culture in Modern Ireland*, 2nd edition. Field Day, 2007, pp. 76–110.

—. *Literature, Partition and the Nation State: Culture and Conflict in Ireland, Israel and Palestine*. Cambridge University Press, 2002.

Coleridge, Samuel Taylor. *Biographia Literaria, or Biographical Sketches of My Literary Life and Opinions*, edited by George Watson. J. M. Dent and E. P. Dutton, 1975.

Connolly, James. *Labour in Irish History. Collected Works*, 2 vols, introduction by Michael O'Riordan. New Books, 1987.

Coughlan, Patricia and Alex Davis, editors. *Modernism and Ireland: The Poetry of the 1930s*. Cork University Press, 1995.

Culler, Jonathan. "Lyric, History and Genre." *New Literary History*, vol. 40, no. 4, Autumn 2009, pp. 879–99.

Curtis, L. Perry. *Apes and Angels: The Irishman in Victorian Caricature*. Smithsonian Institution Press, 1971.

D'Arcy, Margaretta and John Arden. *The Non-Stop Connolly Show: A Dramatic Cycle of Continuous Struggle in Six Parts*. Pluto Plays, 1977–8.

da Silva, Denise Ferreira. *Toward a Global Idea of Race*. University of Minnesota Press, 2007.

Davis, Alex. *A Broken Line: Denis Devlin and Irish Poetic Modernism*. University College Dublin Press, 2000.

Davis, Thomas. "Irish Songs." *The Nation*, January 4, 1845, p. 314.

Dayan, Colin. "Melville, Locke and Faith." *Raritan*, vol. 25, no. 3, Winter 2006, pp. 30–44.

Deane, Seamus. "Civilians and Barbarians." *Ireland's Field Day*. University of Notre Dame Press, 1986, pp. 33–42.

—. *Strange Country: Modernity and Nationhood in Irish Writing Since 1790*. Oxford University Press, 1997.

Deleuze, Gilles. *The Fold: Leibniz and the Baroque*, translated by Tom Conley. University of Minnesota Press, 1993.

Deleuze, Gilles and Félix Guattari. *Kafka: pour une littérature mineure*. Éditions de Minuit, 1975.

Derrida, Jacques. *Otobiographies: l'enseignement de Nietzsche et la politique du nom propre*. Éditions Galilée, 1984.

—. *Otobiographies: The Teaching of Nietzsche and the Politics of the Proper Name*, translated by Avital Ronell. University of Nebraska Press, 1985.

—. "Shibboleth: For Paul Celan." *Sovereignties in Question: The Poetics of Paul Celan*, edited by Thomas Dutoit and Outi Pasanen. Fordham University Press, 2005, pp. 1–64.

—. *Specters of Marx: The State of the Debt, the Work of Mourning and the New International*, translated by Peggy Kamuf. Routledge, 1994.

Diepeveen, Leonard. *The Difficulties of Modernism*. Routledge, 2013.

Dobbins, Gregory. "Whenever Green is Red: James Connolly and Postcolonial Theory." *Nepantla: Views from the South*, vol. 1, no. 3, 2000, pp. 605–48.

Doerksen, Victor G. *Ludwig Uhland and the Critics*. Camden House, 1994.

Donnell, Alison, Maria McGarrity, and Evelyn O'Callaghan, editors. *Caribbean Irish Connections: Interdisciplinary Perspectives*. University of the West Indies Press, 2015.

Dorward, Nate, editor. *The Fly on the Page*, special issue of *The Gig*, no. 3, November 2004.

Duffy, Charles Gavan. *Young Ireland: A Fragment of Irish History, 1840–1850*. Cassell, Petter, Calpin and Co., 1880.

Eagleton, Terry. *Heathcliff and the Great Hunger: Studies in Irish Culture*. Verso, 1995.

Emmerson, Charles. *1913: In Search of the World Before the Great War*. Public Affairs, 2013.

Empson, William. *Seven Types of Ambiguity*. New Directions, 1966.

Enright, Anne. *The Forgotten Waltz*. McLelland and Stewart, 2011.

Esty, Jed. *A Shrinking Island: Modernism and National Culture in England*. Princeton University Press, 2004.

Fadem, Maureen E. Ruprecht. *Medbh McGuckian: Iterations of Silence and the Borders of Articulacy*. Lexington Books, 2019.

Falci, Eric. "Carson's City." *Continuity and Change in Irish Poetry, 1966–2010*. Cambridge University Press, 2012, pp. 120–51.

Fanon, Frantz. *Black Skin, White Masks*, translated by Charles Lam Markham and introduction by Homi Bhabha. Pluto Press, 1986.

—. *Peau Noire, Masques Blancs*. Éditions du Seuil, 1952.

—. *Towards the African Revolution: Political Essays*, translated by Haakon Chevalier. Grove Press, 1988.

Feldman, Allen. *Formations of Violence: The Narrative of the Body and Political Terror in Northern Ireland*. University of Chicago Press, 1989.

Flax, Jane. *Thinking Fragments: Psychoanalysis, Feminism, and Postmodernism in the Contemporary West*. University of California Press, 1991.

Flynn, Leontia. *Reading Medbh McGuckian*. Irish Academic Press, 2014.

Fortunati, Leopoldina. *The Arcane of Reproduction: Housework, Prostitution, Labor and Capital*, edited by Jim Fleming and translated by Hilary Creek. Autonomedia, 1995.

Fryatt, Kit. "The Poetics of Elegy in Maurice Scully's *Humming*." *Irish University Review*, vol. 46, no. 1, Spring/Summer 2016, pp. 89–104.

Gibbons, Luke. *Transformations in Irish Culture*. Cork University Press, 1996.

Gilonis, Harry. "The Spider, the Fly and Philosophy: Following a Clew through Maurice Scully's *Livelihood*." Dorward, pp. 29–43.

Gilroy, Paul. *The Black Atlantic: Modernity and Double Consciousness*. Harvard University Press, 1993.

Glissant, Édouard. *Caribbean Discourse: Selected Essays*. University Press of Virginia, 1989.

Golden, Sean. "Post-Traditional English Literature: A Polemic." *The Crane Bag*, vol. 3, no. 2, 1979, pp. 7–18.

Gordon, Avery F. *Ghostly Matters: Haunting and the Sociological Imagination*, 2nd edition, foreword by Janice Radway. Minnesota University Press, 2008.

Greaves, C. Desmond. *The Life and Times of James Connolly*. International Publishers, 1971.

Gregory, Lady, editor. *Ideals in Ireland*. Unicorn Press, 1901.

Harrington, Joseph. *Poetry and the Public: The Social Form of Modern U.S. Poetics*. Wesleyan University Press, 2002.

Hauser, Arnold. *Mannerism: The Crisis of the Renaissance and the Origin of Modern Art*, 2 vols. Routledge and Kegan Paul, 1965.

Heaney, Seamus. *Door into the Dark*. Faber and Faber, 1972.

—. "The Placeless Heaven: Another Look at Kavanagh." *The Government of the Tongue: Selected Prose, 1978–1987*. Farrar, Straus and Giroux, 1989, pp. 3–14.

Heidegger, Martin. *What is a Thing?*, translated by W. B. Barton, Jr. and Vera Deutsch, with analysis by Eugene T. Gendlin. University Press of America, 1967.

Hewett, Waterman T. *Poems of Ludwig Uhland*. Macmillan, 1904. https://arch ive.org/details/3358018 (last accessed July 29, 2021).

Holt, Thomas C. *The Problem of Freedom: Race, Labour, and Politics in Jamaica and Britain, 1832–1938*. Johns Hopkins University Press, 1992.

Horkheimer, Max and Theodor W. Adorno. *Dialectic of Enlightenment*, translated by John Cumming. Continuum, 1972.

Howe, Susan. "Melville's Marginalia." *The Nonconformist's Memorial: Poems*. New Directions, 1993, pp. 83–150.

—. *My Emily Dickinson*. North Atlantic Books, 1985.

Huk, Romana. "'Out Past/Self-Dramatization': Maurice Scully's *Several Dances*." *Irish University Review*, vol. 46, no. 1, Spring/Summer 2016, pp. 105–18.

Hutton-Williams, Frank. "Against Irish Modernism." *Irish University Review*, special issue on "Irish Experimental Poetry," vol. 46, no. 1, Spring/Summer 2016, pp. 20–37.

"The Individuality of a Native Literature." *The Nation*, August 21, 1847, p. 731.

Jakobson, Roman and L. G. Jones. "Shakespeare's Verbal Art in 'Th'Expence of Spirit.'" *Roman Jakobson, Language in Literature*, edited by Krystyna Pomorska and Stephen Rudy. Harvard University Press, 1987, pp. 284–303.

Jeffares, A. Norman. *A Commentary on the Collected Poems of W. B. Yeats.* Stanford University Press, 1968.

Johnston, Dillon. *The Poetic Economies of England and Ireland, 1912–2000.* Palgrave, 2001.

Joyce, James. *A Portrait of the Artist as a Young Man*, edited by Seamus Deane. Penguin, 1992.

Joyce, Stanislaus. *My Brother's Keeper.* Viking Press, 1985.

Joyce, Trevor. "'Approach of Bodies Falling in Time of Plague' and 'Proceeds of a Black Swap': Some Explanatory Notes." Dorward, pp. 17–18.

---. *Fastness. A Translation from the English of Edmund Spenser.* Miami University Press, 2017.

—. "Irish Terrain: Alternative Planes of Cleavage." *Assembling Alternatives: Reading Postmodern Poetries Transnationally*, edited by Romana Huk. Wesleyan University Press, 2003, pp. 156–68.

—. "Mirror: of Glazier Velazquez." *The Lace Curtain*, vol. 6, Autumn 1978, p. 8.

—. "On stone floods: A Commentary from a Letter to Michael Smith." Dorward, pp. 3–15.

—. *Pentahedron.* New Writer's Press, 1972.

—. "The Phantom Quarry: Translating a Renaissance Painting into Modern Poetry." *Enclave Review*, vol. 8, Summer 2013, pp. 5–8. Archived at http://enclavereview.org/the-phantom-quarry-translating-a-renaissance-painting-into-modern-poetry/ (last accessed July 29, 2021).

—. *The Poems of Sweeny Peregrine: A Working of the Corrupt Irish Text*, edited by Michael Smith. New Writers' Press, 1976.

—. "Poetry, Form and Meaning." *Cork Caucus: On Art, Possibility & Democracy.* National Sculpture Factory and Revolver—Archiv für aktuelle Kunst, 2006, pp. 371–8.

—. *Rome's Wreck.* Cusp Books, 2014.

—. *stone floods.* New Writers' Press, 1995.

—. *with the first dream of fire they hunt the cold.* New Writers' Press and Shearsman, 2001

Kant, Immanuel. *The Critique of Judgement*, translated by James Creed Meredith. Clarendon Press, 1982.

Kavanagh, Patrick. *Collected Poems.* Martin Brian and O'Keeffe, 1972.

Keating, Kenneth. *Contemporary Irish Poetry and the Canon: Critical Limitations and Textual Liberations.* Palgrave Macmillan, 2017.

Kiberd, Declan. *Irish Classics.* Harvard University Press, 2001.

Kiely, Robert. *Incomparable Poetry: An Essay on the Financial Crisis of 2007–2008 and Irish Literature.* punctum books, 1996.

Kinsella, Thomas. *The Dual Tradition: An Essay on Poetry and Politics in Ireland.* Carcanet Press, 1995.

—. "The Irish Writer." *Davis, Mangan Ferguson: Tradition and The Irish Writer.* Dolmen Press, 1970, pp. 57–71.

Kirby, Peadar. *Celtic Tiger in Collapse: Explaining the Weaknesses of the Irish Model*, 2nd edition. Palgrave Macmillan, 2010.

Knowlson, James. *Damned to Fame: The Life of Samuel Beckett*. Simon and Schuster, 1996.

Lacan, Jacques. *The Four Fundamental Concepts of Psychoanalysis: Book XI of The Seminar of Jacques Lacan*, edited by Jacques-Alain Miller and translated by Alan Sheridan. W. W. Norton, 1981.

Leavis, F. R. *New Bearings in English Poetry*. Faber and Faber, 1932.

LeGuin, Ursula. *The Left Hand of Darkness*. Futura, 1981.

Linebaugh, Peter. *Red Round Globe Hot Burning: A Tale at the Crossroads of Commons and Closure, of Love and Terror, of Race and Class, and of Kate and Ned Despard*. University of California Press, 2019.

Lloyd, David. "Countering Legitimacy: Prison Protest and the Colonial Welfare State." *States of Welfare*, special issue of *Occasion*, vol. 2, December 2010. http://arcade.stanford.edu/journals/occasion/articles/countering-legitimacy -prison-protest-and-colonial-welfare-state-by-david-lloyd (last accessed July 29, 2021).

—. "Frames of *Referrance*: Samuel Beckett as an Irish Question." *Beckett and Ireland*, edited by Seán Kennedy. Cambridge University Press, 2010, pp. 31–55.

—. "An Impressive Collection." Review of *with the first dream of fire they hunt the cold* by Trevor Joyce. *Irish Times*, September 8, 2001, p. 10.

—. *Ireland After History*. Cork University Press, 1999.

—. *Irish Culture and Colonial Modernity, 1800–2000: The Transformation of Oral Space*. Cambridge University Press, 2011.

—. *Irish Times: Temporalities of Modernity*. Field Day, 2008.

—. "Kant's Examples." *Representations*, vol. 28, Fall 1989, pp. 34–54.

—. *Nationalism and Minor Literature: James Clarence Mangan and the Emergence of Irish Cultural Nationalism*. University of California Press, 1987.

—. "Nationalism and Postcolonialism." *W. B. Yeats in Context*, edited by David Holdeman and Ben Levitas. Cambridge University Press, 2010, pp. 179–92.

—. "The Pathological Sublime: Pleasure and Pain in the Colonial Context." *The Postcolonial Enlightenment: Eighteenth-Century Colonialism and Postcolonial Theory*, edited by Daniel Carey and Lynn Festa. Oxford University Press, 2009, pp. 71–102.

—. "The Poetics of Decision: Yeats, Benjamin and Schmitt." *Études Anglaises*, vol. 68, no. 4, October–December 2015, pp. 468–82.

—. "The Poetics of Politics: Yeats and the Founding of the State." *Anomalous States: Irish Writing and the Post-Colonial Moment*. Lilliput Press, 1993, pp. 59–87.

—. "Republics of Difference: Yeats, MacGreevy, Beckett." *Beckett's Thing: Painting and Theatre*. Edinburgh University Press, 2016, pp. 27–84.

—. "Rethinking National Marxism: James Connolly and 'Celtic Communism.'" *Irish Times: Temporalities of Modernity*. Field Day, 2008.

—. *Under Representation: The Racial Regime of Aesthetics*. Fordham University Press, 2019.

Lloyd, David and Paul Thomas. *Culture and the State*. Routledge, 1997.

Longley, Edna. "'Altering the past': Northern Irish Poetry and Modern Canons." *Irish Writing Since 1950, The Yearbook of English Studies*, vol. 35, 2005, pp. 1–17.

—. *The Living Stream: Literature and Revisionism in Ireland*. Bloodaxe Books, 1994.

Longley, Michael. *Collected Poems*. Jonathan Cape, 2006.

Lukács, Georg. *The Theory of the Novel: A Historico-Philosophical Essay on the Forms of Great Epic Literature*, translated by Anna Bostock. MIT Press, 1983.

Luxemburg, Rosa. *The Accumulation of Capital*, translated by Agnes Schwarzschild, introduction by Tadeusz Kowalik. Routledge, 2003.

Mangan, James Clarence. "Anthologia Germanica, No. XVI: Ballads and Miscellaneous Poems." *Dublin University Magazine*, vol. 18, no. 103, July 1841, pp. 19–36.

—. "Chapters on Ghostcraft." *Prose Writings*, centenary edition, edited by D. J. O'Donoghue. M. H. Gill, 1904, pp. 160–98.

—. *James Clarence Mangan: Autobiography*. Dolmen Press, 1968.

—. "Sketches of Modern Irish Writers: James Clarence Mangan." *Irishman*, August 17, 1850, p. 28.

Marin, Louis. *To Destroy Painting*, translated by Mette Hjort. University of Chicago Press, 1995.

Marx, Karl. *Capital: A Critique of Political Economy*, vol. I, translated by Samuel Moore and Edward Aveling. Lawrence and Wishart, 1954.

Marx, Leo. "Melville's Parable of the Walls." *Sewanee Review*, vol. 61, no. 4, Autumn 1953, pp. 602–27. Reprinted in McCall, pp. 239–56.

Mauss, Marcel. *A General Theory of Magic*, 1950 edition, translated by Robert Brain. Routledge and Kegan Paul, 1972.

Mays, J. C. C. "Flourishing and Foul: Six Poets and the Irish Building Industry." *Irish Review*, vol. 8, Spring 1990, pp. 6–11.

—. "The Third Walker." *Irish University Review*, vol. 46, no. 1, Spring/Summer 2016, pp. 48–62.

McCall, Dan, editor. *Melville's Short Novels*. W. W. Norton, 2001.

McCarthy, Conor. *Modernisation: Crisis and Culture in Ireland, 1969–1992*. Four Courts Press, 2000.

McCormack, W. J. "Austin Clarke: The Poet as Scapegoat of Modernism." Coughlan and Davis, pp. 75–102.

McGuckian, Medbh. *Captain Lavender*. Wake Forest University Press, 1995.

McNaughton, James. *Samuel Beckett and the Politics of Aftermath*. Oxford University Press, 2018.

Melville, Herman. "Bartleby the Scrivener: A Tale of Wall St." McCall, pp. 3–34.

"Memory, Modernism and Media: Ireland 1913–1916." *NUI Maynooth*, June 2013, Conference Program. http://memorymodernismmedia.wordpress.com/ (last accessed July 25, 2013; subsequently deleted).

Mitchel, John, editor. *Poems of James Clarence Mangan*. P. M. Haverty, 1859.

Molloy, E. "Racial Capitalism, Hauntology and the Politics of Death in Ireland." *Identities: Global Studies in Culture and Power*, 2019, pp. 1–18.

Moretti, Franco. "The Long Goodbye: *Ulysses* and the End of Liberal Capitalism." *Signs Taken for Wonders: Essays in the Sociology of Literary Forms*. Verso, 1983, pp. 182–208.

Morin, Emilie. *Beckett's Political Imagination*. Cambridge University Press, 2017.

Morrison, Toni. *Playing in the Dark: Whiteness and the Literary Imagination*. Vintage Books, 1992.

Mulhall, Anne. "The Ends of Irish Studies? On Whiteness, Academia, and Activism." *Irish University Review*, vol. 50, no. 1, Spring/Summer 2020, pp. 94–5.

Nairn, Tom. "The Modern Janus." *The Break-Up of Britain: Crisis and Neo-Nationalism*. New Left Books, 1977, pp. 331–50.

Nancy, Jean-Luc. "Painting in the Grotto." *The Muses*, translated by Peggy Kamuf. Stanford University Press, 1996, pp. 69–79.

Ngũgĩ wa Thiong'o. *Decolonising the Mind: The Politics of Language in African Literature*. James Currey, 1986.

Nixon, Rob. *Slow Violence and the Environmentalism of the Poor*. Harvard University Press, 2013.

O'Brien, Flann. "A Bash in the Tunnel." *Stories and Plays*. Penguin Books, 1977.

O'Connor, Emmet. *A Labour History of Ireland, 1824–1960*. Gill and Macmillan, 1992.

O'Malley, Ernie. *On Another Man's Wound*, edited by Cormac O'Malley, revised edition. Mercier Press, 2002.

O'Neill, Peter D. and David Lloyd, editors. *The Black and Green Atlantic: Cross-Currents of the African and Irish Diasporas*. Palgrave Macmillan, 2009.

Obert, Julia. *Postcolonial Overtures: The Politics of Sound in Northern Irish Poetry*. Syracuse University Press, 2015.

Olson, Charles. "Projective Verse." *Modern Poets on Modern Poetry*, edited by James Scully. Fontana, 1973, pp. 271–82.

Oppenheimer, Paul. *The Birth of the Modern Mind: Self, Consciousness and the Birth of the Sonnet*. Oxford University Press, 1989.

Patten, Eve. "Medbh McGuckian." *British Council*, British Council, 2021. https://literature.britishcouncil.org/writer/medbh-mcguckian (last accessed July 29, 2021).

Philip, Marlene Nourbese. *She Tries Her Tongue, Her Silence Softly Breaks*. Ragweed Press, 1989.

Pilkington, Lionel. *Theatre and the State in Twentieth-Century Ireland: Cultivating the People*. Routledge, 2001.

Pound, Ezra. *ABC of Reading*. Faber and Faber, 1973.

—. *The Cantos*. New Directions, 1972.

—, translator. *Sophocles: Women of Trachis*. Faber and Faber, 1956.

Quigley, Mark. *Empire's Wake: Postcolonial Irish Writing and the Politics of Modern Literary Form*. Fordham University Press, 2013.

—. "White Skin, Green Face: House of Pain and the Modern Minstrel Show." O'Neill and Lloyd, pp. 64–80.

Quinn, Justin. *The Cambridge Introduction to Modern Irish Poetry, 1800–2000*. Cambridge University Press, 2008.

Renan, Ernest. "What is a Nation?," translated by Martin Thom. *Nation and Narration*, edited by Homi Bhabha. Routledge, 1990, pp. 8–22.

Rogin, Michael Paul. *Subversive Genealogy: The Politics and Art of Herman Melville*. Alfred A. Knopf, 1983.

Said, Edward W. "Introduction: Secular Criticism." *The World, The Text and the Critic*. Harvard University Press, 1983, pp. 1–30.

Sakai, Naoki. "Distinguishing Literature and the Work of Translation: Theresa

Hak Kyung Cha's *Dictée* and Repetition without Return." *Translation and Subjectivity: On "Japan" and Cultural Nationalism*. University of Minnesota Press, 2008, pp. 18–39.

Satris, Marthine. "An Interview with Maurice Scully." *Contemporary Literature*, vol. 53, no. 1, 2012, pp. 1–30.

—. "Interview with Trevor Joyce." *Journal of British and Irish Innovative Poetry*, vol. 5, no. 1, 2013, pp. 11–30.

Scully, Maurice. "As I Like It." *The Beau*, no. 3, 1983/4, p. 10.

—. *Livelihood*. Wild Honey Press, 2004.

---. *Things That Happen*. Shearsman Books, 2020.

Shakespeare, William. *The Tempest. The Riverside Shakespeare*. Houghton Mifflin, 1974, pp. 1606–38.

Sharman, Adam. "Vallejo, Modernity and Poetemporality." *Tradition and Modernity in Spanish American Literature: From Darío to Carpentier*. Palgrave Macmillan, 2006, pp. 85–107.

Sisson, Elaine. "'A Note on What Happened': Experimental Influences on the Irish Stage, 1919–1929." "Forum Kritika: Radical Theatre and Ireland (Part 2)." *Kritika Kultura*, vol. 15, 2010, pp. 132–48.

Smyth, Gerry. *Decolonisation and Criticism: The Construction of Irish Literature*. Pluto Press, 1998.

Spenser, Edmund. "The Ruines of Rome." *The Poetical Works of Edmund Spenser*, edited by J. C. Smith and E. De Selincourt. Oxford University Press, 1912, pp. 509–14.

Stafford, Barbara Maria. *Body Criticism: Imaging the Unseen in Enlightenment Art and Medicine*. MIT Press, 1991.

Stewart, Susan. "Notes on Distressed Genres." *Crimes of Writing: Problems in the Containment of Representation*. Duke University Press, 1994, pp. 66–101.

Szondi, Peter. *Celan Studies*, edited by Jean Bollack and translated by Susan Bernofsky and Harvey Mendelsohn. Stanford University Press, 2003.

Tuchman, Maurice. "A Talk with Avigdor Arikha." *Arikha*, edited by Richard Channin. Hermann, 1985, pp. 43–9.

Uhland, Ludwig. *Dichtungen, Briefe, Reden: Eine Auswahl*, edited by Walter P. H. Scheffler. J. F. Steinkopf, 1963.

Walcott, Derek. *Omeros*. Farrar, Straus and Giroux, 1990.

Walsh, Catherine. *Astonished Birds* and *Cara, Jane, Bob and James*. hard-Pressed Poetry, 2012.

—. *City West*. Shearsman Books, 2005.

—. *Optic Verve: A Commentary*. Shearsman Books, 2009.

Wang, Dorothy. *Thinking Its Presence: Form, Race and Subjectivity in Contemporary Asian American Poetry*. Stanford University Press, 2014.

Wilkinson, John. "The American Tract." Review of *Souls of the Labadie Tract* by Susan Howe. *Notre Dame Review*, vol. 27, Winter/Spring 2009, pp. 241–7.

Williams, Raymond. *Marxism and Literature*. Oxford University Press, 1977.

Wills, Clair. *Improprieties: Politics and Sexuality in Northern Irish Poetry*. Oxford University Press, 1993.

Wills, James and Freeman Wills. *The Irish Nation: Its History and Its Biography*, vol. I. A. Fullerton and Co., 1876.

Wood, Michael. *Yeats and Violence*. Oxford University Press, 2010.

Wyatt, Thomas. "They flee from me, that sometime did me seek." *Silver Poets of the Sixteenth Century*, edited by Gerald Bullett. J. M. Dent, 1947, pp. 14–15.

Yeates, Pádraig. *Lockout: Dublin 1913*. Gill and Macmillan, 2000.

Yeats, W. B. "Four Years: 1887–1891." *The Autobiography of W. B. Yeats*. Macmillan, 1953, pp. 69–120.

—. "A General Introduction for My Work." *Essays and Introductions*. Gill and Macmillan, 1961, pp. 509–26.

—. *The Poems: A New Edition*, edited by Richard J. Finneran. Macmillan, 1983.

Index